African Perspectives on Adult Learning

Research Methods for Adult Educators in Africa

Other books in the Series

African Perspectives on Adult Learning

Research Methods for Adult Educators in Africa

Bagele Chilisa • Julia Preece

Co-published by the UNESCO Institute for Education, Feldbrunnenstr. 58, 20148, Hamburg, Germany, and Pearson Education South Africa, corner of Logan Way and Forest Drive, Pinelands, Cape Town, South Africa, in collaboration with the Institute for International Cooperation of the German Adult Education Association, Obere Wilhelmstr. 32, 53225 Bonn, Germany, and the Adult Education Department of the University of Botswana, Private Bag 0022, Gaborone, Botswana.

First published 2005

ISBN 9282011186

Acknowledgements
Rob Nagel for the photo of the Hoodia cactus on p. 20; the Newark Musuem for the Art of Africa Knowledge Cards on p. 55; Sandy Grant/Phuthadikobo Museum for the photos on pp. 150 and 159

Published by David Langhan
Editorial manager: Lisa Compton
Project manager: Anita van Zyl
Symbol research and selection: Sandie Vahl
Editor: Elmien Wolvaardt
Proofreader: Rachel Bey-Miller
Book design by Graham Arbuckle
Cover design and artwork by Toby Newsome
Typesetting by Robin Taylor
Printed by CTP Book Printers, Cape
N5889/28175

Contents

ADINKRA SYMBOLS

For the icons in this Series, we have chosen Adinkra symbols that are associated with learning and community in some way. These striking and expressive symbols are used by the people of Ghana and the Ivory Coast in textile and jewellery design, architecture, wood carvings, etc., and represent only one of a number of writing systems found in Africa.

	Symbol	Meaning	Interpretation
	bese saka	sack of cola nuts	abundance, plenty, affluence, power, unity, togetherness
	dame-dame	name of a board game	intelligence, ingenuity, strategy, craftiness
	dwennimmen	ram's horns	humility, strength, wisdom, learning
	mate masie	what I hear I keep	wisdom, knowledge, learning, prudence, understanding
	nkonsonkonson	chain link	unity, human relations, brotherhood, cooperation
	nsaa	hand-woven fabric	excellence, authenticity, genuineness
	sesa woruban	morning star inside a wheel	life transformation

The authors

Bagele Chilisa

Bagele Chilisa received her doctorate from the University of Pittsburgh, USA and is now Associate Professor and head of Department of Educational Foundations at the University of Botswana. She teaches research methods and evaluation courses to undergraduate and graduate students in the Faculty of Education. She has supervised research projects for numerous post-graduate students and was lead researcher in several research projects sponsored by UNICEF, DFID, UNDP and FAWE (Forum for African Women in Education). Her research focuses on research methodologies, educational policies, indigenous knowledge systems and HIV/AIDS. She wrote chapters 2, 3, 5, 6, 7, 8, 9 and 13.

Julia Preece

Julia Preece is Professor of Adult and Life-long Education at the University of Glasgow, UK. She worked at the University of Botswana, Department of Adult Education from 2000 to 2004. Her special areas of interest and expertise include gender, social exclusion, adult education and lifelong learning, citizenship, community education and poverty development. She has also taught at the Universities of Surrey and Lancaster in the UK. She was an inner-city community education and development worker from 1978 to 1990. She wrote chapters 1, 4, 10, 11, 12 and 14.

Foreword

The remedial strategy of borrowing textbooks conceived in contexts of and for students from developed countries with well-established traditions of adult education is no longer viable. The present textbook series, African Perspectives on Adult Learning, represents the outcome of a venture initiated three decades ago by the Institute for International Cooperation of the German Adult Education Association (known by its German acronym as IIZ/DVV). Bringing together non-governmental and civil society organisations, the IIZ/DVV turned this venture into a creative partnership with academia, aimed at building the training and research capacities of African universities that serve the adult education community. It has become a means of fruitful cooperation with several leading African universities, all partners being concerned with providing textbooks for university departments and institutes of adult education relevant for the African context.

The abiding interest, as well as growing financial support and substantive input of the IIZ/DVV, has provided a key ingredient for the success of this project, along with

establishing its potential for expansion. The University of Botswana has been another major contributor right from the beginning. Its Department of Adult Education has given the academic and institutional support needed for such an ambitious undertaking, graciously shouldering the Editorial Secretariat of the Series. The third pillar of this endeavour – and a decisive one – was furnished by the UNESCO Institute for Education (UIE), an international centre of excellence in adult learning enjoying the full backing of UNESCO and boasting extensive publishing experience in the field. UIE brought in vital international and inter-regional expertise coupled with the vision of the Fifth International Conference on Adult Education (CONFINTEA V). The Institute has also mobilised sizeable financial resources of its own, led the Series Editorial Board and assumed responsibility for managing often difficult matters entailed by such a complex venture.

The present Series recommends itself through many distinctive features that reflect the unique manner in which it has come about. One of these has to do with the professional guidance and technical

nkonsonkonson

advice provided by the competent, sensitive and broadly representative Series Editorial Board, whose members have displayed the capability and wisdom required to steer a project of this kind. Their intellectual resources, experience and know-how made it possible for the Series to take on its actual form. We wish to express our deep gratitude to all the members of the Editorial Board for their profound involvement, the optimism they brought to the Series and their dedication to its successful completion.

The co-publisher with UIE is Pearson Education South Africa, which has proven to be a partner highly committed to the goals of the project, one prepared to engage in a collaboration of a different order and take risks in exploring new paths in publishing. As a full member of the Series Editorial Board, the co-publisher has offered invaluable assistance, especially in the writers' workshops and in coaching the authors throughout the composition of the chapters. The creative way in which Pearson Education South Africa has integrated the project into its work and its firm dedication to fostering editorial and authorial capacities in Africa deserve special mention.

Without this sense of mission, the Series would not have seen the light of day.

The authors of the works in this Series have themselves been selected on the basis of proposals they submitted. We took pleasure in working with all of these devoted partners, and the project greatly benefited from their combination of individual conviction together with teamwork, collective analysis and decision-making. We wish to thank all the authors for their hard work as well as their adherence to a demanding schedule. Their professionalism and competence lie at the heart of this Series and were instrumental in its realisation.

Finally, and most importantly, special recognition is due to Professor Frank Youngman, the Series Managing Editor, and his Assistant, Dr Gabo Ntseane of the University of Botswana, who constitute the Editorial Board Secretariat. Frank Youngman initiated the idea for this Series in 2001, and the Secretariat has been in the front line at all times, carefully guiding the process, monitoring progress and ensuring the quality of the work at all stages without compromise.

This Series addresses the critical lack of textbooks for adult education and the alienating nature of those currently in use in Africa. We have sought to develop a new set of foundational works conceived and developed from an African perspective and written mainly by African scholars. An African perspective, however, is not mere Afrocentrism, although some degree of the latter is required to move beyond the reigning Eurocentrism and general Western domination of all scientific domains and adult education in particular. Injecting a dose of Afrocentrism without prejudice to universal values, elementary scientific knowledge and other cultures, and without complacency in the face of retrograde and discriminatory values and traditions, has proven to be a significant challenge. In essence, the African perspective has revealed itself to be both a renaissance of the continent and its manifold traditions, as well as the birth of its own new vision and prospects in the context of a fast-growing, ever-changing and increasingly globalised world.

For the initial volumes in this evolving Series, the following five titles were selected: *The Psychology of Adult Learning in Africa; Foundations of Adult Education in Africa;*

Research Methods for Adult Educators in Africa; Developing Programmes for Adult Learners in Africa; and *The Social Context of Adult Learning in Africa.* We will certainly judge the success of these volumes by taking into account the reactions and responses of their users, and we will make any necessary adjustments while striving to widen the scope of the venture to cover other linguistic areas of Africa and to explore new thematic fields for deepening the African perspective. There is no question that IIZ/DVV and UIE are committed to lending their intellectual and financial support to this endeavour. Furthermore, the University of Botswana is committed to providing the academic and administrative base for the Series, while Pearson Education South Africa foresees the ongoing viability of the project. In opening up new approaches to adult education and learning in Africa, the Series meets the needs of governments, non-governmental and civil society organisations, and academia in an area of great importance to UNESCO and the community of nations.

Adama Ouane
Director, UNESCO Institute for Education

Preface

During the 1990s it became clear that adult learning must be an important part of all strategies for development. In a series of world conferences between 1990 and 1996, various agencies of the United Nations addressed the issues of education for all, the environment, human rights, population, social development, the status of women, human settlements and food security. Each of these conferences recognised that progress would be dependent on adult members of society transforming their life circumstances and gaining greater control over their lives. To achieve this change, adults require new knowledge, skills and attitudes. This significant insight was highlighted by the Fifth International Conference on Adult Education (CONFINTEA V) that was organised by UNESCO in 1997. CONFINTEA V affirmed that adult learning is potentially a powerful force for promoting people-centred development. It concluded that the education of adults is key to sustainable development in the twenty-first century.

The concept of adult learning articulated by CONFINTEA V is a broad one, embracing formal, non-formal and informal learning processes in all areas of people's lives. This concept is relevant in African contexts, where the learning of adults takes place across their various social roles, in the home, the community, and the workplace, as well as in formal educational and training institutions. Opportunities for learning are availed by a wide variety of providers. The state has a central responsibility to promote and facilitate adult learning. In some countries this responsibility has been diminished by the impact of structural adjustment policies. But in others the state continues to play an important role, with a wide range of government departments organising programmes that involve adult learning. These programmes are multi-sectoral, including activities as varied as agricultural extension, health education, business training, consumer education, community development, and wildlife education. Also, the organisations of civil society are significant sites of adult learning, providing their own educational programmes as well as a context in which adults acquire new competencies through their active involvement in running such organisations. For example, in many countries the trade union movement is an important source of adult learning. Increasingly, the private sector is a major provider of learning opportunities for adults. Its role has two dimensions. Firstly, companies are expanding their training and development for employees as they respond to the challenges of technological change and global competition. Secondly, there is a rapid growth of commercial educational institutions such as colleges, academies, and institutes, which are responding to market demands for learning opportunities, especially in work-related fields such as information technology, tourism and business. These institutions are to be found in all the urban centres of Africa. Public and private universities also cater for many adult learners, especially through their part-time, evening, and distance learning programmes. The education and training of adults in Africa therefore takes place in many settings, embraces many content areas and modes of learning, and is provided by many different types of organisations. It is a complex and diverse field of activity.

The successful implementation of adult learning policies and programmes depends in large measure on the availability of knowledgeable, skilful, and socially committed educators of adults. Because they are key agents in the realisation of adult learning, the quality of their initial and continuing training is crucial. The educators of adults in Africa work in a wide variety of organisational and social contexts, from government bureaucracies to community-based projects. They play multiple roles as programme planners, organisers, teachers, researchers and counsellors. While this diversity of situations and roles reflects the reality of adult learning settings, it presents significant conceptual and practical problems in terms of training those who educate adults. One example is that those who work with adults in learning activities don't always identify themselves as adult educators. Rather, they identify themselves as health promoters, business advisers or community workers. Nevertheless, whatever the nomenclature of a particular cadre, it is important that they are proficient in their work of helping adults to learn. The development of their expertise includes a body of knowledge, skills and values that is centred on adult education as a field of study and practice.

The professional training of educators of adults in Africa takes place in institutions of tertiary education across the continent, primarily at diploma and degree level. For example, in every country there are colleges of agriculture that prepare agricultural extension workers, health institutes that train community-based health workers and technical colleges that train vocational teachers. In particular, many African universities have departments or institutes of adult education that train personnel for fields as varied as adult basic education, prison education and human resource development. Although the areas of content specialisation vary from agronomy to literacy, the curricula of the training programmes have many common topics, such as the psychology of adult learning, programme development, communication skills and research methods. This is because all educators of adults require a common body of knowledge (such as an awareness of the historical and philosophical dimensions of adult education practice) and a number of generic skills (for example, in teaching and research). A key learning resource in these training programmes is the prescribed course textbook. However, those who teach these programmes often have difficulty in finding textbooks that are relevant to the work situations and social contexts of their students.

A review of English-language curriculum materials used in the professional training of adult educators in Africa reveals that the majority of textbooks for the courses are published in the United States or the United Kingdom. The content of these books seldom reflects issues of African development or the realities of adult education policy and practice in Africa. The social and organisational contexts, theoretical underpinnings and practical examples are derived largely from the experience of adult education in the advanced industrialised countries of the West. Hence the textbooks currently being used in the training of adult educators in Africa are at best lacking in relevance and, at worst, actively promoting inappropriate models of adult education. Furthermore, because of the cost of these books, student access is often limited.

The post-colonial history of adult education as a field of study in African tertiary education institutions shows that very few indigenous textbooks have been produced over the years. Useful individual books, such as the *Adult Education Handbook* (edited by the Institute of Adult Education, Dar-es-Salaam, 1973) and *A Handbook of Adult Education for West Africa* (edited by Lalage Bown and Sunday Hezekiah Olu Tomori, London, 1979), have been one-off publications that were not followed up and were not widely available. When an institution in one country has consistently produced relevant materials, such as the Department of Adult Education at the University of Ibadan in Nigeria, they have been difficult to obtain in other countries. The problem of a lack of appropriate and accessible textbooks for use in the training of African adult educators remains.

There is, therefore, a need to develop relevant, affordable and available textbooks that reflect African social realities, theoretical and cultural perspectives, policies and modes of practice. This is the need that the series African Perspectives on Adult Learning seeks to meet. The books in the Series place the African context at the centre of discussions on adult education topics. They take into account the impact of colonialism, liberation struggles, neo-colonialism and globalisation. They show the importance to adult learning of African philosophies, indigenous knowledge systems, traditions and cultures. They demonstrate that the realities of class, gender, race and ethnicity in African societies shape the nature of adult learning activities. They provide examples of the policies and practices that characterise adult education across the continent. While referring to international discourses on adult learning, their presentation of issues in adult education is Africa-centred. The Series therefore contributes to the endogenisation of education within the perspective of the African Renaissance.

The books in the African Perspectives on Adult Learning Series cover important subjects for the training of educators of adults in Africa. They are intended to be course textbooks that will be used in face-to-face teaching environments in a way that encourages interactive learning. Each book is designed to provide an overview of the subject, to introduce appropriate theory and to provide discussion and examples rooted in professional practice, policies and research from African contexts. Each chapter features clear learning objectives, practical examples, activities for the reader to do individually or in small groups, a summary, key points, further questions and suggested readings. It is hoped that the use of the books will promote the development of relevant curricula and interactive teaching approaches in adult education training programmes across the continent.

Each book in the Series provides an African perspective on an important area of knowledge and practice for the educator of adults. In *Research Methods for Adult Educators in Africa*, Bagele Chilisa and Julia Preece consider the subject of research methods for adult educators in African contexts. The book provides Africa-centred rationales for research methodologies, and provides exercises and examples that are embedded in African contexts. It explores and critiques some of the dominant research paradigms using African counter-arguments, contexts and examples. Theoretical concepts draw on critical theories such as post-colonial theory and relevant feminist literature, as well as literature that privileges the African experience and voice. The focus throughout is on critiquing and adapting existing research methodologies and, where appropriate, proposing methodologies that are more appropriate for African contexts. Research methodologies are thus presented in ways that challenge the reader to examine the approaches they adopt for research to see whether they are inclusive of marginalised groups and worldviews embedded in the African people's experiences, histories and cultures. The thrust of the argument throughout the book is that the current dominant research paradigms should be continuously reviewed to accommodate other ways of conducting research and reporting findings that are embedded in African realities, values and ways of knowing.

The aims of the book are:

- To provide a practice-based textbook on research for the educators of adults.
- To emphasise the need for strategies of carrying out research that privilege previously marginalised groups, and to name and communicate their experiences in ways that allow for the creation of new concepts, terms, categories of analysis and knowledge that are responsive to the needs of the researched.

The book identifies three paradigms, namely the positivist/post-positivist paradigm, the interpretive paradigm and the emancipatory paradigm. It then demonstrates how to carry out research using designs from each of these paradigms.

Chapter 1 introduces some key research concepts, contexts for adult education in Africa, and potential research agendas. Chapter 2 discusses each of the three paradigms. Each paradigm is discussed in terms of the philosophies that inform its approaches and the way questions about reality, knowledge and values are understood, explained and incorporated in research processes and procedures. It further details the characteristics of each paradigm and illustrates research studies that use designs within each paradigm.

Chapter 3 explores other ways of approaching research that are embedded in African philosophical perspectives. It suggests techniques of gathering data that utilise knowledge systems from the marginalised and formerly colonised nations. Chapter 4 provides some insights into how the first three chapters might influence the practicalities of organising and critiquing material from an African perspective.

Chapter 5 suggests ways of writing a research proposal such that the worldviews of those who have suffered a long history of oppression are given space to communicate from their frames of reference and worldviews. Chapters 6–9 provide the nuts and bolts of carrying out and presenting quantitative and qualitative research in ways that accommodate multiple worldviews. Chapter 10 shows how one can justify and use a combination of quantitative and qualitative research in adult education contexts.

Chapters 11 and 12 focus on research designs derived from the emancipatory paradigm. The first, action research, focuses on participatory rural appraisal; the second highlights feminist research approaches for their focus on giving voice to the marginalised and the way they are able to highlight gender inequalities (a dominant issue in

African contexts). Chapter 13 demonstrates the particular features of conducting Africa-centred ethics in order not to undermine or humiliate the very people who are providing the research data. Finally, Chapter 14 completes the research process by discussing the write-up and dissemination phases, always with an awareness of audience and purpose.

The ability to undertake research is an essential skill for educators of adults, who continually need to gather, analyse and present data related to their work. *Research Methods for Adult Educators in Africa* provides an excellent resource for developing and enhancing these skills.

Frank Youngman
Department of Adult Education

Acknowledgements

Both authors sincerely thank everyone who provided input for the development of this book. Our gratitude goes to the Series Managing Editor, Frank Youngman of the University of Botswana, who offered suggestions, reading materials and constructive feedback throughout the writing of the book. Our gratitude also goes to the anonymous external reviewer whose insights helped the content and shape of the book. We would like to thank the following reviewers for their valuable comments: Wolfgang Leumer, German Adult Education Association; Adama Ouane, UNESCO; Christopher Macintosh, UNESCO; Stanley Mpofu, University of Namibia; Gabo Ntseane, University of Botswana; Eddie Turay, University of Sierra Leone; Mantina Mohasi, University of Lesotho; Antony Okech, Makerere University; and Martin Kamwengo, University of Zambia. I would also like to thank David Langhan, our publisher at Pearson Education, for his outstanding skills in coordinating the writing process, his insights into the layout and production of the book, and for his support and encouragement throughout the writing of the book.

Bagele Chilisa and Julia Preece

Bagele Chilisa would further like to thank the following people and organisations: I am indebted to faculty in the Research Methodology Department at the University of Pittsburgh for their training in quantitative methods. Faculty in the Department of Administration and Policy Studies at the University of Pittsburgh helped me to move beyond quantitative to qualitative, interpretive studies. In particular I would like to thank R. T. Eichelberger, W. W. Cooley and W. Bickel. Working with them at the Learning Research and Development Centre, University of Pittsburgh, was very valuable and has contributed very much to my way of looking at educational inquiry. In addition, I am indebted to the many

nsaa

students who have taken my research courses at the University of Botswana over the years. I have learnt a great deal from their questions and their research studies. Some of the examples in the book come from their work. The help of my colleagues and friends is gratefully acknowledged. Musa W. Dube, University of Botswana, and Michelle Commeryas, University of Georgia, commented on specific parts of the manuscript. Nnunu Tsheko, University of Botswana, assisted me with Chapter 7. Finally, I thank members of my family for their support, encouragement and inspiration throughout the writing of this book.

Chapter 1

Contexts

OVERVIEW

This chapter introduces some key concepts for the book. It offers a definition of research and explains some personal skills that are needed for conducting a study. Some features of adult education research in contemporary society are introduced and the contexts for adult education in African societies are considered. This involves looking at some of the historical and contemporary influences on African nations, including the concepts of development, lifelong learning and globalisation, and also how African perspectives have a bearing on the adult education research process. A summary of adult education research agendas – and the politics of those agendas – introduces you to some ideas for your own research, finishing with a practical exercise: creating a research question from a research topic.

LEARNING OBJECTIVES

By the end of this chapter, you should be able to:

1 Distinguish some key concepts and personal skills necessary for conducting research.
2 Understand the influence of African contexts on adult education research.
3 Have a critical awareness of the politics of adult education research in African situations.
4 Identify relevant African adult education research agendas.
5 Formulate a research question that is relevant to adult education.

dame-dame

KEY TERMS

applied research   Research that produces findings that are useful in practice.

basic research   Research that develops new theory.

civil society   Organisations that operate independently from the state.

data   Information.

democracy   A form of management and leadership that embraces participation, accountability, respect for human rights, and the right of citizens to form independent organisations.

globalisation   Increased global interaction as a result of economic and technological advancements.

impact studies   Studies that explore the outcome of policies or interventions such as donor aid.

lifelong learning   Learning that is continuous throughout life.

method   The way in which data is collected.

methodology   The research design, which encompasses both worldview and method.

qualitative   Based on interaction and dialogue with research participants.

quantitative   Based on statistics.

research   A systematic form of inquiry.

research paradigm   A way of interpreting the world and the rules for investigating it.

⊞ BEFORE YOU START

Have you ever tried to experiment with your teaching style? Have you ever conducted an evaluation of a learning programme? Maybe you have applied for funding to support a new income-generating project and have had to collect or show evidence of a need for the project. If you have, you have probably engaged in some aspect of research. Based on your experiences of what you did in these activities, write down your own definition of research.

KEY RESEARCH CONCEPTS

Research is a systematic method of inquiry to expand our knowledge about a particular issue of interest. Systematic means that you have a system for, or recognisable pattern of, doing things. You ask the same questions of everyone so you can compare answers. You use the same technique with everyone when asking those questions so that you can compare like with like. This definition needs to be expanded:

- As researchers, people adopt a particular strategy or set of principles that will guide them in their detailed search for deeper understanding of a problem.
- There is no single, correct way of conducting an enquiry. The nature of the problem and the questions you want to ask will influence how you go about it.

Furthermore, your choice of how you approach your research problem and what you expect to find out will be influenced by your own *worldview*, which is your philosophical framework for seeing the world. Chapter 2 will show how this framework is grounded in different perceptions of social reality and may vary according to the researcher's own cultural, gender or class background and experiences.

Irrespective of your choice of topic, the process of planning and conducting research is essentially the same. First you identify a research problem or question (you will get a chance to do this towards the end of this chapter). Then you establish a conceptual framework – the way you want to interpret and understand the world and the associated rules of investigating through this conceptual framework. This is your *research paradigm*. There are three paradigms discussed in Chapter 2. They are positivist/post-positivist (a scientific approach that looks for a single, provable reality), interpretive (looking for different interpretations of reality amongst people) and emancipatory (an approach that privileges views of reality from marginalised social groups).

The research paradigm helps determine your *methodology* (the theoretical perspective of your research, and the design or process which encompasses your worldview). This in turn influences which method to use – your data (information) collection techniques. A methodology might be *quantitative* (based on statistics) or *qualitative* (where the researcher interacts more directly with people and tries to get as close to their reality as possible). A methodology might also be termed an approach, such as a case study, action research or survey.

So a quantitative study that uses a survey approach will use *methods* such as questionnaires. A qualitative study might choose to use a method such as a face-to-face interview. Chapters 6 and 8 discuss these methodologies and methods in much more detail.

The purpose of your research will also influence which methodology or approach you use. If your purpose is primarily to create new knowledge or theory that does not require immediate practical application, then your purpose will be what is known as *basic* or pure *research*. If your goal is to improve existing practice in the near future, then your purpose will be *applied research*. Applied research might use approaches such as action research, a form of evaluation or a case study. In any case you might choose a methodology that is quantitative or qualitative. Your research design (an explanation of your methodology) has to justify which methods to use based on your overall conceptual framework (research paradigm and research purpose). Once you have studied the principles of doing a research project through qualitative and quantitative methodologies, Chapters 11 and 12 look at two complementary research approaches that are particularly relevant to African adult education contexts and the emancipatory paradigm.

ACTIVITY

Write down your understanding of these concepts:
1 Research paradigm
2 Methodology
3 Method.

PERSONAL SKILLS

Your personal skills are those qualities and competencies within you that can be used in a variety of situations. There are different kinds of skills, of course. For instance, knowing how to sew, or plough, or drive, are all skills. But they are practical skills for a particular purpose. You cannot drive without knowing how to use the clutch, the brake, the accelerator pedal and the steering wheel. Knowing how to drive enables you to do jobs that require the ability to drive. A personal skill, however, is an internal quality that is useful in any situation. Patience, for instance, is a personal skill. It is useful when driving, when looking after children, when serving a customer, when waiting in a queue. Another personal skill is the ability to organise. Someone who knows how to organise can apply that skill in the home and at work – whether they are married, have children, or are farmers, extension workers, lorry drivers or teachers. Perhaps it is time for you to anticipate some problems you might face when doing a piece of research and then think up some personal skills and qualities that might be useful for helping you manage those chal-

lenges effectively. Before you read on, do this activity.

ACTIVITY

1 List some problems that you might anticipate in conducting a research project.
2 List some personal skills or qualities that can be used in several different situations to overcome those problems.

Perhaps your list included the following:

■ Problems: Timing your workload, getting permission to see people, keeping appointments, persuading people to take part, organising your material and work schedule.
■ Useful skills: Patience, organisation, planning, communication, analysing, problem solving, politeness, timekeeping.

All these personal skills, in their different ways, will help to overcome potential problems that might arise during the inquiry. Conducting an investigation can be fraught with little problems. No matter how well you think you have planned, some things will always happen unexpectedly. But it is possible to minimise these problems if you plan ahead properly.

The main focus of this book is on research contexts that respect African value systems. Its other focus is on adult education research in African contexts. To research such forms of education requires a particular understanding of context, including learner expectations and their relationship to wider political concerns.

AFRICAN CONTEXTS

Other books in this series will give a more detailed account of African contexts for adult education. Some key features will be summarised here. To understand African contexts we must start with their pre-colonial and colonial pasts.

Traditional African adult education

Adult education in Africa has always been concerned with many of the same matters that other educationists are concerned with. This has usually been exercised through an oral tradition under the leadership of chiefs, headmen and elders over the community as a whole. A particular feature of this learning has been the initiation training into adulthood, and instruction in crafts through apprenticeships. Moral and historical education has also been conducted through storytelling, music and proverbs. Some of these traditions were interrupted by colonial and missionary intrusions into Africa.

Colonial influences

The division of Africa in 1884 by European colonial powers introduced regulations and colonial languages, such as English, French and Portuguese. The colonial goal of adult education and literacy was primarily to support the colonial administration. Mulenga (1999) states that certain men were given selective education for particular skills that would ensure they fitted into society and promoted the social stability and continuity of the colonial regime. In British colonies women were treated in the same way that women in Victorian England were treated. So their education was confined to domestic matters that reinforced their subordinate status to men.

The post-independence initiatives in many countries included the establishment of government adult education agencies – usually for literacy and distance education. In universities, departments of extramural education emerged, following the patterns of the country of origin of their colonial masters.

These two histories have influenced both the style and nature of today's adult education provision and subsequent research agendas. They set the pattern for development around a number of key concerns.

Adult education and development

Development is associated with nation building and the goals of economic prosperity. In adult education contexts, development programmes in most African countries include agricultural extension, productivity and efforts to reduce malnutrition and enhance skills training. This includes the promotion of literacy and income-generation projects in order to reduce poverty and increase women's involvement in public affairs and general democratic participation.

Poverty, gender and inequality

Coy (2002) states that, by 1998, 66% of the world's poor lived in Africa. African women share the biggest burden of poverty. Snyder and Tadesse (2002) argue that their present unequal share of the economy is attributed in part to the colonial treatment of women as home makers rather than farmers, thus bypassing their educational needs for the skills required to take part in a modern, technological and wage-based economy:

> *Colonial officials tended to visualize women in terms of a Victorian image of what a woman ('a lady') should be, instead of observing women's actual functions. Colonials equated 'men' with 'breadwinner' and, as a result, introduced*

technologies to men and recruited men for paying jobs, which often took them off the farm (Snyder and Tadesse, 2002: 76).

This trend continued with the expansion of an international market economy. Men migrated to work in the mines, plantations and towns. Men were favoured for education, employment and access to resources. Even land settlement schemes gave title deeds to men. This meant they had automatic rights to the proceeds of the land, including the products of women's labour. So the colonial period set the scene for unequal education and subsequent access to economic sustainability.

Education policies designed by international agencies and national governments often focus on literacy. Policies are based on the premise that universal literacy can accelerate national development and reduce the dependency of emerging economies on Western resources (World Bank, 1988; UNESCO, 1976). Egbo (2000) argues, however, that the issue of literacy is not that simple. It can mean different things to different people. Literacy alone does not seem to change women's economic status, for instance. She argues for something more – a 'critical literacy' that would stimulate women to recognise and question the sources of their oppression. The effect of different literacy activities needs further research and development in different African contexts. Poverty and gender inequality are interrelated issues that affect adult education interventions across a number of fronts, and ultimately the nature of research activities that need to be undertaken. In the light of Africa's colonial heritage, it is significant that literacy projects, like most development programmes, depend on the policies and expectations of donor funding.

Donor aid and adult education

Aid is not neutral. Youngman (2000: 96) states that aid makes African countries relatively weak within international politics. Aid therefore 'provides a channel for external influence over their development policies and programmes'.

Leach (2000) points out that the World Bank often provides the lead on education policy. Other donor agencies, such as USAID and DFID, simply follow suit. Different countries have their aid specialities (Sweden's is basic education, Germany's is technical/vocational education) so development policies in the recipient country often have to be tailored to fit in with the ideology of the donor country. Aid therefore has strategic significance. It influences research, policy and practice.

A typical example is cited by Baylies and Bujra (2000: 152) on the way HIV/AIDS support has been managed: 'The virtues of decentralisation were extolled by the World Bank to Tanzanians as a means of bringing the battle against AIDS to local people. In practice, it has often dissipated and fragmented efforts'.

So aid becomes a form of neo-colonialism where the aid itself enforces dependency on an ideology and a practice dictated from outside the recipient nation. This limits a nation's sense of freedom and ability to function as a true democracy because it is never completely in control of its own destiny.

Concepts of democracy and civil society

A simple definition of *democracy* can be embedded in the phrase 'the right to be heard and the right not to be excluded' (Hoskyns, 1999: 84). It is seen as a form of management and leadership that embraces participation, accountability, respect for human rights, and the right of citizens to form independent organisations. The emerging nature of many democracies across the world, including Africa, is often said to coincide with the emergence of organisations that operate independently of the state, known under the umbrella term *civil society*.

Civil society consists of groups and organisations that sometimes have the potential to influence government policy. However, they are separate from the state; they function within the country's political system and play various roles in adult education. Their role and effectiveness within African contexts is under-researched.

Globalisation

The concept of *globalisation* represents the constriction of time and space brought about by technological advancement. It also drives economic development and further technological advancement. Communication systems are now global and very fast. Businesses can exchange and sell goods electronically. People can travel more quickly to other countries and rely more heavily on international goods and services as part of their daily lives.

The main drivers for globalisation come from advanced industrialised countries, resulting in increased marketisation of their commodities, skills and knowledge, and international competitiveness. Global influences of culture, values and language also come from those same key players. Africa and other emerging economies, therefore, are experiencing new forms of domination by multinational corporations and international institutions, such as the World Trade Organisation.

Some of the consequences of this are the blurring of national boundaries, conflicts in identity and reduced power of nation states. Resistances to globalisation are manifested in regional efforts to reinforce local identities and belief systems. The effect on poorer countries is exploitation of natural resources and under-payment of labour. Africa is caught up in a double bind of being subject to powerful economic demands that try to influence the continent's own economies; at the same time these demands ignore the indigenous economic strengths and cultural beliefs that make up African identities. So the continent is experiencing a new form of colonialism that reinforces economic differences. Debt, cheap labour and aid are all created largely by external agendas.

Adult education has a primary responsibility to raise awareness of these effects and to stimulate new thinking about how Africa can be a more assertive player in, rather than merely a recipient of, globalisation. One way is to establish a dialogue about what lifelong learning means in African contexts.

Lifelong learning and African value systems

The concept of *lifelong learning* (as a development of the term lifelong education) has been well documented (Faure, 1972; UNESCO, 1996, 2002). Its origins are based on the principle that learning is a continuous process that occurs from the cradle to the grave. One part of this process is to create various opportunities for post-initial education so that learning is seen as a continuation of what has already begun. It is linked to the understanding that we can no longer rely on initial education to carry us through all our learning needs at the workplace and in society. We live in a world of rapid change and must continually update our skills, attitudes and knowledge to enable us as individuals to compete effectively in constantly changing environments. In advanced industrialised countries lifelong learning is also based on capitalist arguments that everyone should be self-sufficient and marketable so as to reduce the burden of dependency on the State. A further factor influencing these values is the changing *demographics* (the share of different age groups in society). We now have an increasingly ageing population that needs to remain active and useful as far into their later years as possible.

Avoseh (2001) makes a number of observations about the traditional African value system and lifelong learning. The lifelong learning heritage in most of Africa is essentially a collective, rather than individual, concept. Its emphasis, therefore, is on building social capital (for community development) rather than human capital (for economic prosperity). African lifelong learning consists of the following dimensions and values:

- *Spiritual*: participation that is influenced by the metaphysical world, resulting in a sense of obligation to the community – but encapsulated in spiritual obligation to one's ancestors and God.
- *Communal*: commitment to the interests of the 'corporate existence of the community'
- *Political*: duties that serve the interests of the nation before oneself through community, family and spiritual responsibilities (from Avoseh, 2001: 480).

These African values are encapsulated in a number of African languages. For instance, in Kenya it is *Harambee*, in South Africa the word is *Ubuntu* and in Botswana it is *Botho*. These words encompass ideas of respect for human life, mutual help, generosity, cooperation, respect for older people, harmony and preservation of the sacred. Commitment to the family includes an obligation to the living and the dead and those yet to be born. Avoseh points out that the African traditional pedagogy for lifelong learning is encapsulated in beliefs, ceremonies, and rituals, cultural and sub-cultural forces that mould the individual as a social being. While these values do not address current issues of gender or poverty imbalances, they indicate that there is a potential conflict of interest with Western notions of lifelong learning where acquisition of qualifications is promoted more than acquisition of traditional social values.

The African voice is relatively weak in the lifelong learning debate. There are still only a few centres in Africa devoted to lifelong learning, for example at the University of the Western Cape in Cape Town, South Africa. The external image of African countries is that they are still developing, their initial schooling infrastructure is incomplete and that literacy is the main focus for adult education. Without intervention from African sources, the concept of lifelong learning will be confined to something suitable for Western and advanced industrialised countries, while low and middle-income countries will be expected to focus their resources on a less all-embracing concept: basic education. UNESCO has summarised this issue as follows: 'Lifelong learning must not be a luxurious goal won in the rich countries, but a goal also for the poor aiming at empowering themselves' (UNESCO, 2002: 2).

⚙ ACTIVITY

Discuss:
1 **The local adult education needs in your region (for example, literacy, changing technologies, agriculture).**
2 **In which fields of adult education is donor aid given?**

3   How do donors influence the kind of
    education that takes place in African
    contexts?

From these contexts we can see there is
a political need for the adult education
research agenda to take a lead role in stimu-
lating both debate, and curriculum and
policy initiatives in the field of lifelong
learning in Africa. The politics of adult
education research in Africa is entwined in
its colonial past, its development plans and
struggles to compete on a level playing field
in the globalised world.

POLITICS OF RESEARCH

Research is never neutral. It is influenced by
stakeholders. These include funders, policy
makers, practitioners and the researchers
themselves. So when research agendas are
drawn up, there is always a tension between
the ideologies and personal agendas of all
parties involved. Moreover, as Omolewa
(2000) states, there is no agreed meaning
for the term 'adult education'. This can
result in indecisive policies on structure and
management of adult education, lack of
responsiveness to research and a preference
among practitioners to rely on experience,
not research. One of the responsibilities of
research is that it should draw attention to
both the gains and shortcomings of current
initiatives. Then it can make policy recommendations that can be heeded in future
plans. There are several ways in which
research needs are addressed in Africa.

Commissioned research

Commissioned research is research that
is identified by policy makers as an area
of need. It is often advertised and people
are invited to 'tender' or apply for the
job of addressing a pre-defined research
problem (such as the role of literacy in
poverty reduction). Many people have com-
plained about the nature of commissioned
research (Noel and Ramatsui, 1994; Mannathoko, 1994). Research for evaluation or
planning purposes is often commissioned
to expatriate advisors and used by policy
makers and donor agencies to inform their
decisions. While governments also fund
research 'the country's national goals and
priorities are often determined or strongly
influenced by the agenda and priorities of
foreign donors' (Mannathoko, 1994: 253).

Commissioned research often has a
double bind for developing countries. Firstly,
the commissioner defines the research
agenda, and secondly, outsiders conduct the
research. The result is that the practitioner
is barely visible in the whole process. Adult
educators have a responsibility to ensure
that their voices are heard in commissioned
research by talking to policy makers about
the problems, frustrations and benefits for
them of commissioned research.

Collaborative research

One alternative to the above problem is
collaborative research. That is, research
which is conducted between a practitioner
and a researcher or between two or more
institutions. But it is often the case that
such research may well result in an unequal
power relationship between the more powerful institution and its partner, or between
researcher and practitioner. So collaboration through a multi-pronged strategy must
be achieved through continued dialogue
and joint activities between practitioners,
policy makers and researchers. Some
examples include: collaboration regarding
provision of technical expertise for local
researchers; dialogue with donors about
providing core support for sustainable use
of indigenous knowledge; development
of inter-country research proposals and

research issues that are decided by African practitioners and researchers together.

International networking

One perceived problem for African countries is that there are not enough indigenous people who understand how to deal with all the research problems that need to be addressed. This is the reason given for why external researchers are recruited. One way to overcome this argument is to build local research capacity. This is often achieved through international dialogue between different African countries and the development of research networks. There are a number of African regional networks: for example the Educational Research Network for Eastern and Southern Africa (ERNESA) and the Educational Research Network for West and Central Africa (ERNWACA). These are groupings of nationally recognised associations or networks of educational researchers, policy makers and practitioners. They are committed to collaboration and information sharing among themselves as well as to the dissemination of research findings to educational policy makers and practitioners within and across countries in the region. These organisations try to ensure that unequal and exploitative partnerships do not develop between members and external agencies. You may wish to establish similar research networks in your region.

Planning and policy

Noel and Ramatsui (1994) point to a worldwide demand that researchers, policy makers and practitioners listen to each other and understand the constraints under which each is working. In the case of developing countries this means expansion in the use of local educational researchers by governments and international agencies to assist in tasks of policy formulation, planning and implementation. You might like to consider why governments and donors fail to use existing research or local skills. Some arguments are discussed below.

Research findings are often presented in a form that is not easily understood by the layperson. Research is usually done on an unplanned, ad hoc basis. Furthermore, the relationship between policy, research and practice is not necessarily clear cut. Practitioners often feel that researchers and policy makers are too far removed from the reality at grass-roots level. The practitioner is often the last to be consulted about a problem they are directly involved in. Researchers want policy makers and practitioners to believe their results and act upon them. Yet research itself can come up with contradictory viewpoints (for example, about the effectiveness of different teaching methods). Policy makers want very simple, unambiguous answers which they can implement, such as the optimum number in a class for effective teaching, although research does not always give clear-cut answers.

All those involved need to be realistic about what can be done. As Burchfield (1994) states, research can shape the perceptions of policy makers and their frame of reference, but the outcome is likely to be of long-term, rather than short-term, value. Factors that influence policy decisions, in addition to hard facts, are public opinion, resource availability, political expediency, and organisation capacity and the opinion of donors who may not understand the complexity on the ground.

There is, therefore, ongoing tension between researchers and policy makers. They serve different constituencies and priorities, and have different people to please. Chapter 14 will discuss some of these issues in more detail when you look at how to disseminate your research.

⊞ ACTIVITY

1 Discuss the issues covered in the preceding sections. Do you recognise them as relevant to your country?
2 Find out about a recent policy decision resulting from research about adult education in your field of work (you may have personal experience of this).
3 Who asked for the research? Who conducted the research? What role did practitioners play?
4 What sort of tensions arose in the research process when the findings were produced? What changes were made as a result?

RESEARCH AGENDAS

In 1996 UNESCO produced a position paper in Dakar at the African Regional Consultation on Adult and Continuing Education. It stated:

> Adult and continuing education in Africa is part of a world system in which the dominant development paradigm has been based on the path of Western industrialisation. Within this development theory the human capital factor is the dominant educational theory. The implementation of these ideas has had adverse effects on the Africa region. ... What is urgently needed is an alternative approach to development and adult and continuing education which is people-driven and based on African values, principles and experience' (p. 12) ... research institutions and practitioners are called upon to commit themselves to undertaking research that is relevant, participatory, based on indigenous culture and language of the people and that would serve the needs of local communities (UNESCO, 1996).

The suggested research agendas that follow are based on these arguments. That is, the African value systems of connectedness to the earth and ancestral spirits, and their oral traditions and indigenous knowledge systems have to be part of the methodology and research questions. At the same time researchers must attend to the political agenda of pre-colonial, colonial and post-colonial influences on adult education policy and practice within African settings. To address all these concerns, some research will be pure or 'basic' while other forms will be in the applied mode for immediate applicability.

Such research will explore the planning, management and practice of adult education and provide feedback for improved development at local and national levels. It will also suggest guidelines for new models that stimulate and sustain bottom-up, learner-led programmes. Some outstanding areas to address might include those listed below.

Donor aid and adult education

Research should identify the consequences of aid for the adult education sector (*impact studies*). Questions might include: How do the external influences interact with what adult education does? What is the pattern of aid for activities where adult education plays a part? What type of research is funded?

Issues of empowerment

There is a trend to develop participatory and collaborative community initiatives that encourage communities to solve their own problems. Yet the practice does not always match its ideology. Small-scale action research interventions might help to analyse local realities in order to improve strategies for community empowerment.

Chapter 10 will look in detail at one type of action research, participatory rural appraisal, that tries to address this issue.

Inequality and access

Adult education is not equally available to all sectors of the population. Qualitative and quantitative designs might identify systems of inequality and their impact on participation, including prevailing assumptions about women (poverty, gender and power relations). But to address inequality, the research design must consider the disadvantaged first, rather than rely on reaching simply those most easily accessible. Chapters 12 and 13 will elaborate on this.

Building national data systems

There is a need to identify problems of programme delivery and to develop improved processes and methods; there is also a need for up-to-date *data* on populations to enable proper planning for their needs. Large-scale enquiries that do research for national development plans, such as national literacy statistics, and that predict possible outcomes of planned educational activities, will be discussed in more detail in Chapter 6.

Curriculum and quality

The types of research that inform curriculum policy are often evaluation and action research. These help to determine whether objectives have been achieved and address issues of accountability of programme implementation. Another aspect of curriculum and quality is the issue of curriculum relevance as a means of consciousness-raising. This might include the use of national languages and the role of adult education in promoting an African values-based civil society. In other words,

this is research that explores whether the curriculum addresses the development needs of the target population.

⌗ ACTIVITY

Discuss:
1 Whether the research agendas discussed in this section are relevant to your country.
2 Can you identify examples of research topics for your own situation that might fit under these headings?
3 Are there other issues not covered here that are relevant to your adult education context?

RELATED TOPICS

The above issues mean that many research topics have interrelated agendas. So a study of literacy programmes might include analysis of opportunities for post-literacy activities, how they are taught and why. It might include an evaluation of the relevance of locally developed materials to learner needs. Alternatively, the focus might be on guidance and counselling, organisation issues, and the effectiveness of practitioner training for literacy education.

A study of income-generation projects also has a relationship to literacy in respect of who is targeted and how to support the development needs of such projects.

Investigations into HIV/AIDS may include a study of what adult education strategies are used to intervene in the crisis, and whose agenda is being promoted in projects like home-based care or in the way that educational material is disseminated.

A focus on remote-area dwellers may include studying their participation in national life, their access to national resources, and the effect of development plans on their traditional values.

Community action plans and their relationship to community development and participatory rural appraisal may take different theoretical and political positions on the notion of empowerment, democracy and civil society or how well prepared extension workers are in the issues of health or adult education theory.

Deciding on a relevant research topic

The ensuing chapters, in particular Chapter 5, will show you how to put together a piece of research according to a particular research paradigm and methodology. At this stage, however, you might like to 'brainstorm' some research ideas. Here are some ideas that other students have used:

■ Education for people with disabilities
■ Poverty reduction programmes
■ Participation in literacy classes.

How many of these ideas can be relevant to adult education, do you think? The answer is that all of them could be, depending on how you frame the investigation question.

✖ ACTIVITY

Try turning each of the above topics into a research question.

RESEARCH QUESTIONS

The following are some possible questions for these topics. In each case the problem has become focused, to make it realistic for a small study. This means narrowing the location for the inquiry and making the question as specific as possible. The biggest mistake beginner researchers make is to think of a very broad question, because that is how the world seems. But when you do research or small-scale inquiries, you need to do just the opposite. You can investigate only a very small piece of the world by asking several questions around a tiny piece of the problem. There are many other possible research questions for these topics. These are just examples:

■ Education for people with disabilities: What are the adult education experiences of people with disabilities? (Implications for adult education and policy: if their experiences are bad, learning providers can find out what issues are of greatest concern to people with disabilities, and then correct these problems.)
■ Poverty reduction programmes: Does the income-generation training programme meet the expectations of people enrolling in it? (Implications for adult education and policy: the findings can inform policy makers on how to improve income generation training programmes.)
■ Participation in literacy classes: What factors encourage or prevent adults from participating in literacy classes? (Implications for adult education and policy: information from this survey can enable providers to promote their programmes more effectively and therefore more effectively encourage potential learners.)

Chapter 5 will refer to the issue of identifying a research problem in more detail in relation to writing your research proposal.

SUMMARY

Research is a systematic method of inquiry. The precise choice of method and focus of inquiry will depend on the nature of the problem and the philosophical framework of the researcher. Research may have a pure or applied purpose. It may choose quantitative or qualitative methodologies. A research paradigm can derive from the positivist, interpretive or emancipatory perspective. Adult education research is grounded in assumptions about adult learners and the role of adult education as either compensatory, developmental or for consciousness-raising.

Adult education in Africa has to be understood as an accumulation of its pre-colonial, colonial and post-colonial experiences. While Africa had its oral tradition of adult education, colonial interventions produced a selective education system to support the colonial project. This has impacted on gender inequalities in terms of literacy and economic activity. Development initiatives are still often controlled by donor agendas that do not always appreciate the realities of African contexts and value systems, particularly in terms of lifelong learning, civil society and globalisation. Adult education research must therefore take cognisance of the ways in which research needs are addressed in Africa. It should be conscious of its relationship to policy and practice. African adult education research agendas cover a broad spectrum of issues from impact studies regarding donor aid to small-scale action research to the building of national data systems. The research questions themselves must be focused and specific to the chosen topic.

KEY POINTS

- The way research is conducted depends on the researcher's worldview and purpose.
- Adult education research in African contexts should be vigilant to the influence of colonialism and neo-colonialism: it should notice the interface between

African values and the impact of colonial and neo-colonial interventions on research practice and outcomes.
- Research in African contexts has to be aware of the relationship between stakeholders and research participants: the researcher should consider whose agenda the study itself is promoting and for whom the researcher is doing the inquiry.

▩ ACTIVITY

Work in small discussion groups for this activity. Allow about 45 minutes. The following texts provide summaries of different studies on literacy levels in an African country. They address the problem from very different perspectives. The first text represents a commissioned study by an external evaluator and the second text represents a report that was undertaken by people living in the same country in which the study took place.

Your task is to look for differences in style, attitude and approach. Identify how literacy is defined in each report. Describe how the information is collected and explain what kind of information is revealed in each study. Discuss and explain how the language used in each report helps to define the value base of the people in the study. Make suggestions on how each study could have been conducted differently. How might a different approach influence the research conclusions?

Text 1

In today's modern age it is essential for everyone to be able to read and write; to regularly update themselves on new skills and knowledge so they can be part of the developed world. Literacy in this context is described as functional literacy. That is the ability to read and write simple words and phrases that are necessary for everyday living. The research team were commissioned by the Government to investigate the scale of literacy problems in the country. Their primary task was to establish the number of illiterates in the country and to formulate proposals for eradicating the problem.

A test was therefore devised to identify the minimum standard of reading, writing and numeracy skills of individuals in two sub-districts, totalling 2 000 adults ranging in age from 18 to 45. The test asked people to write their name, calculate simple addition and subtraction exercises and to identify key words relevant to their culture, such as cow, goat, maize, and field. The exercise was conducted in English and the local language, and details of initial schooling, if any, were obtained.

The results of the survey revealed that only 60% of men and women had received initial schooling up to Grade 7. Few were utilising reading or writing skills in their daily activities and 50% were completely illiterate. This means that a literacy development programme on a mass scale is required. Recommendations include:

- Providing regular publicity campaigns through radio and extension workers emphasising the need to gain literacy skills.
- Providing textbooks that are relevant to the needs of adult learners. Where these are not available, school reading books are recommended.
- Teaching to be through the English language medium as much as possible, since most public material is written in English, though initial education classes may be in the mother tongue.
- Numeracy to focus on basic calculations with money and the ability to read bills, such as electricity, water, etc., so that immediate applicability can be utilised.

- A target of 100 000 people per annum to be reached, with a goal of complete eradication of illiteracy within five years.

Text 2

Literacy is a contested concept. It can mean the ability to read and write simple words. It can mean the strategies people use to store and retrieve information. In some contexts people may appear illiterate, while in others those very same people will demonstrate considerable communication skills and the ability to make use of words, signs, symbols and relevant mathematical calculations for their needs. As university academics in the country we therefore took the approach that first we must find out how people interact in their daily lives and what activities require them to develop or use communication methods beyond oral interaction. We talked to headmen and heads of households in six villages and six towns across the country. We explained that our purpose was to find out how people were using, storing and passing on knowledge and information in families, to the wider community and further afield. Meetings were held separately with male and female adults to discuss the purpose of our research and to ask for ideas as to what contexts would best demonstrate people's use of information and skills. We used both observation and in-depth interviews, employing, as co-interviewers, trusted contacts who could communicate in the local language.

In town we found that the women who worked as informal street sellers would employ rapid mental arithmetic in the exchange and selling of goods to customers and to each other. A system of signs indicated fixed prices that customers would read from and judge whether to buy, barter or not. Similarly, public notices were read by certain key people and announced at local gatherings so all could obtain the relevant information.

In the villages women would exchange news and advice at the village standpipe. Messages that needed to be relayed on paper would be a combination of pictures, signs and symbols. Strategies for memorising key dates or events were evident inside houses by pictures, objects or written notices. Most households obtained news regularly from the radio. Awareness of, and critical analysis of, current affairs was disseminated and discussed through local networks. A cooperative system of support for particular needs was available through word of mouth based on general awareness of individual skills, aptitudes and knowledge. Individual interviews revealed that while formal schooling was not easily available in villages, informal learning took place through family gatherings, the repeated use of proverbs, folk tales and religious meetings. The degree to which people required an understanding of the written word or numbers was decided individually. In most cases those individuals would seek out relevant information as and when they needed it from people who were known to have been to formal school. However, there was increasing interest in the idea of more formal learning, since changing lifestyles and connections with town life required a more sophisticated, individualistic use of letter writing to loved ones and purchasing of new kinds of consumables.

Our recommendations, therefore, were:

■ To conduct a needs analysis within people's natural locations, asking people what kind of information they most needed to utilise in written format.
■ To develop locally designed learning materials around key topic areas that the learners themselves construct with the facilitative support of a teacher.

■ To devise a popular theatre or other local mechanism for conveying informal messages that will publicise people's knowledge and their strategies for obtaining it, and be a means of inviting new learners to construct their own needs analysis for literacy studies.

FURTHER QUESTIONS

1 Which kinds of organisations deliver some form of adult education?
2 List an adult education research problem for each organisation you have named.
3 Do civil society organisations provide the same kind of adult learning programmes that government departments provide?
4 If not, describe some of the differences.
5 List some examples of commissioned research and some examples of indigenous (home-grown) research.
6 Which of these examples influenced policy decision-making in your country?

SUGGESTED READINGS

Burchfield, S. (ed.). 1994. *Research for educational policy and planning in Botswana*. Gaborone: Macmillan Botswana.

Indabawa, S. A. and Mpofu, S. 2006. *The social context of adult education in Africa*. Cape Town: UNESCO and Pearson Education.

Indabawa, S. A., Oduaran, T., Afrik, T. and Walters, S. (eds.). 2000. *The state of adult and continuing education in Africa*. Bonn: DNFE Namibia and IZZ/DVV.

Nafukho, F. M., Otunga, R. N. and Amutabi, M. N. 2005. *Foundations of adult education in Africa*. Cape Town: UNESCO and Pearson Education.

Youngman, F. 2000. *The political economy of adult education and development*. London: Zed Books.

Chapter 2

Foundations of inquiry

OVERVIEW

This chapter explains the role of research in development and puts forward the argument that current dominant research traditions exclude other knowledge systems in the production of knowledge. Three conventional research paradigms – namely positivist/post-positivist, interpretive and emancipatory – are explained and contrasted, and their connection to Western thought and Western values is discussed. The implications of these paradigms for the research process are also discussed.

The chapter will demonstrate that each paradigm implies a methodological approach with a philosophical base that points to assumptions about perceptions of reality, what counts as truth, and value systems. It will show that the researcher's worldview on what counts as knowledge, truth, reality and values impacts on:

- The way research questions are conceived and framed
- Choices on research designs and the way they are articulated
- Decisions about research instruments and procedures
- Analysis, interpretation and dissemination of the research findings.

The place of African knowledge systems within each of these paradigms is also highlighted.

LEARNING OBJECTIVES

By the end of this chapter, you should be able to:

1 Explain the role and impact of research on development in Africa.
2 Comment on the conventional research paradigms.
3 Critically appreciate the influence of philosophical and theoretical perspectives on the research process.
4 Understand and apply the different philosophical assumptions about reality, knowledge and values to the research process.

nkonsonkonson

KEY TERMS

axiology The nature of values and their role in the construction of knowledge.

epistemology The nature of knowledge and how to establish truth in the construction of knowledge.

hermeneutics Interpretation of social texts.

hypothesis An informed guess about an event, the existence of a phenomenon or the relationship between variables.

ontology The essential characteristics of what it means to exist, or the nature of reality.

operational definitions Defining a variable according to the way it is measured in a study.

phenomenology Studies that focus on the meanings people attach to their experiences.

variable A characteristic that the researcher is interested in investigating.

⊞ BEFORE YOU START

Discuss the following concepts:

- Philosophy
- Theory
- Paradigm
- Ideology.

Do you have a personal philosophy? If so, write it down and after you finish reading this chapter decide in which of the philosophies discussed in this chapter yours fits. Does this philosophy play any role in your life?

Do you know of any theories that are popular in adult education? List them. What role do these theories play in adult education research? After you finish reading this chapter compare your list to the list of theories mentioned in the chapter.

SITUATING KNOWLEDGE SYSTEMS

Development has relied exclusively on one knowledge system, namely the modern Western one. The dominance of this knowledge system has dictated the marginalisation and disqualification of non-Western knowledge. In this latter knowledge system ... researchers and activists might find rationalities to guide social action away from economistic and reductionistic ways of thinking (Escobar, 1995: 13).

Research continues to play an important role in the lives of adult people. For example, it informs policy and practice in community projects earmarked to bring about developmental change. Research is involved in building a body of knowledge to inform decision-making and action, and in building theories and principles that become sources of reference in daily activities. It is also concerned with creating new knowledge and deciding which knowledge is credible, trustworthy, true or legitimate. The question to ask is, whose knowledge has

been legitimised? Who participates in the production of new knowledge?

Consider the research that has been carried out in African communities. What does the body of knowledge reveal about the nature of these communities? Has the theory and knowledge led to informed practice or improved standards of living for the people in these communities? Where is this body of knowledge? Has it been communicated to the people? Or is it lying in the libraries where only intellectuals can retrieve it 'to play games with'?

Mshana (1992), for instance, shows that in Tanzania the capitalist mode of production suppressed the peasant communities' knowledge production, political action, social organisation and ecological management. He shows that peasant communities are regarded as primitive and ignorant and continue to receive directives from above. Consequently, research-driven projects to bring about developmental change have failed to bear fruit. Seepe (2000) shows that the Western researchers and their Western-trained African counterparts, through tactics of omission and exclusion, continue

The Hoodia cactus plant

to leave out the contribution of Africa to knowledge production.

The stealing of African indigenous knowledge of local resources, such as plants and herbs, by Western-trained researchers and Western companies shows how African indigenous knowledge systems continue to be marginalised.

The Hoodia cactus plant grows in the Kalahari Desert, a vast area of land that cuts across Botswana, Namibia and South Africa. This land is the original home of the San. The San, through observation and experiments, discovered that the Hoodia cactus has medicinal properties that stave off hunger. Generation after generation of the San have thus chewed the plant on long hunting trips. According to Commey (2003), Phytopharm – a United Kingdom based company working with the South African Council for Scientific and Industrial Research – isolated the active ingredients in the cactus that enable the San to go on long hunting trips without eating. This property, long known to the San, has been renamed P57 by the company. P57 has been manufactured into a slimming pill that fetches large amounts of money for pharmaceutical companies. The San had to fight to claim their intellectual property of the qualities of the Hoodia cactus plant.

The disillusionment with research-driven projects that fail to address the needs of people, and malpractices such as the appropriation of indigenous knowledge by Western-trained researchers, continue to raise questions about the nature of research and how to best carry out research. Scholars continue to debate whether research is neutral or value free. There is general agreement that conventional social science research approaches are embedded in the thinking of Western philosophers working in the context of their cultures, histories and experiences. Research in this context cannot be viewed as neutral. It is also important to

note that, even though Western knowledge is dominant and dictates the 'marginalisation and disqualification of non-Western knowledge' (Escobar, 1995) it doesn't signify a single system of thought. Western philosophers have for a long time differed in their views on research and how to best approach the research process. These differences have led to three distinct research approaches called research paradigms.

The word *paradigm* denotes the researcher's worldview (ways of thinking about and seeing the world), conceptual framework or theoretical orientation that informs the choice of the research problem investigated, the framing of the research objectives, research designs, instruments for collecting data, data analysis and reporting of the research findings. The three paradigms discussed in this book are the positivist/post-positivist, interpretive, and emancipatory research paradigms. These paradigms compete for recognition, acceptance and supremacy. They all claim to be producing valid, reliable, trustworthy and dependable knowledge. Today researchers from diverse cultures continue to debate about the best way to conduct research. In addition, questions are asked about the appropriateness of applying the research procedures, techniques and categories of analysis embodied in these paradigms across all cultures and situations. The following are some of the issues raised:

■ There is a growing argument that women and other marginalised groups, such as the disabled and minority groups, may fail to participate fully in a research process because standard topics in the research do not reflect their experiences or are communicated in a language that they do not connect with their experiences. Take, for example, the HIV/AIDS epidemic. It is taking a long time for the poor in the rural areas in Botswana to connect the name HIV/AIDS, which is widely discussed in the media, with the disease, named differently in their communities, that continues to kill many of their family members. Feminists such as Devault (1999) observe that language may in other cases reflect male experiences and thus fail to communicate the experience of women in general.

- Countries that suffered from imperialism and colonisation critique research processes and procedures on the basis that they are informed by, and rely on, literature and a worldview that continues to perceive the coloniser as the knower and the colonised as ignorant. The history of imperialism and colonialism, for instance, enabled a dichotomous construction of the world along the binary opposites of coloniser/colonised, centre/periphery, Black/White, self/other and legitimate knowledge/indigenous beliefs. In all these configurations the colonised, who form a large part of what is named the Third World, remained peripheral. The colonised could not be credited with the production of knowledge, nor could the knowledge and value system that informed knowledge production be considered legitimate (Smith, 1999). It is for this reason that some researchers believe the process of framing research questions, gathering data, data analysis and interpretation may, if not carefully examined, exclude the colonised worldviews and ways of knowing and thus fail to communicate their experiences.

- Another criticism centres on what is researched and how it is researched. Research is often expensive. Most developing countries do not have the funds to finance research. Thus, international donor agencies and external research funding institutions in most cases provide the funds for research. Samoff (1992) specifically shows how aid agencies use funds to promote intellectual hegemony. He argues that aid agencies prefer to fund research problems in developing countries that can be addressed through uniform methodologies. This criticism raises questions about how research problems are identified and how the methodologies adopted in the studies are chosen. It brings into question the relevance of the research projects that researchers embark on under the pretext of informing policy and decision-making.

- Bias in research may arise because of the social position of the researcher in the community where the research is conducted. There are many categories that illustrate the social standing of a researcher in the community where the research is carried out. A researcher's position or social standing in the community may be defined in terms of geographic location (e.g. Western versus non-Western), race, religion, ethnicity, social class, educational background, gender, history, colour or even age, weight and height, depending on how these categories are perceived or valued in the society. Each of these categories implies or carries with it some power. It is this power that defines what is true, credible, trustworthy and legitimate. Truth is thus a matter of power (Foucault, 1980). It is this power that further guides and shapes the researcher's relationship with members of the community where the research is carried out. The power position informs the researcher's worldview, shaping what they research, how they research it and what they select to report. The power position of the researcher will also determine the type of experiences that the researched can communicate to the researcher.

You will find that some of the problems raised are addressed by the methodologies employed in the three paradigms, while others are not. The problems raised are an indication that the paradigms are not in any way perfect and that the process of finding the best ways to conduct research continues. Scholars continue to:

■ Find ways of conducting research in such a way that the worldviews of those who have suffered a long history of oppression are given space to communicate from their frames of reference and worldviews
■ Improve on the techniques of gathering data and adding to the existing body of knowledge and techniques that utilise knowledge systems from the marginalised and former colonised nations
■ Find strategies for carrying out research that allow previously marginalised languages to name and communicate their experiences in ways that create new concepts, terms and categories of analysis
■ Adopt theoretical frameworks that accommodate different modes of seeing the world
■ Find new ways of reporting research findings.

The emphasis in this book on an African perspective is an attempt to discuss the research methods in ways that challenge you to examine the approaches you adopt to research so you can see whether it is inclusive of marginalised groups and worldviews embedded in the African people's experiences, histories and cultures. It is important therefore that you fully understand the paradigms and their implications for the way you choose to conduct research. What follows in this chapter is a description of each paradigm in terms of the philosophies that inform its approaches and the way questions about reality, knowledge and values

are understood, explained and incorporated into research processes and procedures. The differences in these paradigms can be understood by looking at:

■ The philosophies and theories that inform each approach
■ How each approach perceives or explains the nature of reality (*ontology*), knowledge (*epistemology*) and values (*axiology*)
■ The methodology used in the research.

⌗ ACTIVITY

List as many of the marginalised worldviews embedded in the African people's experiences, histories and cultures as you can, and consider ways these can be acknowledged and integrated into the research process.

POSITIVIST/POST-POSITIVIST PARADIGM

Philosophical underpinnings

Positivism is a position or approach which holds that the scientific method is the only way to establish truth and objective reality. Can you imagine using scientific methods to carry out research on witches? The positivists would conclude that, since the scientific method does not yield any tangible results on the nature of witches, they do not exist. Positivism is based upon the view that natural science is the only foundation for true knowledge. It holds that the methods, techniques and procedures used in natural science offer the best framework for investigating the social world (Hitchcock and Hughes, 1995).

Many philosophers, among them Aristotle (383–348 BC), Francis Bacon (1561–1626) and John Locke (1632–1704), contributed to what is known as positivism today. Aristotle believed that the world operates on fixed natural laws, which could be discovered through observation and reason. He also believed that these fixed laws could be tested, measured quantitatively and the results verified. He is considered a realist and his thinking classified the philosophy of realism. Realism takes the stand that reality is viewed in material terms. Realism assumes an external reality that can be objectively investigated. The basic tenet of this philosophy is that if something exists, it exists in a quantity and can be measured. The realist maintains that truth exists in nature, that is, the physical world is discoverable by people through the utilisation of scientific methods. Knowing begins with sensory intake, which is then ordered and organised by means of intellect.

Francis Bacon (1561–1626) and John Locke (1632–1704) also added to our understanding of positivism as it is known today. Their thinking has been labelled empiricism. Empiricists believe that the senses and empirical data are the most important sources of knowledge. According to empiricists, people know things by seeing, hearing, touching, smelling and observing them. Empiricists use deductive methods to generate generalisations from specific sensory data.

It was, however, Augustine Comte (1798–1857), a nineteenth-century French philosopher, who summed up these related ideas by different philosophers as positivism. Like the empiricists and realists, he believed that genuine knowledge is based on sensory experience and can be advanced only by means of observation and measurement.

The middle part of the twentieth century saw a shift from positivism to post-positivism.

Post-positivism is influenced by a philosophy called critical realism (Trochin, 2002). The post-positivists, like the positivists,

believe that there is a reality independent of our thinking that can be studied through the scientific method. However, they recognise that 'all observation is fallible and has error' and that 'all theory is revisable'. Reality cannot be known with certainty. Observations are theory laden and influenced by researchers' biases and worldviews.

Objectivity can nevertheless be achieved by using multiple measures and observations and triangulating the data to get closer to what is happening in reality. You will learn more about triangulation in Chapters 8 and 9. It is important to note that the post-positivists have a lot in common with positivists. Most of the research approaches and practices in education today would fit better into the post-positivist category. The two will therefore be treated as belonging to the same family. It is important to note that a number of philosophers working over a long period of time contributed towards the thinking and the body of knowledge and worldviews embodied in each paradigm.

Every philosophy has a distinct way of explaining the nature of reality (ontology), knowledge (epistemology) and values (axiology). Philosophies that inform the three research paradigms provide different answers to these questions.

Assumptions

Below are positivist/post-positivist assumptions about the nature of reality (ontology), knowledge (epistemology) and values (axiology).

Ontology: Ontology is that body of knowledge that deals with the essential characteristics of what it means to exist. For instance, if one says witches are real, the next question one has to address is: 'In what form do they exist?' On the question of what is the nature of reality, the positivists hold that there is a single, tangible reality that is relatively constant across time and in different settings. Part of a researcher's duty is to discover this reality. Reality is objective and is independent of researchers' interest in it. It is measurable and can be broken into *variables*. Post-positivists concur that reality does exist but that it can be known only imperfectly because of the researcher's human limitations. The researcher can discover reality within a certain realm of probability (Mertens, 1998).

Epistemology: Epistemology inquires into the nature of knowledge and truth. It asks:

■ What are the sources of knowledge?
■ How reliable are these sources?
■ What can one know?
■ How does one know if something is true?

For instance, some people think that the notion that witches exist is just a belief. Epistemology asks further questions: Is a belief true knowledge? Or is knowledge only that which can be proven using concrete data? If one says witches exist, what is the source of evidence? What methods can be used to find out about their existence? For the positivist, the nature of knowledge is inherent in the scientific paradigm. Knowledge is those statements of belief or fact that can be tested empirically, can be confirmed, verified or disconfirmed, and are stable and can be generalised (Eichelberger, 1989). Knowledge constitutes hard data, is objective and therefore independent of the values, interests and feelings of the researcher. Researchers only need the right data-gathering instruments or tools to produce absolute truth for a given inquiry.

The positivists borrowed their experimental methods from the natural sciences. Within this context, the purpose of research is to discover laws and principles that govern the universe and to predict behaviours and situations. Post-positivists believe that perfect objectivity cannot be achieved but is approachable.

Axiology: Axiology refers to the analysis of values to better understand their meanings and characteristics, where they originate, their purpose, whether they are accepted as true knowledge and their influence on our daily experiences. It deals with the nature of values and their role in the construction of knowledge. For the positivist, all inquiries should be value free, and researchers should use the scientific method of gathering data in order to achieve objectivity and neutrality during the inquiry process. Post-positivists modified the belief that the researcher and the subject of study were independent by recognising that the theories, hypotheses and background knowledge held by the investigator can strongly influence what is being observed. These assumptions about the nature of reality, knowledge and values influence the research process. An example of positivist/post-positivist study is presented in Sample Study 2.1. Refer to it to confirm some of the research processes within this approach.

Research methodology

The research problem

The purpose of research is to predict, test a theory, and find the strength of relationships between variables or a cause and effect relationship. Quantitative researchers begin with ideas, theories or concepts that are operationally defined to point to the variables in the study. A variable is a trait, concept or characteristic that the researcher is interested in measuring or observing. The problem statement at minimum specifies variables to be studied and the relationships between them. Variables are operationally defined to enable replication, verification and confirmation by different researchers. Operationally defining a variable means that the variable is defined according to the way it is used or measured or observed in the study.

In a literacy study by Botswana's Central Statistics Office (CSO, 1997) a sample survey design was adopted. Variables, for instance 'literacy' and 'ability', were operationally defined. Research questions, research objectives and *hypotheses* were constructed to further clarify the research problem. The researchers constructed these independently of the participants. They were therefore pre-determined and fixed.

Researchers use either research questions or hypotheses, depending on the type of research design. A research hypothesis is an informed guess about an event, the existence of a phenomenon or a relationship between variables. A research question can be written as a hypothesis and vice versa (see Chapter 7 for illustrations). Researchers are most likely to use research questions or objectives with survey research, and hypotheses with experimental and quasi-experimental designs. In the Botswana literacy study (CSO, 1997) (summarised in Example 2.1), research objectives and procedures were built around the definition of literacy used by UNESCO. Tests were used to measure reading and numeracy. Skills measured in numeracy and reading are clearly delineated and are again limited by the definition of literacy. How relevant do you think this definition is to the life experiences of the people? Do you think the people being researched share the researchers' definition of literacy? In most cases, research within the positivist/post-positivist paradigm is more about what researchers want to know – what knowledge and theory they want to legitimise. The researchers in the Botswana literacy study note:

The narrow definition of literacy currently held by the Botswana National Literacy Programme may, to some extent, have

influenced the development of tests for this survey [...] Advanced functional literacy skills were not tested (CSO, 1997: 9).

Commeyras and Chilisa (2001) have questioned the value of the study in providing information on the development of literacy in Botswana. They argue that the survey results reveal very little about the actual literacy gained by the people in Botswana and the variety of literacies that exist. Neuman (1997) notes that researchers in the positivist/post-positivist research paradigm adopt a technocratic approach where they ignore questions of relevance, ethics and morality to follow orders, or to satisfy a sponsor or a government. It is thus generally viewed as a 'legitimating ideology of dominant groups' (Neumann, 1997: 45).

Research design

The research plan is highly structured. There is concern about how variables are measured and about sampling procedures that minimise error and allow for generalisation of the research findings to the population from which the sample is drawn. Context-ual variables that might introduce error in the study are controlled. For instance, demographic variables such as sex and location may introduce error if the data is treated as if it comes from a homogenous population. These variables are included in the study.

Instruments for gathering data include questionnaires, tests, observations or experiments; all aimed at producing numbers as data. Probability samplings, including simple random sampling, stratified random sampling, cluster sampling and multi-stage sampling, are used. Note for instance the precision with which sampling was effected in the Botswana literacy study (CSO, 1997). Also note the emphasis on probability sampling. This was done so the results could be known within a certain probability and could be generalised to the population from which the sample was drawn. See Chapter 6 for a discussion of sampling procedures.

Data analysis

Data analysis starts after data collection. Statistical procedures are essential tools for analysing, summarising and presenting results. Statistics, as well as tables and graphs, are used to report findings. The researcher uses impersonal language to report the findings and omits statements about values from the written report.

⚏ ACTIVITY

Read through Example 2.1 and identify where and how the positivist/post-positivist paradigm was used.

EXAMPLE 2.1
(Adapted from CSO, 1997)

Statement of the problem

The survey was designed to measure the country's literacy, not only by the number of years spent at school (formal school), but also through the testing of objective literacy skills. In this survey, 'objective literacy' was defined as 'The ability to read and write in either Setswana, English or both; and the ability to carry out simple mathematical computations.' 'Ability' was ascertained through results of literacy tests in Setswana, English and Mathematics.

Specific objectives were:

■ To assess gender and age literacy differentials
■ To assess factors influencing school

attendance
■ To assess the impact of literacy programmes and factors relating to accessibility of educational facilities
■ To identify the most pressing needs in terms of educational policies and provision in order that the priorities can be set for the future direction of adult literacy programmes in Botswana
■ To assess socio-economic and cultural factors that may be associated with literacy problems in the adult population.

Research design

Sample survey.

Sampling procedures

Enumeration areas (EA) were identified. These are small geographic areas which represent an average workload for an enumerator. The average EA was 120–150 dwellings. EAs were subdivided into blocks. An average block was 50 households. Blocks were organised by type of area. Urban blocks were grouped into strata of their own. Rural areas were organised into the following strata: villages, lands, cattle posts and freehold farms. Probability sampling was carried out at block level, type of dwelling, household and individual level. Total sample size was 46 129 households.

Instruments and procedure

Questionnaires and tests were used. An individual questionnaire was administered to Botswana citizens in the age group 12–65 with an educational attainment of Standard 4 or lower and not currently attending school.

In this study the process of decoding was assessed through tasks that required respondents to read out loud some words and sentences and that required them to identify and match words with pictures, in both Setswana and English. The process of writing was assessed through tasks that required respondents to write down dictated sentences in both languages.

The numeracy tests covered the skill of number naming, in which the respondents were required to read given numbers aloud; number writing, by requiring the respondents to write down dictated numbers; and solving of written arithmetic problems. In the latter task respondents were given written problems to read and solve. The problems involved addition of a number of cattle to that of donkeys and the numbers are embedded in the prose text. Other numeracy skills tested in this study included the ability to solve arithmetic equations involving the concepts of addition and subtraction ($50 - 20 =$; $10 + 40 =$) and that of reading time. The survey came up with a pass mark of 50% to determine the literate and illiterate, based on a two-point scale of correct and incorrect answers to test items.

Results

The survey found that 68.9% of the adult population are literate in either Setswana or English. Females had higher literacy rates: 70.3% compared to males: 66.9%. A total of 193 662 persons aged 12 years and over had never attended formal school.

THE INTERPRETIVE PARADIGM

Philosophical underpinnings

The positivist/post-positivist paradigm today remains under criticism by the interpretive paradigm. The interpretivists differ with the positivists on assumptions about the nature of reality, what counts as knowledge and its sources, and values and their

role in the research process. The interpretive approach can be traced back to Edmund Husserl's philosophy of phenomenology and to the German philosopher Wilhem Dilthey's philosophy of hermeneutics (Eichelberger, 1989; Neuman, 1997).

Phenomenology: Phenomenologists use human thinking, perceiving and other mental and physiological acts, and spirituality to describe and understand human experience. From the phenomenological perspective, truth lies within the human experience and is therefore multiple; it is time, space and context bound. Under these assumptions, a belief or claim coming from a culture one does not understand is consistent and correct. In contrast to the positivist/post-positivist paradigm, phenomenologists/interpretivists believe that research should produce individualised conceptions of social phenomena and personal assertions rather than generalisations and verifications.

Hermeneutics: The term comes from the name Hermes, a god in Greek mythology who had the power to communicate the desires of the gods to mortals (Neuman, 1997). Hermeneutics involves a reading and interpretation of some kind of human text. The text of our social world is complex. Hermeneutics is therefore the process whereby it is possible to come to an understanding of a given social text and choose between two or more competing interpretations of the same text. In reading and interpreting the text, one can look at the relation of parts to the whole and do it in a dynamic and interactive way that would lead to a fuller and newer understanding of the actual life situation (Eichelberger, 1989). Interpretations occur within a tradition; within space, time and a specific situation. Phenomenology and hermeneutics thus largely inform assumptions on the nature of reality, knowledge and values in the interpretive paradigm.

Ontology: On the question of what reality is, the interpretivists believe that it is socially constructed (Creswell, 1994; Mertens, 1998) and that there are as many intangible realities as there are people constructing them. Reality is therefore mind dependent and a personal or social construct. If you believe, for instance, that witches exist, it is your personal reality, a way in which you try to make sense of the world around you. Reality in this sense is limited to context, space, time and individuals or groups in a given situation and cannot be generalised into one common reality. These assumptions are a direct challenge to the positivist's assumption about the existence of a tangible external reality. The assumptions legitimise conceptions of realities from all cultures. The question, however, is: How many of the realities from the African perspectives have been considered to be valid? The majority of the Botswana communities' understanding of reality, for example, is influenced by their connectedness to earth (*lefatshe*) and the spirits (*Badimo*) (Chilisa, 2003). There are individual realities as well as group-shared realities. Of interest is how these assumptions about the nature of reality are built into the research process. In Chapter 3 possible ways in which assumptions about the nature of reality in African contexts can be built into the research process will be explored.

Epistemological assumptions

Interpretivists believe that knowledge is subjective because it is socially constructed and mind dependent. Truth lies within the human experience. Statements on what is true and false are therefore culture bound, and historically and context dependent; although some may be universal. Within this context, communities' stories, belief systems and claims of spiritual and earth connections should find space as legitimate knowledge. Often, however, even intrepretivist research operates within the mode of a Western historical and culture-bound research framework and treats these belief systems as 'barriers to research or exotic customs with which researchers need to be familiar in order to carry out their work without causing offence' (Smith, 1999: 15).

Axiological assumptions

Intepretivists assert that, since reality is mind constructed and mind dependent and knowledge subjective, social inquiry is in turn value bound and value laden. The researchers are inevitably influenced by their values, which inform the paradigm chosen for inquiry, the choice of issue, the methods chosen to collect and analyse data, and the interpretation of the findings and the way the findings are reported. The researcher admits the value-laden nature of the study and reports values and biases. An example of the interpretive study is presented in Example 2.2. Refer to it to confirm some of the research processes within this paradigm.

Methodology

Purpose of research

The purpose of interpretive research is to understand people's experiences. The research takes place in a natural setting where the participants make their living. The purpose statement of the study expresses the assumptions the interpretivist uses to understand human experiences. Assumptions on the multiplicity of realities also inform the research process. For instance, the research questions cannot be established before the study begins, but rather evolve as the study progresses (Mertens, 1998). The research questions are generally open ended, descriptive and non-directional (Creswell, 1994). A model consisting of a *grand tour question* followed by a small number of sub-questions may be used. The grand tour question is a statement of the problem that is examined in the study in its broadest form, posed as a general issue not to limit the inquiry (Creswell, 1994). Imagine that you are carrying out research among adults in your community. What are some of the issues that might still limit the inquiry process? In Africa, colonial rule created a dichotomy of the coloniser as knower and colonised as ignorant. It also created a midway space of the educated as better than those who did not go to school, though still lesser than the colonisers. Within this context, the position of the researcher as more educated than the majority of the adults still limits the inquiry process, as the researched are most likely to suppress indigenous knowledge in favour of acquired knowledge from the media. Within the interpretivist assumptions, researching in African contexts should involve questioning even the language used in the research process. Should one speak of research questions, for instance? Some of these issues are addressed in Chapters 8 and 9.

Research design

The researcher gathers most of the data. In recognition of the assumption about the subjective nature of research, researchers describe themselves, their values, ideological biases, relationship to the participants and closeness to the research topic. Access and entry to the study site are important and sensitive issues that need to be addressed. The researchers have to establish trust, rapport and authentic communication patterns with the participants so that they can capture the subtle differences and meanings from the participants' voices (Denzin and Lincoln, 1998). Ethics is an important issue

that the researcher addresses throughout the study whenever it arises. For instance, in a study on community youth and HIV/AIDS, Ntseane (2002) notes that one of the participants started crying when they related stories about the loss of their relatives. Ntseane in turn cried. The ethical dilemma here is what to do next. Should the researcher make an appointment for another meeting to continue the interview, advise the participant on professional counselling or simply forget about the participant?

Common designs include ethnography, phenomenology, biography, case study and grounded theory (Creswell, 1994). These are explained in Chapters 8 and 9. Data gathering techniques are selected depending on the choice of design, the nature of the respondents and the research problem. They include interviews, observations, visual aids, personal and official documents, photographs, drawings, informal conversations and artefacts. Three other ways of collecting data are based on ways of perceiving reality, knowledge and values in African contexts. These are theorised as:

- Democratic and community-centred ways of knowing
- The story-telling framework
- Language as a bank of knowledge.

It is also shown how divination can inform the research process. In theorising about these techniques, there is now a focus on what knowledge is produced by whom and for whom, the spaces where the knowledge is produced, and language as a bank of knowledge (see Chapter 3).

Non-probability sampling is employed. Purposive sampling is the most common sampling strategy used. This strategy allows the researcher to choose participants who are judged to be knowledgeable on the topic under study. The different approaches under purposive sampling include intensity sampling, homogenous sampling, criterion sampling, snowball sampling and random purposive sampling. Sampling and data collection end when no new information comes from the participants. These procedures are discussed in detail in Chapter 9. Consider the implications for purposive sampling when researching adults in African contexts. Who are the most likely knowledge experts and whose knowledge is it? In Chapter 3 you will learn about African indigenous intellectuals called sage philosophers.

Data analysis

Data analysis continues throughout the data collection process. Findings may be in the form of dense descriptions that include direct quotations from the participants and documents, diagrams and tables rather than statistics and graphs. Creativity in reporting the findings is to be promoted. The report of findings can adopt many forms that include poems, drama, stories, videotapes and even songs. Imagine reporting findings to a community of adults in an African country. What will be the most effective way to present these findings? Chapter 14 discusses ways of disseminating data among adults in African contexts.

⊞ ACTIVITY

Read Example 2.2 and discuss the features that make it an interpretive design.

EXAMPLE 2.2
(Summarised from Mabongo, 2002)

Research problem

The major purpose of the study was to understand the training needs in occupational health and safety of caregivers pertaining to their involvement in the provision of basic health care to terminally ill people, including those with HIV/AIDS, at home. The study entailed the collection of data in areas such as the caregivers' ability to relieve patients' distressing symptoms, precautionary safety measures, personal hygiene, coping mechanisms with the burden of care, and the motivational skills of caregivers.

Research questions

- What is the community-based caregivers' understanding of occupational hazards associated with health care at home, including the disposal of clinical waste?
- What is the caregivers' knowledge of the provision of quality of care provided at home?
- Are caregivers experiencing 'emotional stress and burnout syndrome' and, if so, how can they be assisted?

Method

The study employed a qualitative research design utilising a phenomenological approach. A phenomenological approach was specifically selected because it focuses on individual experiences as well as on human interaction.

Participants

Ten caregivers directly involved in care giving for eight terminally ill people were purposively selected.

Instruments and procedures

In-depth interviews, group focus interviews and observation guides were used to gather data. Focus group interviews lasted between thirty and sixty minutes. The participant observation method was used because it allowed the researcher to triangulate information collected during interviews with the actual behaviours and actions that occurred during caregiving. For rigorous and effective observation, a guide or checklist of what to look for was drawn up. Where necessary the researcher participated in caregiving. In this study the researcher acknowledged the following factors as potential bias that the readers should take cognisance of, when interpreting the findings:

■ HIV/AIDS issues arouse painful feelings with a tendency to over-sympathise with caregivers, who carry the burden of care.
■ The researcher's participation in the caregiving affected the relationship with the researched.

Results

Some caregivers expressed the view that they suspected that there was a risk of contracting HIV, an infectious agent causing AIDS. They expressed concern about the poor quality of the gloves used for protection and that the sizes were too short. The researcher confirmed that surgical gloves were used for different purposes of protection. Caregivers also attended to distressing symptoms of patients such as breathlessness, coughing and any form of pain. A caregiver was observed rubbing the chest and back of a breathless patient. Although this action was aimed at alleviating the discomfort, an upright position was appropriate to relieve the breathlessness.

Caregivers reported that they were not trained in their duties, as they revealed that they used their experience and common sense. Some caregivers declined the offer made by the researcher to assist in providing care such as bathing. One patient required supporting the back with pillows to assist breathing. Another caregiver had no idea how to manage a patient with a urinary catheter due to an incontinence problem. The patient was unable to control urine and as a result a catheter had been inserted to protect bed linen. Further to these, none of the caregivers whose patients were on TB treatment knew the reason for ensuring that the patients should have meals before administering these drugs. It must be noted that making meaning includes giving the reasons for actions. In the study, a ten-month-old sick infant, whose mother was also in the terminal stage of illness, was taken care of by the youngest caregiver. The researcher wondered whether the special needs could have been addressed. Generally, caregivers did not report most of the occupational risks associated with caring. This could explain limited information among caregivers in this area. Culture discourages disclosing what is considered family information to outsiders. Also, caring for a close blood relation is viewed as an obligation, so that associating care with hazards could be unacceptable.

THE EMANCIPATORY PARADIGM

There are scholars who criticise both the interpretive and positivist/post-positivist paradigms. Some scholars (Gillan, 1982) argue that most research studies that inform sociological and psychological theories were developed by white male intellectuals on the basis of studying male subjects. In the United States, African Americans argue that many research-driven policies and projects have not benefited them because they were racially biased (Mertens, 1998). In Africa, scholars (Chambers, 1997; Escobar, 1995; Mshana, 1992) argue that the dominant research paradigms have marginalised African communities' ways of knowing and have thus led to the design of research-driven development projects that are irrelevant to the needs of the people. A third paradigm has emerged, which has been labelled critical social science research by Neuman (1997), action participatory and feminist designs by Merriam and Simpson (2000), research with the aim to emancipate by Lather (1991) and emancipatory paradigm by Mertens (1998). The term *emancipatory paradigm* is adopted in this book to denote a family of research designs influenced by various philosophies and theories with a common theme of emancipating and transforming communities through group action (Mertens, 1998). One of the influential theories is Marxism, which was originated by the German philosopher Karl Marx. Karl Marx believed that those who controlled the means of production, that is, the ruling class, also controlled the production of knowledge and ideas. Inevitably the knowledge produced perpetuates the domination of other social classes by the ruling class. The theory also helps to explain the dominance of Western-based research paradigms and the marginalisation of knowledge produced in other cultures. Other theories include critical theory, feminist theories, Freierian theory, race-specific theories and post-colonial theories. Some of these theories are discussed in Chapters 3, 11 and 12.

Ontological assumptions

The emancipatory paradigm adopts the stance that social reality is historically bound and is constantly changing, depending on social, political, cultural and power-based factors (Neuman, 1998). Like the positivists/post-positivists, scholars within this paradigm adopt the stance that reality is out there to be discovered. They differ with the positivists/post-positivists in their belief that social reality is constantly changing. Reality has multiple layers, the surface reality and the deep structures that are unobservable. Theories and a historical orientation help to unmask the deep structures. An example of a study with a strong theory base and historical orientation is the study on the political economy of adult education by Youngman (2000). In this study the history of adult education and its interface with colonisation, post-colonisation, globalisation, class, ethnicity and gender is explored.

Critical theories are used to explore oppressive ideologies, myths that support and reproduce the status quo, and distortions and false appearances that stand in the way of change. Youngman believes that adult educators adopt theoretical stances and biases on the meaning of development that impact on their work. He argues, for instance, that adult educators reproduce class, gender and ethnic inequalities through the hidden curriculum, thus perpetuating poverty among the already disadvantaged majority of the adult population. His theoretical stance and analysis in unmasking surface reality and revealing inequalities come out in an analysis of a class discussion of family welfare educators (FWE), a cadre of village-level health educators, and their tutor regarding environmental sanitation and the building of toilets in the village.

The discussion was as follows:

Tutor: You want to talk to the community about toilets – that there are no toilets in the village so you can call them together so that …

FWE: If people tell me that they cannot afford to build toilets because they haven't got the means, what do I do? …

FWE: Most of my clients tell me they have no money to pay for things like contraceptives.
Tutor: That's not true. They have money; they spend it on beer drinking.

Youngman adopts a critical stance in his analysis of the transcript. He writes that 'the tutor expressed an ideology of class superiority in relation to the poor' (Youngman, 2000: 195) by comparing them to cattle and describing them as liars who deny they have money for contraceptives when they actually spend it on beer. An interpretive researcher would most likely describe these views and treat each as true, while an emancipatory researcher adopts a stance that exposes the power dynamics in social relations.

Epistemological assumptions

On the question of what is truth, the researchers within this paradigm maintain that knowledge is true if it can be turned into practice that empowers and transforms the lives of the people. Theory is the basic tool that helps the researcher to find new facts. The facts are built into a theory that is consistently improved by relating it to practice (Neuman, 1998). Take, for example, some of the collective stories, myths, language use and indigenous knowledge systems on gender relations (refer to Chapter 3). In the context of this paradigm, some of the meanings may reveal only surface reality. True knowledge in this context lies in the collective meaning made by the people that can inform individual and group actions that improve the lives of the people. Knowledge is constructed from the participants' frame of reference. The

relationship between the researcher and the researched is not based on a power hierarchy as in the interpretive paradigm, but involves the transformation and emancipation of both participant and researcher. In a study on literacy in Nigeria by Omolewa et al. (1998) the researchers relinquish conventional literacy methods for those based on the indigenous knowledge systems. The participants undergo a transformation and are empowered through a realisation of their potential as teachers, renewed confidence in their culture, its values and what they already know. Knowledge is built directly through practice as it unfolds in the participation of the people and the researchers.

Axiological assumptions

Researchers who adopt the emancipatory paradigm view research as a moral and political activity that requires them to choose and commit themselves to a value position. Researchers achieve objectivity by reflecting on and examining their values to ensure that they are appropriate for carrying out the research study. Unlike in the interpretive paradigm where every viewpoint is correct, some views will be wrong while others will be right.

Research methodology

Research process

The purpose of research is to destroy myth, illusions and false knowledge, and to empower people to act to transform society. Quantitative as well as qualitative methods are used in the research process. Techniques of collecting data and sampling procedures used in quantitative and qualitative studies are used. Participants are involved in identifying the problem, defining the problem, collecting and analysing the data, disseminating the findings and using the findings to inform practice. In the study by Omolewa et al. (1998), for instance, the survey method as well as oral texts, focus group interviews and individual interviews were used. The meanings of literacy evolved from the people's experiences and eventually informed the changes in the literacy programme. Common designs are the participatory rapid appraisal approach and action research (discussed in more detail in Chapter 11).

▨ ACTIVITY

Read Example 2.3 and do the following:

- Identify the features that place the sample study in the emancipatory research paradigm.
- What commonalities does the study share with those in the positivist/post-postivist research paradigm and the interpretive paradigm?

EXAMPLE 2.3
(From Omolewa, 1998)

Research problem

While there has been an increasing involvement of government in literacy promotion activities, it is observed that literacy has been constrained by the problem of non-growth, which includes an inability to replicate activities, an increasing pattern of wastage, the problem of learner reluctance and rejection, and the neglect of the ultimate objective of asking learners to take over the literacy venture. All the agencies involved in literacy promotion have had their share of these problems, thus making necessary the search for an alternative.

Research objectives

- Identify alternative strategies for the promotion of literacy in Nigeria, especially in rural settings.
- Provide a solution to the intractable problem of non-growth.
- Improve the replicability of literacy programmes.
- Reduce the pattern of wastage and learner apathy.
- Promote learner empowerment as literacy's ultimate goal.

Method

Combined elements of qualitative and quantitative research designs, combining a survey of the village with a historical analysis and a qualitative approach.

Instruments and procedures

Questionnaires, oral texts such as stories, language, proverbs, sayings and interviews.

Results

During the research it was established that the indigenous apprenticeship system offered an attractive alternative training programme. First, the system demanded that people should begin to serve as guides (teachers) soon after basic skills had been acquired. The guides, however, continue to serve under others who themselves continue their own learning.

There is a need to use aspects of the indigenous culture and practices to attract learners and to consolidate their interest. It is not enough to attract learners. It is more important to retain learners in the programme and to use them to publicise the value of the programmes to the hitherto unreached. Tradition encourages the cultivation of the virtues of tact, sympathy, understanding, courtesy, patience, punctuality, doing by example and practicability, all of which seek to enhance adult learners' commitment.

Discussion

The learners have cultivated an attitude that restores learning to its status in pre-colonial times, when education was continuing and lifelong and promoted even beyond death in stories and songs. The suspicion of learning, resulting from intervention of Islamic traders and Christian teachers, has given place to a revival of learning for learning's sake. Thus the participants in our project contend that learning is by no means a once-and-for-all affair, found only in pages of books and ending with the award of certificates. Rather, they contend that even the songs of birds teach lessons and the colour of the sky conveys a message to one who is eager to learn. The pride

in learning is thus a return to the roots of the indigenous society that took pride in the art of learning. It is also a rejection of the wrong ideas about Western education. For in the West, one is told, even in a village school, that the truly educated person knows how little he or she knows and that there is no end to learning (Omolewa, 1998).

SUMMARY

The framework adopted in this chapter and throughout the book is that the current dominant research paradigms should be continuously reviewed to accommodate other ways of conducting research and reporting findings that are embedded in African and other marginalised groups' realities, values and ways of knowing. The diagram below illustrates the framework (Figure 2.1). What the diagram shows is that as an adult educator you will choose

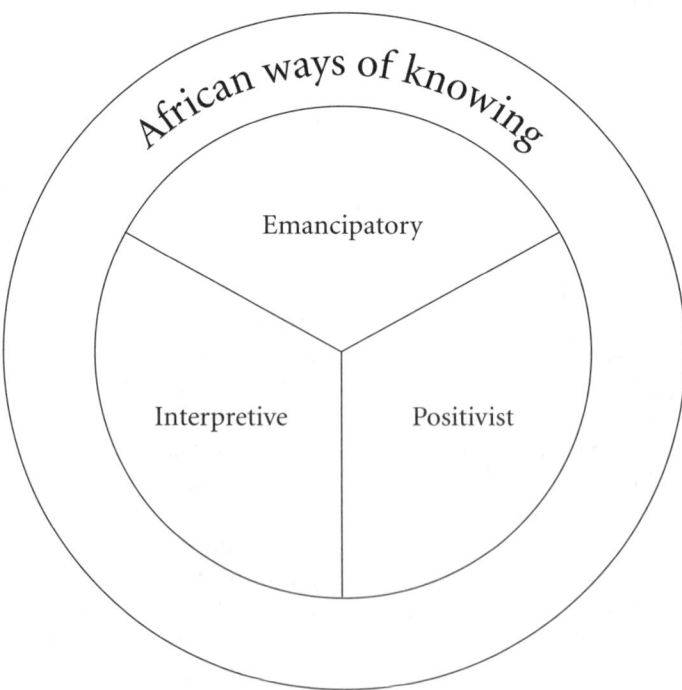

Figure 2.1

	Positivist paradigm	Interpretive paradigm	Emancipatory paradigm
Reason for doing the research	To discover laws that are generalisable and govern the universe	To understand and describe human nature	To destroy myths and empower people to change society radically
Philosophical underpinnings	Informed mainly by realism, idealism and critical realism	Informed by hermeneutics and phenomenology	Informed by critical theory, post-colonial discourses, feminist theories, race-specific theories and neo-Marxist theories
Ontological assumptions	One reality, knowable within probability	Multiple socially constructed realties	Multiple realties shaped by social, political, cultural, economic, race, ethnic, gender and disability values.
Place of values in the research process	Science is value free, and values have no place except when choosing a topic	Values are an integral part of social life: no group's values are wrong, only different	All science must begin with a value position; some positions are right, some are wrong
Nature of knowledge	Objective	Subjective; idiographic	Dialectical understanding aimed at critical praxis
What counts as truth	Based on precise observation and measurement that is verifiable	Truth is context dependent	It is informed by a theory that unveils illusions
Methodology	Research designs: quantitative; correlational; quasi-experimental; experimental; causal comparative; survey	Research designs: qualitative; phenomenology; ethnographic; symbolic interaction; naturalistic	Research designs: combination of quantitative and qualitative action research; participatory research
Techniques of gathering data	Mainly questionnaires, observations, tests and experiments	Mainly interviews, participant observation, pictures, photographs, diaries and documents	A combination of techniques in the other two paradigms

Table 2.1 Beliefs associated with the three paradigms (adapted from Neuman and Social, 1997; Mertens, 1998; Merriam and Simpson, 1998)

a research design informed by any one of these paradigms, depending on the nature of the problem you are investigating and your worldview. In addition, you will have to critically assess the research process and procedures to see if they allow the researched people to communicate their experiences from their frames of reference and whether they allow you to credit them with the production of knowledge. For a summary of the characteristics of each paradigm discussed in this chapter, refer to Table 2.1.

KEY POINTS

- Research practices are dominated by Western modes of thinking.
- Researchers should continuously search for methodologies that emphasise complementarity of knowledge systems and participation in knowledge production by previously marginalised groups.
- Research is value-laden, and the choice of a methodology used in a study implies a worldview or way of thinking about the topic of research, the community researched, the data collection procedures, analysis and reporting.

ACTIVITY

1 Visit the library and find journals on adult education or lifelong learning.

Select a journal and categorise studies done within a five-year period according to the three paradigms. Debate the visibility of African ways of knowing in these research studies.

2 Identify quantitative and qualitative studies that were done in your community during the twentieth century (1901–2000). Take, for instance, census surveys. What were the strengths and limitations of these survey studies?

FURTHER QUESTIONS

What is your worldview and how do you think it is likely to influence your research study?

SUGGESTED READINGS

Eichelbeger, R. T. 1989. *Disciplined enquiry: Understanding and doing research.* New York: Longman.

Mertens, D. M. 1998. *Research methods in education and psychology*. London: Sage Publications.

Neuman, W. L. 1997. *Social research methods*. Boston: Allyn and Bacon.

Samoff, J. 1992. 'The intellectual/financial complex of foreign aid'. *Review of African Political Economy*, Vol. 53, pp. 60–75.

Chapter 3

African perspectives

OVERVIEW

This chapter discusses imperialism and colonisation as processes that justified the dismissal of African ways of knowing. The chapter further explains post-colonial discourses as a body of texts and knowledge and engages in a discussion to dispute the description of post-colonial societies from Western perspectives. Perceptions of social reality, truth and values in the African contexts are discussed to show how they can inform the way research is carried out. Specific methods of gathering evidence based on some of the African worldviews are discussed. The aim is to explore processes through which African indigenous peoples can have greater autonomy in research and construct their own social realities in ways not so mediated by Western knowledge systems, which are framed solely within the boundaries of Western history, culture and worldviews. African philosophies and their assumptions about the nature of reality, knowledge and values are discussed. Their implications for research are discussed from the perspective of the following: ethnophilosophy, sage philosophy, professional philosophy, and political and ideological philosophy.

Four ways of doing research based on African philosophical assumptions are discussed.

LEARNING OBJECTIVES

By the end of this chapter, you should be able to:

1   Comprehend African philosophies and their implications for the research process.
2   Compare and contrast African philosophical assumptions about the nature of reality, knowledge, truth and values to Western-based philosophies.
3   Utilise African ways of knowing in carrying out adult education research studies.
4   Critically evaluate knowledge bases that are embedded in African traditions.

dwennimmen

KEY TERMS

Africanisation   Placing the African world-view at the centre of analysis.

African Renaissance   Africans' redefinition of themselves in their own terms.

ethnophilosophy   The collective world-views encoded in folklore, language, myths, metaphors, taboos and rituals as a unified form of knowledge.

philosophic sagacity   The analysis of accepted practices, beliefs and world-views in African communities.

political and ideological philosophy   Post-colonial discourses that seek to justify Africa as an equal partner in the global world.

post-colonial discourses   A body of knowledge engaged in the description and analysis of the colonised and their resistance to colonial rule.

professional philosophy   This subjects the definition of philosophy to Western categories of analysis and argues that African philosophy is still at the definition stage.

sage   A man or woman regarded as wise and knowledgeable in the culture and practices of his or her community.

⌗ BEFORE YOU START

Discuss the questions that follow.

1   What is your opinion on the existence of African philosophy and traditional African philosophers?
2   Do you think there are any philosophers in the adult populations in your communities?
3   What have they done to be called philosophers?
4   Have these philosophers and their philosophies played any role in the production of knowledge?
5   Discuss the quotation below and demonstrate its applicability to adult education.

… when philosophical foundations and the history of education are discussed, only one educational thought and practice is legitimised, that which is steeped in the European culture and tradition … (Goduka, 2000: 63).

41

RESEARCH METHODS: AFRICAN CONTEXTS

In Chapter 2, it was shown that research methodologies have been influenced by philosophies and theories developed by Western scholars in cultures totally different from those in Africa. In this chapter, philosophies and theories that can inform the process of knowledge production are explored against the background of Africa as a historically marginalised continent that suffered oppression and dehumanisation during colonisation and is still operating at the margins of the global economy. This chapter discusses how the history of colonialism and imperialism should frame what is researched and how it is researched. African philosophies and theories that seek to assert the African identity are explained and their implications for the research process discussed.

IMPERIALISM AND COLONIALISM

Imperialism is 'the practice, theory and the attitudes of a dominating metropolitan centre ruling a distant colony' (Said, 1993: 8). In 1884, the European powers, namely Britain, Belgium, France, Germany, Italy, Portugal and Spain, met at the Berlin Conference and divided Africa amongst themselves. African states became colonies of European powers and assumed names related to the colonial power, the settlers, explorers or missionaries. For example, present-day Zimbabwe was named Southern Rhodesia and Zambia was named Northern Rhodesia. European explorers, travellers and hunters were notorious for claiming discovery of African lands, rivers, lakes, waterfalls and many other of Africa's natural showcases and renaming them. This was a violent way of dismissing the indige-

nous people's knowledge as irrelevant and a way of disconnecting them from what they knew and how they knew it. Not only were the indigenous people's epistemological assumptions dismissed, also in dispute was the ontological question of what a person is. Most colonised people were considered primitive, barbaric and therefore sub-human. Smith notes:

> One of the supposed characteristics of primitive people was that we could not use our minds or intellects. We could not invent things, we could not create institutions or history, we could not imagine, we could not produce anything of value, we did not know how to use land and other resources from the natural world, we did not practice the arts of civilisation (Smith, 1991: 25).

Consequently, African indigenous knowledge systems were ignored and today remain an untapped resource that researchers can harness to contribute to knowledge production (Makgoba et al., 1999). African indigenous knowledge systems refer to the processes and technologies of producing, validating, storing, retrieving, disseminating and applying the knowledge embodied in the languages, legends, folk tales, and cultural experiences of African people. This knowledge is symbolised in cultural artefacts such as sculptures, basket weaving and house painting, and in music, dance and other practices such as farming, medicine, worshipping and so on. It is knowledge imprinted in the cultural practices of the peoples of Africa. This knowledge is useful for the adult education researcher because it:

- Provides useful data that enables researchers to challenge stereotypes about Africans
- Provides data that complements data

obtained through conventional research methods such as interviews and questionnaires, and sometimes allows the researcher to check and validate this data

- Allows the researcher to come up with new topics, themes, processes and categories of analysis, and modes of reporting and dissemination of information not obtainable through conventional research methods but responsive to the culture of the researched people
- Gives the researcher an opportunity to explore topics and themes missing in the literature that is written predominantly from the perspective of Western-trained researchers
- Gives the researcher an opportunity to theorise about methods and research processes from the perspective of the cultures and values of African people
- Makes visible the knowledge that was previously ignored, thus enabling the researcher to close the knowledge gap that resulted from colonisation, imperialism and the subsequent subjugation of indigenous knowledge systems.

It is not an easy process for African researchers to believe that the thought processes embedded in their cultural beliefs and practices, which have been labelled barbaric by the West, have a value, and that they can inform new ways of theorising the research process. Imagine that most of the knowledge systems informed by Western thinking have been exhausted. Imagine that Aristotle's realism, for instance, has been overused. Imagine that Africa has a reservoir of knowledge systems, worldviews and philosophies that can enable the theorising and practice of research. Or imagine the world as a global village where the international values of equality and social justice invite Africans to participate in the theorising and building of knowledge about ways of con-

ducting research that is responsive to the needs of the people. Take into account an Africa currently operating on the fringes of the global economy, with the majority of adults living in the rural areas, cut off from the participation process, except as consumers in the global market. Think of your role as a researcher who has to involve them in the production of knowledge. The change in your mindset is possible if you are able to understand imperialism as a process through which the colonial powers constructed, described, named, represented and ruled the African people through systems and strategies of distorted knowledge production, violent subjugation of indigenous voices, and political conquest under the guise of intentions to bring civilisation to the world. Imperialism marked the stagnation of development and the beginning of the process of underdevelopment in Africa (Rodney, 1979).

Post-colonial discourses

In reaction to imperialism, *post-colonial discourses* have emerged. These discourses constitute a body of knowledge engaged in the documentation, description and analysis of the experiences of the colonised and their resistance to colonial rule. They are engaged in a redefinition of self in relation to the global world and a 'search for answers and change in the face of entrenched global structures of oppression and exploitation' (Dube, 2002: 103). They are systems of thought that seek to analyse and expose Western colonising hegemonies of knowledge, norms, values and technology. For instance, 'in writing back, and talking back' to the metropolis and in counter-narratives that redefine Africans, Makgoba defined Africans as:

a people with a particular history, a people from a particular civilisation, a people who are unique in their socialisation and their way of interpreting the world; a people distinct but interdependent with other peoples; a people with originality; a people that gave birth to humanity, language, science, technology, philosophy, wisdom, and so forth (Makgoba, 1999).

The term post-colonial covers the pre-colonial, colonial and post-independence period (Ashcroft et al., 1998). This is so because colonialisation is still ongoing. While in the past the colonisers sought to control resources, today the competition is about control of the production of knowledge (Friedman, 1999). Globalisation has become a substitute for colonisation. Today the metropolis seeks to define, legitimise and control the right to know and what to know through the Internet, media, technology and the market system.

⌘ ACTIVITY

Discuss how globalisation (the 'metropolis') controls or limits what you know. Who sets the agenda for the information that is disseminated through various media?

AFRICAN PHILOSOPHY

What is African philosophy? When speaking of the ethnic or cultural origin of the philosophy in question, it may be more appealing to speak of African philosophies (Eze, 1997). In this context we may speak of the Bakalanga of Botswana's philosophy or the Igbo people of Nigeria's philosophy. Even within this context, some still deny that there is any such thing as African philosophy, let alone individuals who can be called African philosophers. Oruka observes that such thinking:

arises from the implicit belief that philosophy is an activity of some races and civilisations but not of others. Philosophy is 'Greek or European' – it is white. … it is white male (Oruka, 1998: 99).

Philosophy emphasises logic, rigour and critical analysis. Oruka goes on to note:

Postulating that logic, science, critique, and so on are un-African and typically accidental is an unconscious way of advancing imperialism, albeit a different form of imperialism, namely academic and intellectual imperialism (Oruka, 1998: 104).

In this book, African philosophy is perceived as a counter-argument to the Western philosophy agenda. It is perceived as 'part of our total package of liberation from the apron of Western intellectual colonisation' (Sogolo, 1993: XII). It is an engagement of discourses that claim back lost identities, create spaces for significant selfhoods, 'write back and talk back' to the West in modes couched in the histories, cultures, linguistic and life experiences of the people in post-colonial Africa (Eze, 1997; Sogolo, 1993). In the research process, how do participants claim back dignity, respect and self-identity, their knowledge and values? In what ways can a researcher in Africa plan and carry out research in ways that are not defined and limited by traditions of Western philosophy? In most cases, researchers operating within the mode of Western philosophy have dismissed knowledge systems couched in African indigenous peoples' social realities and value system as false, irrelevant and not offering valid explanatory models for managing and solving problems and improving life. In return, the researched have resisted the knowledge produced by the researchers for their own knowledge, based on their own ways of producing knowledge. This knowledge continues to inform their practices.

⊞ ACTIVITY

Think of the innovations and projects that are informed by Western knowledge systems. What counter-knowledge has been created by the people in your community? How does the knowledge affect the projects? What can be done?

PERCEPTIONS OF REALITY

The ontological question of the nature of reality in African contexts comes out more clearly when the question addressed is: 'What is a person?' To this question, the common answer is: 'I am because we are.' Among the Zulu of South Africa the expression is 'Umuntu ngumuntu ngabantu' ('I am a person through other persons'). Among the Bakalanga of Botswana the expression is 'Nthu, nthu ne bathu'. The people referred to here are the living as well as the dead (Louw, 2001). The dead are the ancestral spirits who form part of our extended families, are connected to us, are with us and talk to us in our daily experiences. African reality thus includes a spiritual belief system. It includes a connection and a respect for all the inhabitants of the earth, such as animals, birds and the vegetation. This respect is often explained through historical encounters that the people had.

For example, the Bangwato, an ethnic group in Botswana, do not eat the duiker because it is their totem. According to the legend, the duiker saved Ngwato in a war with his brother Kwena. Ngwato is said to have taken shelter in a bush where the duiker was grazing. When Kwena and his followers saw the duiker they concluded

that Ngwato could not be anywhere near. Since then the Bangwato, the descendants of Ngwato, do not eat the duiker. These experience-based realities also point to African respect for socially constructed realities. Thus realities such as those in the interpretivist paradigm are multiple and therefore differ depending on persons or groups of people's interaction with the environment, and their experiences, values and cultures. The difference with the interpretivist paradigm is that, while there is emphasis on a temporal, individual, constructed reality, in African contexts individual as well as group realities are accommodated. The reference to group realities points to the community-centredness of most activities. The community spirit is nurtured through a common value system.

Axiology

The value system of most African societies is built around respect for others and oneself. This respect is built around the concept of botho in Setswana. Botho in Setswana means 'humanness or personhood' (Segobye, 2000: 3) or respect. According to Segobye (2000) this concept can be tied to the Bantu language family and its people who form the majority in Africa. She notes:

> From proto-Bantu language originates the noun stem -tu meaning person. In Setswana this translates to -tho which, when prefixed with personal pronoun n- or mo-, gives us the word ntu / motho (Segobye, 2000: 3).

The value system ties in well with African worldviews on reality. To exist is to respect others and oneself: Nthu, nthu ne bathu. Often the questions asked in research are: What is the place of values in the construction of knowledge? What is the relationship between the researcher and the researched? From the African view of reality, knowledge is value-laden, as in the interpretive paradigm. The relationship between the researcher and the researched is one of respect for one another and oneself, empowerment of oneself and the other, and interdependence of the two because the welfare and existence of one is dependent on the other.

While ontological and axiological characteristics are general to African philosophy, four categories of African philosophies have emerged, or are 'in the process of doing so' (Kaphagawani, 2000: 88), each with distinct epistemological implications for the research process. These are as follows:

- *Ethnophilosophy*
- *Philosophic sagacity*
- *Nationalistic-ideological philosophy*
- *Professional philosophy*.

These, according to Kaphagawani (2000: 88), 'represent types of African philosophy on the one hand, and methods of philosophising in Africa on the other'. What follows is a discussion of these philosophies, their assumptions about the nature and sources of knowledge, and the implications for the research process.

Ethnophilosophy

Ethnophilosophy 'is a specialised and wholly custom-dictated philosophy that requires communal consensus' (Emagalit, 2001). It is a system of thought that describes, analyses and tries to understand the collective worldviews of diverse African peoples as a unified form of knowledge. It is based on 'the myths, folk wisdom and the proverbs and language of the people' (*Weekly Review*, 1996: L). Proponents of this school of thought, such as Placida Temple, Alex Kagame and John Mbiti, emphasise community spirit,

cooperation, collectiveness, democracy and consensus-building as values espoused through this philosophy. The contribution of this philosophy is on the following epistemological questions: What is knowledge? Who creates knowledge? How is it created? Who owns it? Knowledge from this perspective is the experiences of the people encoded in their language, folklore, stories, songs, culture, values and experiences. This knowledge is important ethnographic data for researchers. Emphasis on teamwork, cooperation, collectiveness and community spirit implies that knowledge is produced by the community, validated by the community and owned by the community. The language, stories, songs and folklore are the banks where the knowledge is stored, and can be retrieved and disseminated. Most contemporary songs, for instance, cannot be credited to one individual, nor can contemporary stories, which Western-trained researchers eventually label as myths, be credited to one individual.

Philosophic sagacity

The starting point for this philosophy is to dismiss as hegemonic the argument that a philosopher is one who received formal education and applies Western logic and principles of analysis. The contention is that in Africa there are philosophers even among those who did not go to school. Sagacity is a 'reflective system of thought based on the wisdom and the traditions of people' (Emagalit, 2001: 4). Through sagacity, the wisdom and beliefs of individuals who have not been schooled in the formal education system are exposed (*Weekly Review*, 1996). *Sages* are well versed in the wisdoms of their people and have a reputation for their knowledge.

Professional philosophers interview sage philosophers and, in the process, expose the wisdom of critical thinkers in Africa who guide their thought and judgement by the power of reason and inborn sight.

The contribution of this philosophy is to give legitimacy to knowledge articulated by indigenous intellectuals or wise women and men who may not have gone to school. This is an important epistemological assumption given that most African indigenous thought systems are not documented. Adult education researchers thus have a larger body of knowledge to consult in the research process. One of their duties would be to identify the sages in the communities and to work with them throughout the research process. Wise men and women have over a period of time created a system of thinking and practice that can inform the research process. Take, for example, traditional doctors who use divining bones in the consultation with their clients. The space used for consultation – the diviner-client relationship during the consultation process – can inform the researcher-researched relationship in African contexts (Chilisa, 2003).

The main contribution of this philosophy can thus be summarised as follows:

- It departs from the emphasis on communal production of knowledge in ethnophilosophy and focuses on the recognition of individual thought and production of knowledge as revealed by the sages.
- It creates space for researchers to accumulate raw data from community intellectuals or sages on their thoughts about the realities, knowledge systems and values of the people.

Nationalistic-ideological philosophy

This focuses on *political philosophy* and the production of post-colonial discourses. Renowned politicians like Kwame Nkrumah, Julius Nyerere, Leopold Senghor and Thabo Mbeki represent it. It utilises a variety of concepts and worldviews. Only a few concepts that are essential in framing the research process are discussed here, namely *African Renaissance* and *Africanisation*.

African Renaissance

The African Renaissance and its formulation is supposed to have originated from Mbeki's declaration in 1998: 'I am an African' (Nabudere 2002). Others, such as Prah (1999) and Mamdani (1999), trace it back to the nationalist thinkers of the 20th century. They argue that it was also expressed through nationalist movements such as Pan-Africanism and Black Consciousness. Mamdani (1999: 130) defines the African Renaissance as a re-awakening of mind that is driven by 'an African intelligentsia that includes all those who drive creative thought and frame debates, whether in the arts or culture, whether in philosophical or social thought.' The African intelligentsia is thus inclusive of the sage philosopher. The African Renaissance is a search for identity, a redefinition, and re-evaluation of the self and of Africa in the context of a globalising world. The following definition also helps to enhance our understanding of the meaning of African Renaissance:

> The African Renaissance is a unique opportunity for Africans to define ourselves and our agenda according to our own realities and taking into account the realities of those around us. It's about Africans being agents of history and master of our destiny. Africa is in a transformation mode. The renaissance is about African reflection and African redefinition (Makogoba, Shope and Mazwai, 1999: XII).

Africanisation

The Africanisation concept is relevant in addressing questions on the construction of knowledge in Africa about Africans, how it should be constructed and its place in the global context. The questions are justified because Western scholars in the name of anthropologists, historians, travellers, explorers and so on, using Western modes of thinking and conceiving reality, have dominated the production, reproduction and dissemination of knowledge about Africa. We have already noted the shortcomings of this knowledge. In this context, Africanisation refers to 'a process of placing the African worldview at the centre of analysis' (cited in Teffo, 2000: 107). Validating this view Prah notes:

> We cannot in all seriousness study ourselves through other people's assumptions. I am not saying we must not know what others know or think of us. I am saying that we must think for ourselves like others do for themselves (Prah, 1999: 27).

Africanisation does not discourage non-Africans from looking at Africa through their own lenses. It seeks legitimacy for African scholarship embedded in the histories, experiences, ways of perceiving realities and value systems of the African people. Africanisation can thus be viewed as an empowerment tool directed towards the mental decolonisation, liberation and emancipation of Africans, so that they do not see themselves only as objects of research, but also as producers of knowledge; and African researchers as people capable of theorising about the production of knowledge in ways embedded in the cultures and experiences of the African peoples.

Professional philosophy

Professional philosophy in the context of Africa refers to works produced by Africans trained in the field of philosophy (Bodurin, cited in Kaphagawani, 2000). Professional philosophers hold the view that African philosophy, like other philosophies, must be based on an analysis and interpretation of reality in general. Proponents of this school of thought, like Kwasi Wiredu, Paulin Hountondji and Peter Bodunrin, believe that for anything to pass as philosophy proper it must involve 'rigorous, sustained and independent thought' (Emagalit, 2001: 2). African philosophy, they argue, is still at the definition stage where the aim is to explain what it is. This outlook questions the value of not subjecting customs and traditions to questioning. For example, the main criticism it levels against ethnophilosophy is that transmitters of folklore do not, in most cases, develop an argument or thesis to substantiate their standpoint. They are most likely to say that their ancestors said the same thing. While this may be a fair criticism, it should be emphasised that the value of ethnophilosophy is in studying its texts to understand the process through which indigenous people produced knowledge, how it was produced, where it was produced and the modes of dissemination. This is not to argue that this body of texts is faultless. Some of the folklore, proverbs and language are oppressive to marginalised groups and seek to perpetuate the status quo. This body of texts is, however, important as far as it exposes the realities that inform the people's frame of reference. The community has a duty to discuss the value, contradictions and sometimes oppressiveness of some of these texts and create counter-narratives that are in line with the value of *botho* (humanness). Another argument raised is that sage philosophers cannot be called philosophers if they are not trained in the field of philosophy. This view mirrors an attempt to define philosophy from a Euro-centric standpoint which sees philosophy as 'white' and does not escape from Western epistemological hegemony. What proof is there, for example, that those who do not go to school cannot reason and apply logic in their analysis of events? The contribution of this philosophical approach is, however, important. The approach builds into the thinking process critical reflection of what is researched and how it is researched. The contribution of this philosophy is thus on critical reflection of the knowledge that is created and the need to be able to subject knowledge to critical analysis and build an argument that is sustainable.

Implications for research

African philosophies appeal to research that involves communities in the production of knowledge, involves indigenous experts, understands and frames problems in the context of indigenous language, uses contemporary stories, songs, folklores, myths and taboos as a framework for understanding, framing research problems, and researching the indigenous people's perspectives. It seeks a dialogue that invites communities to reflect on the worldviews that inform their practices and to critique and reconcile these with the values of humanness. African philosophies are important tools for analysing and privileging knowledge produced by Africans. They sensitise and equip the researcher with tools to assess representation and visibility of Africans in the knowledge production process. They justify the existence and legitimacy of other ways of researching embedded in African ways of knowing. They empower the African researcher to theorise about other ways of researching not tied to Western conventional methods

of researching. Three ways of creating knowledge based on African philosophical assumptions are discussed:

- Community-centred ways of knowing
- The story-telling framework
- Language as a bank of knowledge.

❖ ACTIVITY

Compare and contrast the four philosophical approaches described above and illustrate how they can contribute to the research process in adult education.

COMMUNITY-CENTRED KNOWLEDGE

There are three characteristics that distinguish these ways of knowing from the conventional methods of carrying out research. The main differences are in the spaces where knowledge is produced, the dialogue during the knowledge production and the power relations between the facilitator and the participants. In most African societies, the production of knowledge occurs in selected spaces that suit the nature of the knowledge to be produced. For example, in Botswana these selected spaces include the *kgotla* (village council or community assembly) in the main village where the facilitator of knowledge production is the chief or the chief's assistants; the *kgotla* in the smaller village where the headman is the facilitator; at ward level where the assistant of the headman is the facilitator; and finally at the extended family level where uncles and aunts have marked roles to play. Other marked spaces of knowledge production are the homes of indigenous professionals, such as traditional healers, carpenters, rainmakers and so on.

One of the characteristics that mark knowledge production in these spaces is the community-centered and democratic ways in which problems were identified, defined, discussed, and solutions found and disseminated to the entire community. In Botswana the process of researching a problem is etched in the concept of *pitso* (a call) and *morero* (dialogue). *Pitso* is the entry point of a *morero* and can be made only by community-selected dignitaries such as the chief, the headmen, elders of the ward and elders in an extended family. Let us take an example where the chief calls the people to the *kgotla* and examine the introduction to the problem and the dialogue process. The chief begins by summarising the nature of the problem. This is equivalent to specifying the statement of the problem in research proposal writing. This is followed by an invitation to the people to discuss the problem. The role of the people in the discussion is etched in the language that guides the discussion. Participation is encouraged through the sayings:

■ *Mmua lebe oa ba a bua la gagwe gore monalentle a ntshe la gagwe* (everyone has a right to a say, for even what might appear like a bad suggestion helps people to think of better ideas).
■ *Mongwe le mongwe o latlhela tlhware legonyana* (everybody throws in a word).
■ *Mafoko a kgotla a mantle otlhe* (every contribution has a value in a gathering).

The role of the chief and their relationship with the people is also etched in common language and proverbs used during the discussions. The proverbs illustrate the democracy that prevails during *morero* and the space occupied by the chief as a facilitator. *Morero* gives power to the participants to redefine the problem in ways that are compatible with the community value system, perceptions of reality and the needs and experiences of the people. The following proverbs underlie the discussion process:

■ *Kgosi ke kgosi ka batho* (a chief can only be successful through the help of the people, thus it is important to solicit their views).
■ *Kgosi thotobolo o latlhelwa matlakala* (all the bad and good views should be heard by the chief).

Advantages of community-centred ways of researching

In the *morero* research framework, the community defines the problem with every participant openly saying what they think. The knowledge produced is by the community and receives ownership by the community, which also takes responsibility to disseminate it. The *kgotla*, the space for the discussion, is a well-respected place with a long history of knowledge production, thus the knowledge produced is most likely to be accepted compared to knowledge produced by outside researchers working with individual research participants whose identities remain hidden.

Disadvantages

The main disadvantage of this framework is that women and the youth were not allowed at some of the spaces where knowledge was produced. Women and the youth were rarely allowed at the community centre. Adult educators work with the youth and with women. African researchers need to work out ways in which community-centred ways of researching can be adapted so that the participants include women and the youth as well as other marginalised groups that traditionally would not be allowed at the community centre.

ACTIVITY

Think of ways in which you can include women, youth and other marginalised groups in community-centred research. How would you avoid the possibility of offending the men in such a community?

STORY-TELLING FRAMEWORK

In Chapter 2 it was indicated that the African philosophical framework belongs to the emancipatory research paradigm. One of the tenets of this paradigm is its reliance on a historical analysis of problems. In the study by Omolewa et al. (1998) in rural Nigeria the researchers constructed the history of the village using stories told by the villagers. Stories are central to the lives of African societies. They have been used to collect, deposit, store and disseminate information. They have also been used as socialisation instruments. This socialisation is an important aspect in the research process because it foregrounds the responses that participants in a research study give. The socialisation stories are thus important in understanding the participants' frame of reference. Stories are also a reflection of the values of a society; they are also teaching instruments and a commentary on society, family or social relations. Given the value of stories in African societies, researchers need to be able to retrieve these stories so that African values, belief systems, and community and family histories are triangulated with other sources of knowledge. The use of these stories in adding information to the construction of knowledge can be illustrated by the stories told by the people of Botswana that reflect the values of society, stories that illustrate the socialisation process, and self-praise stories.

Stories that reflect the values of society

Imagine that a researcher wanted to study gender relations in a community and wanted to trace the history of this asymmetrical relationship between men and women. Most of the participants would locate the unequal relationship in the language, in proverbs like: *ga dinke di etelelwa ke namagadi pele, di ka wela ka le mena* (women cannot be leaders).

The story of origin would, however, defy this worldview. According to the Tswana story of origin, the people came from the hill of Lowe. When they came out, men and women were walking side by side driving sheep, goats and cattle. This story defies explanations that justify inequalities on the basis of traditions and reveals other ways of viewing gender relations based on tradition. It is an important contribution to knowledge production in the area of gender relations and could be used as an important entry point for a researcher who might be looking for intervention strategies to address the inequalities.

Stories as socialisation instruments

In Botswana, some of the most common stories told to boys and girls are the story of Masilo and Masilonyana and the story of Tsananapo. In the story of Masilonyana, boys are socialised to appreciate the value of cattle, while Tsananapo focuses on the value of beauty for girls. They show what boys and girls should want most in the society. A girl needed beauty to attract a man who has property. The stories also teach that one cannot get away with murder. Read the two stories that follow.

Masilo and Masilonyana: killing for cattle

Once upon a time, there were two brothers, Masilo and his younger brother Masilonyana. Masilonyana had a black cow and Masilo did not have one. Masilo was very jealous because he did not have a cow. He wanted to take Masilonyana's cow.

One day, when they were out in the plains, Masilo decided to kill his younger brother so that he would inherit the cow. Just after he killed his brother, he heard a little bird sitting upon the tree, singing and saying:

'*Masilo o bolaile Masilonyana* (Masilo killed Masilonyana)

'*Ka ntlha ya kgomo e tshwaana* (all because of his cow).'

Masilo killed the bird and buried it. In the evening when he brought the whole herd to the kraal, he saw the little bird re-appear. The bird landed by the gatepost and started singing its song again. His father asked him, 'Masilo, where is your younger brother?' Masilo said, 'I do not know.' His father said, 'Do you hear this singing bird?'

Tsananapo: killing for beauty!

Once upon a time, there was a very beautiful princess called Tsananapo. The village girls hated her intensely for her beauty.

One day, some of the girls who were her friends invited her to come with them to gather some firewood. They went deep into the forest. After they had gathered their wood, they built a big fire. One of the girls said, 'Let's play a little game.'

'What kind of game?' someone asked.

'Let us see who can jump over the fire!'

And so the girls started jumping over the fire. Tsananapo's turn came and she jumped over the fire and the girls cheered and said, 'Lets do it again.'

So the girls started jumping over the fire again. When it was Tsananapo's turn, someone pushed her straight into the flames. She died. Tsananapo's dog started singing:

'*Tsananapo, Tsananapo, ba mmolaile …* (They have killed Tsananapo …)'

The girls killed the singing dog and buried it. They picked up their wood and went back to the village. When they arrived, they were asked, 'Where is Tsananapo?'

'We left her resting under the tree,' they said. Right then, her dog reappeared and started singing its song, '*Tsananapo, Tsananapo …*'

Contemporary stories

Stories continue to be created around the social problems that haunt communities. In Botswana currently there are stories on HIV/AIDS. One common characteristic of these stories is that they show how the communities have defined the problem and that often the definition is embedded in the values of the society. The stories encode in them the analysis of the problem and the solution that has been prescribed. A common story in Botswana is that HIV/-AIDS is *Boswagadi,* which means an illness that inflicts those who indulge in love relationships with widows or widowers who have not performed the cleansing ritual. There is no cure for *Boswagadi.* The solution for the problem thus lies in avoiding widows and widowers. Researchers who incorporate these stories in their research process acknowledge the problem identified by the society, the society's analysis and solution to the problem.

In that way the research does not disregard the community or impose knowledge from outside. The stories are community owned and therefore common knowledge. Reflecting on these stories during the research process creates an entry point that enables dialogue where information can be analysed, and false knowledge that impedes progress can be discussed during the research process. Such a framework is important for a participatory research approach where the communities come with solutions to the problem and immediately act on the solutions.

Self-praise and self-identity stories

Self-knowledge and self-identity are cherished and important attributes in most African cultures. In the past, almost every individual knew their *self-praise story*. This is a story that tells the history and family tree of the individual, the valued attributes of the family lineage and any marked historical developments. What is important is that the definition of the self is also in relation to the environment: people, animals, birds and vegetation. Today, a majority of rural adults still recite these self-praises. The self-praises are stories that define their complete existence and mark their self-identities. Conventional research sums up the characteristics of the participants under what is called demographic variables, which normally include age, education and occupation. These demographic variables may add little value to a study, especially in communities in the rural areas where the majority of adults have little or no education and rely on subsistence farming for a living. The demographic variables in the conventional research process are individualistic and seek to understand the participants independent of their environment. Self-praise may be an important complementary technique of gathering information on the informants because it allows the researcher to understand the participants as they define themselves in relation to others around them and the environment. In the understanding of social reality, the self cannot be divorced

from others, the spirits and the environment. Such a worldview has to be built into the research process so that at each point the researcher understands the participants' definition of self.

⊞ ACTIVITY

Example 3.1 shows self-praise stories from one elder in Kopong village in Botswana. Study them and discuss their value in adding to knowledge production in research in African contexts.

EXAMPLE 3.1

Ke Moruakgomo wa ga Rampane (I am Moruakgomo the son of Rampane)
Wa ga Mothafela (Of Mothafela)
Wa ga Sekhutlo (Of Sekhutlo)
Mosimane wa ngoo-Motshwane (Of Motshwane)
Mmina kgodumo ya moselesele (My totem is the buffalo)
Ya re goo! Ya re goo! (Sound of the buffalo)
Monna fa a elosa o ipotsa a ikaraba (You have to think twice if you want to fight the buffalo)
E lathisa monna thobolo (A man would throw away his gun and run away in fear of the buffalo)
A bo aikanye setlhare (A man would climb up a tree)
A lebala gore tlhobolo ke tsala ya gagwe (Forgetting that they have a gun)

The explanation

Msanakgomo: This implies that his totem is a buffalo, which is compared to a cow in this name.
Kgodumo ya moselesele: This phrase is a praise to the buffalo. The phrase describes

the fierceness of a buffalo; it can tear down thorn bushes in anger.

Ya rre goo! Ya rre goo! This is the description of the great noise that the buffalo produces when it is angry.

Monna fa a e losa o ipotsa a ikaraba: As a result of its fierceness, hunting or attempting to shoot a buffalo is always a challenge to any hunter. If one misses it with his bullet it will pursue him and kill him.

Through these descriptions of the strength and fierceness of the buffalo, Mothofela proudly likens himself to this animal. Moreover, the self-praise also depicts his genealogy; his father is Rampape, the son of Mothofela, the son of Ntwayapele, son of Sekhutlo.

CULTURAL ARTEFACTS

Adult educators strive to assist the majority of the poor in the rural areas, marginalised ethnic groups, women and other disadvantaged groups to acquire the skills, knowledge and understanding that can enable them to improve their lives.

These were groups silenced by the oppressive ideology of colonialism and imperialism that always cast them as ignorant.

Today there still remains a danger that their voices may remain unheard because the methods of research, as well as the topics, words, categories of analysis and interpretations that researchers use, exclude their worldviews.

Cultural artefacts such as pottery, sculptures, home painting and basket weaving by ordinary women and men may bring to life topics and other categories of thought otherwise missing in the literature. Figure 3.1 and Figure 3.2 are examples of African cloth that express indigenous knowledge.

The Kente legend

According to Asante legend, weaving began after two hunters observed the spider Anante creating an intricate web. They copied the technique and brought their cloth to their chief, Oti Akenten. Kente (see Figure 3.1) has been worn since the late seventeenth century, when imported silk cloth was unravelled to obtain silk threads for inclusion in local hand-woven textiles.

The Ghanaian legend on the kente communicates African perspectives on production and ownership of knowledge. It is clear from this legend that the Africans recognised collective production and ownership of knowledge by all, including animals and all creatures in the environment. For instance, the contribution of the spider to the weaving of kente is acknowledged. The communication between the spider and the hunters could also illustrate the African value of connectedness with the environment, including living and non-living things. The legend thus opens spaces for new discussions on context in research. The legend would seem to suggest that it would be incomplete to discuss context in a study without describing the non-living and living in the community, and how people relate to the living, the non-living and the environment in general. Westerners often label value systems that connect people with the environment as superstition. Collective production and ownership of knowledge, especially by local communities in Africa, are also ignored. Refer back the production of P57 in Chapter 2. The contribution of the San's knowledge of the cactus and the ingredient that enabled them to go for long distances without eating is completely ignored.

Bamana women of Mali are the creators of the unique cloth design called *bogolanfini* (mud cloth) (see Figure 3.2). This ritual cloth has a pattern of circular motifs. The central panel symbolises motherhood, known as the 'the mother of the cloth'. Each configuration has a name that is descriptive of the beliefs and values of the Bamana.

Letters of the alphabet, Chinese and Arabic letters have remained the recognised ways of communicating in writing. The Bamana cloth design captures other forms of representing and storing information. These forms of writing and storing information have to be recognised, collected, anaysed and interpreted for use as baseline literature on research topics of interest.

LANGUAGE AS KNOWLEDGE

Language stores, upholds and legitimises the value systems of society. For research problems to be understood within the value systems of the researched people, it is important to incorporate in the research process the language that frames the problem. The language may exist in the names that frame the problem, expressions, proverbs and other forms of language. Understanding a problem from an analysis of the language used in discussing a problem is not unique to African contexts. It is commonly used by post-structural researchers and researchers using critical analysis. It is also common among interpretive researchers. It is, however, an important technique that needs to be emphasised in African contexts where research problems have for a long time been defined from the perspective of Western-trained researchers who also use Western language to define the

Figure 3.1 Bogolanfini (mud cloth). Ghana, Asante People, 20th C. Art of Africa Knowledge Cards, Hong Kong: Pomegranate Communications.

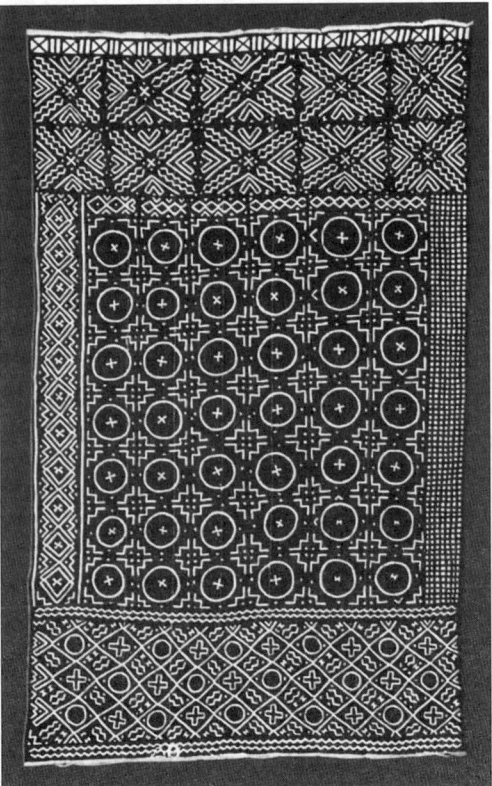

Figure 3.2 Skirt (bogolanfini). Artist: Guacho Diarra, Mali Bamana people, 1985. Art of Africa Knowledge Cards, Hong Kong: Pomegranate Communications.

research problems. Researchers in Africa (Youngman, 1998; Omolewa et al., 1998) have utilised language in the form of proverbs and sayings to explain indigenous people's understanding of researched problems. Youngman (1998) demonstrates how the concept of lifelong learning is encoded in the language of the people by citing proverbs that explain the concepts. The following are proverbs that demonstrate lifelong learning in Botswana:

- *Dilo makwati di kwatabolotswa mo go babangwe* (you get new ideas from others).
- *Noka e tladiwa ke dinokana* (a river becomes full from its tributaries).
- *Botlhale jwa phala bo tswa phalaneng* (the intelligence of an impala comes from its offspring).
- *Thuto gae golelwe* (there is always something to learn no matter how old one is).
- *Kkazena ua kuatua rune zena ua kengeza rune* (do not say that because you were born long ago you know everything) (Youngman, 1998: 10).

Omolewa et al. explain the value of proverbs in the tradition of the Yoruba in Nigeria through sayings. The following sayings explain the functions of proverbs:

Bi owe la nlulu agidigbo (when the agidibo drum is beaten)
Ologbonnii ijo o (proverbs and idioms form the core of its message)
Omaran nii moo (only the informed and wise can react appropriately to it. Only they know its true meaning).
The sayings indicate a deep and hidden meaning in indigenous language that explain experienced realities that experts or sage philosophers can explain (Omolewa et al., 1998: 45).

SUMMARY

This chapter has illustrated how imperialism enabled the suppression, dismissal and trivialisation of African indigenous ways of knowing. It has shown how African philosophy justifies the legitimacy of indigenous ways of knowing. The chapter outlines three ways of doing research that are embedded in practices, experiences, story-telling and language, and recommends that adult education researchers utilise them to ensure that perception of realities inform the knowledge production process.

KEY POINTS

- The need to recognise as legitimate ways of doing research that are embedded in the communities' ways of perceiving reality and value systems.
- The need for the researcher to be able to interpret material from the research participants' frame of reference.
- The need to recognise the value and limitations of oral traditions and the spaces where knowledge was traditionaly produced and be able to adapt these to suit current situations.
- The need to utilise African philosophy and worldviews to inform the research process.

☒ ACTIVITY

Imagine that you are researching the concept of lifelong learning. Incorporate the collected data or knowledge stored in:

- The language of the people
- Community stories that mark the origin of lifelong learning
- The history of the community as it relates to lifelong learning

- A critique of lifelong learning from a community expert, for instance a poet
- Family history of one of the community members that enhances knowledge of lifelong learning.

FURTHER QUESTIONS

1 Do you think it is necessary to create space for indigenous knowledge systems in the research process? What would you do if a member of your research committee or reference group rejected the inclusion of these knowledge systems in your research design?
2 Some scholars believe that the concept of philosophy is a Western one and that it is misleading to use the term philosophy to discuss African knowledge systems. What do you think? How would you respond to such assertions? Think of the examples that you could use to argue your case.

SUGGESTED READINGS

Chukwudieze, E. (ed.). 1997. *Postcolonial African philosophy: A critical reader*. Cambridge, MA: Blackwell.

Kaphagawani, D. N. 2000. 'What is African philosophy?'. In Philosophy from Africa, eds. P. H. Coetzee and A. P. J. Roux, pp. 86–98, Cape Town: Oxford University Press.

Makgoba, M. (ed.). 1999. *African renaissance: The new struggle*. Cape Town: Mafube Publishing and Tafelberg Publishers.

Omolewa, M., Adeola, O. A., Adekanmbi, G. A., Avoseh, M. B. and Braimoh, D. 1998. *Literacy tradition and progress*. Hamburg: UNESCO Institute for Education.

Oruka, H. O. 1998. 'Sage philosophy'. In *Philosophy from Africa*, eds. P. H. Coetzee and A. P. J Roux, pp. 86–98, Cape Town: Oxford University Press, pp. 99–108.

Segobye, A. K. 2000. *Situating the principle of Botho in Botswana society: A historical perspective*. Archaeology Unit, University of Botswana.

Smith, L. T. 1999. *Decolonizing methodologies: Research and indigenous peoples*. London: Zed Books.

Chapter 4

Doing a literature review

OVERVIEW

Chapter 3 discussed views of truth and reality in African contexts and their expression through African knowledge systems. This chapter utilises those concepts as features of the literature review. This includes looking at how alternative sources to the written word can still be part of the literature review. The chapter will discuss how to check the literature for authenticity and bias. In particular, it encourages you to check that the literature reflects African perspectives. You will also learn how to focus your search for information so that it is relevant to your research topic, and how to find, organise and retrieve information once you have collected it.

LEARNING OBJECTIVES

By the end of this chapter, you should be able to:

1 Use a variety of literature sources.
2 Organise and store relevant material for retrieval at a later date.
3 Use references appropriately and accurately.
4 Write a critically analytical literature review about a contemporary adult education issue from an African perspective.

KEY TERMS

Afrocentrism An Africa-centred perspective or worldview.

dichotomous Split into opposites.

epistemology Theory of knowledge.

indigenous knowledge Knowledge that comes from local expertise and experience.

literature review Summary of what has already been written about a particular topic.

OPAC Online public access catalogue.

plagiarism Copying someone else's ideas or work without acknowledging them as your source.

references Details of the authors and texts from which you obtained information used in your own text.

validate Give credibility to something.

🔲 BEFORE YOU START

From your reading so far and your own understanding of where knowledge comes from, make a list of all the different sources of knowledge you could use for a *literature review*.

WHAT IS A LITERATURE REVIEW?

Literature reviews come in many shapes and sizes. For the novice researcher, however, they can be a source of considerable anxiety. Nevertheless, as Chapter 5 will highlight, literature reviews are a crucial feature of any piece of research. They form the basis of the research proposal (the document you prepare before you start collecting data) and, once written, are a reference point for the whole inquiry. They may also form the basis of choosing a researchable topic. Your research questions will both inform and be informed by the literature review. So what is a literature review and what does it entail?

The purpose of a literature review

A literature review is a summary of what has already been written or said about your chosen research topic. Its purpose is to:

- Avoid duplication of earlier studies without knowing that you are doing so.
- Give credit to, and acknowledge the strengths of, previous findings.
- Legitimise (give credence to) your own assumptions.
- Find gaps in the available evidence so far (assess the weaknesses of earlier studies).
- Provide a theoretical basis for analysing your findings, or explaining how you view the world (your worldview, your value systems).
- Help you choose a researchable topic.
- Help you focus your research questions.

The literature review is written primarily in your own words. It refers to, and summarises, what others have said. Occasionally you quote directly from other authors, but the review should be your own story of how you have organised and interpreted existing viewpoints and information. One of the most difficult parts of the literature review is to make sure that what you read and write about is focused on, and relevant to, your own topic. So you have to read selectively. This will be discussed in more detail later.

It depends on the type of study you want to conduct as to whether your literature review is completed at the research proposal stage or after you have written up your findings.

A quantitative piece of research, for instance, will require the literature review to be almost complete before the start of empirical data collection (your fieldwork).

A qualitative study might rely on *action research* (a combined action-, reflection- and analysis-based project – explained in Chapter 10), or *grounded theory* (an exploratory study in a new field of work). It will start with a literature review to frame the study and raise some research questions. It is then likely to include a further literature review in a discussion chapter once the data is examined. For further information regarding the differences between quantitative and qualitative literature reviews, see Creswell (1994).

In most research reports there will be an initial literature review chapter that specifically talks about your topic. There are other phases in your study which will require some form of literature review. For example, if you are doing a study over an extended period of time, you will need to update your literature. There is also likely to be a methodology chapter that refers to relevant methodology literature to explain and justify your research methods. In all cases, however, the literature review is an opportunity to critique and build on previous knowledge.

Critiquing and building on previous knowledge

In Western models of adult education research, most sources of knowledge are perceived as academic texts that have received the status of approval by virtue of their publication or public exposure to other academics. So it is other academics who *validate* (give credibility to) the knowledge. They give it credibility if the knowledge has been presented according to a common set of academic principles. For example, Kane (1990) asks the researcher, when reading other works, to consider the author's reputation in the subject, and how the author explains the basis of his or her findings. This means the information is seen as objective and rational. Most knowledge that has been validated in this way comes from the West. Literature reviews are expected to use similar criteria to judge whether the information is useful or not. Kumar (1999) cites further examples of such criteria. He asks the reader to consider whether the findings can be generalised, whether the knowledge cited in the literature can be confirmed beyond doubt, whether there are other criticisms of the theories used and whether there are gaps in the knowledge.

All these factors must be taken into account, but there are also other considerations when reviewing literature. There is the question of bias. Griffiths (1998: 130) suggests that bias can appear at three levels in research.

- In the research process itself – the methods used
- In the values and politics of the researchers who chose which method to use
- In the wider context of the research – the way it is funded and the way the results are interpreted by others.

In all contexts, there is another source of bias: the assumptions of the authors who have written the texts you read as part of your research. So your reading of texts must include an examination of the underlying assumptions and values of the writer. Are they writing from a dominant, Western perspective? If so, how is this going to influence or represent your own African adult education context?

Earlier chapters have drawn attention to Afrocentric values that should influence both how texts are read, and what kind of texts should be considered. Chapter 3 has discussed, in detail, oral literature (*indigenous knowledge*) as text, and this chapter will also discuss such texts as potential sources of knowledge for the literature review.

Critiquing Western literature from Afrocentric perspectives

Teffo describes *Afrocentrism* thus:

> *Afrocentrism speaks to a mental attitude, a re-awakening that Africans have a perception and conception of reality that is peculiarly theirs, that they themselves are best equipped to articulate this reality* (Teffo, 2000: 108).

Looking at texts from an Afrocentric viewpoint means that texts must be scrutinised not just for their quality of presentation, but also for the degree of bias they show towards African values.

As Chapter 3 discussed African ways of thinking in detail, this serves as a reminder of some of the aspects that need to be considered when reading Western literature. There are a number of African writers who have already critiqued some differences between African and Western perceptions of knowledge (*epistemology*). Nyamnjoh (2002) and Goduka (2000) explain that the dominant Western epistemology perceives the world as *dichotomous*; that is, situations are either one thing or its opposite. So the world is either real and rational or unreal and irrational. It is either scientific and physical or religious and metaphysical. This denies African epistemologies that are based on the interconnectedness between the physical and the spiritual.

> *The popular epistemologies of Africa build bridges between the so-called natural and supernatural, physical and metaphysical, rational and irrational, objective and subjective, scientific and superstitious … making it impossible for anything to be one without also being the other* (Nyam-njoh, 2002: 5).

Omolewa et al. (1998) explain that in adult education terms this means that African academics may also be interested in knowing why something happens, rather than just how. Kanyoro (1999: 19) claims there is always a religious interpretation of events. It is not enough for a tree to fall because of physical causes such as lightning. People might also ask: Why did that tree fall on that particular person at that particular time in that particular way? This is because even the dead are still seen as members of the community; power belongs to the spirits of the ancestors who influence the accomplishments of the present.

While Western education is in some basic respects materialistic in nature, traditional African education is based on an essentially spiritual view of the world (Omolewa et al., 1998). This means that when Western texts discuss African contexts they must be examined in two ways. Firstly, to dismantle their representation of the African in texts and reveal any hidden meanings (Ashcroft et al., 1989), and secondly, for their responsiveness to the notion of connectedness between the earth, the living and the dead. It might

be useful, for instance, to draw on alternative literature – oral, traditional sources of indigenous knowledge – as both an additional resource and a basis from which to judge such texts. The focus of your own research, and worldview, will influence how you interpret these different viewpoints.

Indigenous knowledge sources

Goduka (2000) states that there is no single African voice or text. However, she emphasises that there is an African worldview that values oral traditions of proverbs, myths and legends as essential elements of indigenous wisdoms.

> *[these] provide succinct, easily remembered summaries of important ideas and experiences that are part of the shared cultural knowledge of indigenous communities* (Goduka, 2000: 76).

Other writers (Omolewa et al., 1998) also point to proverbs as a source of critical thinking in adult education contexts. Proverbs and sayings are a means of passing on shared cultural knowledge through generations – they are not static. They are adapted and developed through the telling, through the new experiences of each generation and through interaction with different audiences. But they always represent the connectedness of spiritually centred wisdoms and cultural practices (Goduka, 2000). Omolewa et al. (1998) emphasise how such proverbs also establish the link between traditional forms of education and lifelong learning.

> *From a knowledge of herbs to that of midwifery, from a knowledge of dos and don'ts to that of adjudication: until one dies and joins the ancestors, education continues. Even the dead are still members of the community and have obligations which*

include fostering education (Omolewa et al., 1998: 17).

So in the Nigerian language of Yoruba, the proverb: *'Ogbon ju agbara lo'* means that wisdom is greater than strength. Goduka (2000) points out that in the oral culture of the Shona, Tsumo proverbs form part of Shona legal procedure in Zimbabwe.

Many oral literatures are now available in text form, though it must be acknowledged that once such literature is cast in print, it cannot retain its dynamic nature. Nevertheless, Courlander (1996) and Kaschula (2001) provide a rich array of oral literature from across Africa. These can be drawn on as a way of critiquing more formal texts and as a resource for refining your research questions so they become relevant to a particular African context.

ACTIVITY

Discuss:
1 What proverbs or legends have your relatives passed on to you?
2 What were the main learning points in those sayings?
3 How do they influence your own values or daily behaviour?

WRITING A LITERATURE REVIEW

Literature may be academic or non-academic. It can come from libraries, the Internet or oral contexts, as well as sources such as government or departmental reports and minutes of meetings. But, whatever the source, you need to be systematic and organised about collecting and reviewing it.

Doing an outline plan

There is no single way to do a literature review. You must find a way that works for you. It also depends on what the study is about:

- Presenting a theory to be tested
- Placing a problem within related literature that will be tested and the results compared with that literature
- Presenting a practical, real-world problem that will be studied and analysed in relation to the relevant literature.

In any case, you need to plan what to look for, otherwise much time can be wasted in reading irrelevant material and probably missing key information. The simplest way to start is to brainstorm some key words that seem relevant to your topic. By the time you start a literature review you should have a fair idea of what the main research question is. This is where to start.

Suppose you want to investigate the effectiveness of programme planning in a certain organisation. In this case the research is about studying a problem and analysing it in relation to existing literature. What aspects of programme planning would you be looking at? A brainstorm of key words associated with programme planning in adult education might look like Figure 4.1.

After you have identified some keywords and themes you have to locate the keywords, or the problem, within the literature. A useful start may be theoretical literature on programme planning in adult education; possibly also other studies within Africa that indicate the main issues or concerns that need addressing in relation to their effectiveness. You may also want to explore traditional adult education practices and proverbs that demonstrate what has worked in the past in the region. So there are a

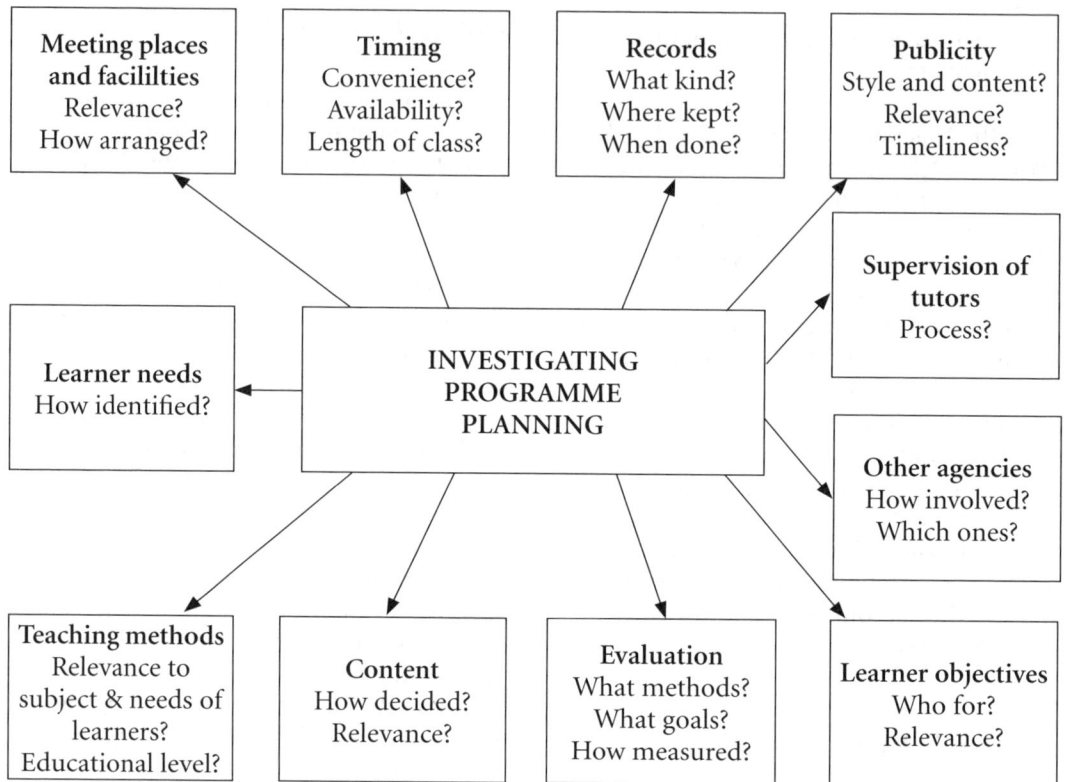

| Meeting places and facililties Relevance? How arranged? | Timing Convenience? Availability? Length of class? | Records What kind? Where kept? When done? | Publicity Style and content? Relevance? Timeliness? |

INVESTIGATING PROGRAMME PLANNING

Supervision of tutors Process?

Learner needs How identified?

Other agencies How involved? Which ones?

Teaching methods Relevance to subject & needs of learners? Educational level?

Content How decided? Relevance?

Evaluation What methods? What goals? How measured?

Learner objectives Who for? Relevance?

Figure 4.1: Keywords planning chart

number of sources from which to obtain literature.

⊞ ACTIVITY

Choose a research topic in adult education and create a suitable key words planning chart.

FINDING THE LITERATURE

Library sources

Most library sources are now recorded on computer databases (CD-ROMs and online). A number of authors of research text books (Creswell, 1994; Kumar, 1999; Merriam and Simpson, 1995) list a range of different databases so they will only briefly be mentioned here. Some useful ones for adult education research are: *ERIC* (Educational Resources Information Centre), *PsycLit* (Psychological abstracts), *Socio file* (Sociological abstracts) and *SSCI* (Social Sciences Citation Index).

Many university libraries also provide facilities for accessing online journals through *EBSCO Academic Search Premier*. The starting point for academic texts, however, is likely to be a university's Online Public Access Catalogue (OPAC). This shows what documents that particular university has available. Figure 4.2 shows what the OPAC screen usually looks like.

```
KEYWORD

AUTHOR/TITLE

SUBJECT

CALL NUMBER

JOURNAL TITLE

RETURN TO MAIN MENU
```

Figure 4.2: Online Public Access Catalogue (OPAC) screen

If you are in the early stages of your research you will probably want to click on the keyword section. By following the instructions on the screen you can access information about some useful texts that exist in your own library. When you have located the book you do not necessarily have to read it from cover to cover. By referring to your keywords planning chart you can often look in the index at the back of library books for these words to help focus your search. Then read only the pages that talk about the topic of your focus.

Books are not the only documents you can use. There can also be unpublished reports that are stored within local organisations.

Reports and other documents

When investigating a particular local activity there may be organisation reports, pamphlets, even minutes of meetings that can prove useful to the literature review. The chairpersons of voluntary organisations or departmental committees will usually give you permission to see these if you explain your purpose. When looking for local information these documents may be the best source.

Government departments and local organisations may also have policy documents or statistics that can help inform the study. From these documents you can analyse whether policies or trends have changed over time or whether organisations adopted particular strategies that proved successful or not. Minutes of meetings can give an idea of how these organisations discuss or think about certain aspects of their activities. They give an indication of how projects developed over a certain timespan. But with all these documents you have to be selective. They are specific to a particular context. They may contain very one-sided (biased) information. They may also contain material that is not relevant for your study.

If you want to broaden your search and make comparisons with international material, then the Internet is a mine of information.

Using the Internet

Nowadays, the Internet is a common source of information for countless purposes. However, it is not always possible to tell whether the information is reliable or not, since anyone can create a website and present their material for the world to read. There are two possible ways in which you can use the Internet.

The first, and most reliable, is to identify websites of international organisations that regularly update their reports and other documents. This can include electronic journals as well as organisations such as the World Health Organisation for information on HIV/AIDS, or the New Partnership for Africa's Development (NEPAD) in relation to poverty issues.

The second way in which you can use the Internet is to go through a search engine. This entails clicking the search button on the computer menu and typing in a key word. Once the screen reveals possible websites, you can decide whether to refine the search or select one of the displayed websites for further information.

The final source, indigenous knowledge, has already been discussed in detail, especially in Chapter 3, so it will only briefly be referred to here.

Indigenous knowledge sources

African societies contain a rich array of knowledge in local languages, which may not be in written form at all. These include legends, local proverbs and mythologies. You will find it useful to visit village elders, traditional doctors and chiefs for additional information that can contextualise the study and enable you to critique other literature from a relevant African perspective.

Depending on the nature of the study, you will need to ensure that this kind of literature is different from your empirical data collection. For instance, proverbs and sayings can be regarded as part of your literature review because they represent information that is passed down through the generations. They are therefore equivalent to written material. However, opinions and facts that relate to the present are not regarded as resource texts. They belong to your findings and data collection phase.

Similarly, if your study actually aims to find out what proverbs exist for a particular theme or society (for example, Youngman's 1998 study of traditional concepts of lifelong learning in Botswana), then your literature review will have to be confined to written material or proverbs from another society. This is because your literature is reviewed in order to set the scene for your study. It is there to enable you to compare and contrast it with the new data that you intend to collect.

ACTIVITY

Do an Internet search for material that is relevant to the key words planning chart you compiled in the previous activity. If you struggle to get useful results, refine your key word search by being more specific.

ORGANISING COLLECTED MATERIAL

Keeping records for future reference

Once you have decided what literature to review and where to get it, the important task is to organise any collected material in such a way that you can use it effectively, both for the immediate purpose and for future studies if necessary.

As with planning the literature review, there are many ways to record what you have read, and to store those recordings so they can be retrieved when required. The important thing is to avoid duplication of effort. Many a writer has spent frustrating hours looking for the exact *reference* or a missing page number for a quotation when the writing has been completed.

Example 4.1 contains some of the essential details that should be recorded for every library reference, Internet website or indigenous knowledge source. It is useful to attach to these essential details a summary of the relevant content in addition to any further page notes you may record. When copying the exact words, remember to insert quotation marks and the page reference.

EXAMPLE 4.1: DETAILS TO RECORD

- Author name
- Year, place of publication, ISBN or ISSN
- Title of article/chapter
- Title of book/journal/report
- Internet website address and date of retrieval
- Indigenous knowledge location (if relevant):
  - Ethnic group
  - Language
  - Country
  - Date of source
  - Source of knowledge
- Summary of whole chapter, legend, proverb or article and personal comments
- Page notes: include page numbers, especially for quoted material.

All this information could be stored on computer diskette, on cards or in a ring binder. Whatever method you choose, be consistent and know where you have put your information.

Remember to allow space for noting down your own critique or interpretation of the text, since the literature review is also an analysis of what you refer to.

⊞ ACTIVITY

Start your own record system for references:
- **Go to the library and identify one or two texts that are relevant to your research.**
- **Find a document on the Internet, using a search engine.**
- **Record the relevant details and main points for each document.**
- **Discuss in class any problems you encountered.**

WRITING ANALYTICALLY

'Critical analysis' in academic writing does not mean you simply criticise what has been written. It entails respecting the writer's viewpoint while looking for gaps or omissions. It involves identifying the strength of the text's argument (the main points and reasons for saying what it does) and then identifying ways in which that argument can be refined, improved or contradicted by alternative evidence. In adult education, literature reviews follow very similar formats:

- *Introduction*: a brief explanation of the topic and (if relevant) theoretical framework to be discussed and how the review will be structured.
- *Description of the problem*: the topic to be reviewed and why you are doing this (its significance).
- *Systematic review of the literature that addresses the topic*: usually broken down into themes. Thematic subtopics will each compare and contrast a body of literature. By comparing two or more separate authors the reviewer shows where there are agreements or disagreements about the topic, and also where certain aspects have not been covered before.
- *Conclusions:* where the reviewer summarises his or her own arguments and identifies potential avenues of enquiry.

The research study *Literacy, Tradition and Progress* (Omolewa et al., 1998) was an action research project carried out in Nigeria to investigate the effectiveness of literacy education embedded in traditional education practices. They identified the following subthemes for their literature review:

- Traditional education as greater empowerment

- Dialogue and language in traditional education
- Participation as return to tradition
- The scope of traditional education
- Conceptualising a return to tradition
- The experiences of Botswana, Kenya and Malawi (from Omolewa et al., 1998: table of contents).

These headings show that the topic has remained focused on traditional education practices from a variety of perspectives. The following example, adapted from one section (on the scope of traditional education) of this study, demonstrates how concepts are introduced and how different authors are discussed in order to build up a picture of the argument, while also acknowledging criticisms of this approach.

EXAMPLE 4.2
(Adapted from Omolewa et al., 1998)

Traditional education can be viewed from various perspectives. One of these is the ability of traditional education to meet all the needs of a society through learning content that is drawn from real-life experiences, rather than through subject-specific disciplines, or what Barrie Brennan has called its cross-disciplinary knowledge (Brennan, 1987: 76). There is also the unique nature of its teaching style (*pedagogy*). This includes its methods, how it uses local resources and how it evaluates the learning. Another perspective is the relationship between the learner and the facilitator of learning (the teacher), a relationship that relies extensively on the value systems that are relevant to the kind of learning taking place and the origin of such values.

In examining the main characteristics of the traditional education system in Africa, Msimuko (1987: 22) observes that, apart from being a lifelong process, it covers a broad range of topics, is applicable to a wide range of situations, and uses a variety of teaching styles. It is also learning that is collaborative, encourages cooperation and is voluntary (Mwondela, 1972: 14). The involvement of the entire family and indeed the locality makes it unnecessary to search for resource persons to help with teaching. When this is compared with the search for resource persons in Western-oriented education programmes, especially when they are outside of the learner's locality, the potential of the traditional education system deserves to be taken more seriously.

As regards the content of the traditional curriculum, Msimuko (1987: 28–29) lists areas such as history, social skills, rural education, language, music and dance, sex education, religious education, technical education and recreation. In a sense, the ultimate goal of traditional education is to re-create society and ensure social progress, and this is a major factor in determining its content. As the learning on offer does not follow a rigid pattern, the entire process becomes a kind of game. As Akinpelu observes: 'Life must be lived as a play … playing certain games' (Akinpelu, 1988: 35).

Academics often challenge the worth of traditional education. It is said that the traditional education system is too multi-disciplinary to warrant serious attention, that it is idealistic, even based on a possible distortion of the truth, because people are even trying to re-create situations that never existed in the past.

Yet others see it as being elitist and think that people in favour of the approach are actually the products of Western education. This criticism, as pointed out earlier, may be based on a lack of proper understanding of the traditional situation, especially in African countries. The reason for this report is to produce a better understanding of the traditional education system.

ACTIVITY

Discuss Example 4.2 in class.

- **How are references introduced or referred to in each paragraph?**
- **How do the writers then interpret the reference?**
- **Which phrases lead the reader into the ideas that follow (e.g. the first sentence)?**
- **How do the writers lead the reader back to their own research question by the end of the section?**

USING REFERENCES

You will see from both this textbook and Example 4.2 that whenever academic writers use information from other authors, they acknowledge their source in the text itself. This is done by citing the author's family name, followed by the year of publication.

In the case of a direct quote (placed in quotation marks) the page number of the original quote is also inserted. This helps the reader see your own work in its proper context. It also means that anyone else can go back to the original source for further details. Furthermore, it protects the writer from being accused of *plagiarism*. Plagiarism is when a writer uses someone else's ideas or writing as if they were the writer's own. An academic's writing is his or her intellectual property, so it is important to avoid being accused of stealing someone else's ideas when they have already been written down and made public. If you omit some words from the text, then these should be replaced by three full stops as Example 4.2 shows. This demonstrates that you feel it is unnecessary to include those particular words for your purpose, but want to avoid misrepresenting the original writing.

Even though you have already referred to authors in your own text, full details of the source must also be provided at the end of your report – like the authors of this book have done in the list of references at the back of the book. Now you can see the importance of keeping accurate records of material during the literature search. This applies equally to website information. The source of oral literature also needs to be explained but, unless your source was a written version, the details within your text should be sufficient.

The exact style for references varies from one document to another. But one of the most common styles used in educational research is the American Psychological Association (2001). This style is the one used in this book. But it is also acceptable to annotate your text with numbers like this[1] and then to use those numbers to list further details in the references. Sometimes the notes are placed as footnotes at the bottom of each page. The examples in the next activity show the differences.

ACTIVITY

Study these styles carefully, paying attention to how the references are set out.

End of the chapter annotated style

... what Barrie Brennan has called its cross-disciplinary knowledge[1] ...

Reference is cited at the end of the chapter:

1. Brennan, B. (1987: 76). Traditional Education ... A Pacific View. *Adult Education and Development*, Vol. 29.

End of the page footnote style

… what Barrie Brennan has called its cross-disciplinary knowledge[1] …

Reference is cited at the foot of the page where the annotation occurs:

---

[1]Brennan, B. (1987: 76). Traditional Education … A Pacific View. *Adult Education and Development*, vol 29.

SUMMARY

This chapter has taken you through the practical steps of conducting a literature review. The emphasis has been on demonstrating that an African perspective requires both critiquing Western texts for bias, and searching for indigenous knowledge that reflects the spirituality and connectedness of African value systems. Where possible, use oral literature that draws on traditional wisdoms and shared cultural knowledge. In all cases record keeping should be organised and systematic, as should the writing process itself. The review requires an introduction, a number of sub-themes that are addressed in turn, and a concluding paragraph that summarises the whole chapter.

KEY POINTS

- When the researcher reviews literature for an African research project the researcher should critically evaluate the literature's use of Western values.
- African indigenous knowledge from oral traditions can be an important resource for formulating and framing the research problem or critiquing dominant literature viewpoints.
- Literature searches and record keeping must be systematic and retrievable

before, during and after project completion.

ACTIVITY

Write a critically analytical literature review. Decide on a topic for yourself. Then:
- Decide on the referencing style.
- Plan the sub-headings or themes.
- Identify relevant literature.
- Keep records of your reading.
- Write your review using appropriate and accurate referencing.
- Develop the academic argument by referring to a number of authors on the same theme.

FURTHER QUESTIONS

1 What forms of indigenous knowledge are you familiar with?
2 Are they relevant as sources of knowledge in today's society?
3 If you can only find Western texts for your literature review, what can you do?
4 What other forms of record keeping, in addition to the examples in this chapter, can you suggest?
5 Look at a variety of literature reviews. Can you identify phrases or link words that are commonly used when discussing different authors?

SUGGESTED READINGS

American Psychological Association. 2001. *Publication manual of the American Psychological Association*, 5th edn. Washington, DC: American Psychological Association.

Courlander, H. 1996. *A treasury of African folklore*. New York: Marlow and Company.

Creswell, J. W. 1994. *Research design: Qualitative and quantitative approaches.* London: Sage Publications.

Higgs, P., Vakalisa, N. C. G., Mda, T. V. and Assie-Lumumba, N. T. (eds.). 2000. *African voices in education.* Lansdowne, South Africa: Juta.

Kashula, R. H. 2001. *African oral literature.* Claremont, South Africa: New Africa Books.

Kumar, R. 1999. *Research methodology: A step-by-step guide for beginners.* London: Sage Publications.

Merriam, S. B. and Simpson, E. L. 1995. *A guide to research for educators and trainers of adults.* Malabar: Krieger.

New Partnership for African Development (NEPAD). 2003. http://www.nepad.com/

World Health Organisation (WHO). 2003. http://www.who.int/en/.

Chapter 5

Getting started

OVERVIEW

This chapter demonstrates a model of conceptualising and writing a research proposal that engages in multiple epistemologies while at the same time situating the African worldview at the centre of analysis. The chapter starts by problematising the position of the adult education researcher in the research process. An understanding of the researched, the researcher's worldviews, and theoretical and methodological biases, as well as knowledge of the discipline, are discussed as factors that contribute to the process of selecting a problem. Ways of identifying problems and writing research proposals that are inclusive of African worldviews are discussed.

LEARNING OBJECTIVES

By the end of this chapter, you should be able to:

1 Identify the main elements in a research proposal
2 Evaluate and critique a research proposal
3 Write a research proposal that accommodates African worldviews.

sesa woruban

KEY TERMS

definition of the self   Researchers define themselves in terms of their perception of reality, beliefs and values; and in relation to the researched.

research proposal   A plan of how a research study will be executed, and an estimate of the time and costs involved during the study. The purpose of a research proposal is to convince the reader that there is a problem that is worth addressing.

BEFORE YOU START

Summarise the characteristics of adult education that were presented in Chapter 1, then discuss the following:

1 From the research studies and reports on adult education that you have read, what are the common research designs used in the discipline?
2 Some people think that adult education researchers use qualitative research methods and should not bother themselves learning about quantitative methods. What do you think?
3 What are the common theories in the discipline of adult education?
4 Discuss the different types of adult learners.
5 Some people think adult education excludes children as learners. How relevant is this thinking in Africa today, given the large populations of orphans who are not in regular schools?

Answers to these questions will help you to come up with your own definition of adult education that is relevant to your country. The answers will also help you to think about and prioritise problems in adult education that are urgent, topical and need immediate attention. They will also help you to think of the relevant research designs for the problems you are researching and the theories that you can use as tools of analysis for the data. This thinking process is what you need for writing a *research proposal*.

POSITIONING THE RESEARCHER

The adult education researcher in Africa works with adults and out-of-school youths, the majority of whom live in rural areas. This has implications for the research process in many ways. First, the adult education researcher has to address misconceptions that adults, especially those in rural areas, are ignorant because of the low literacy rates. Post-colonial perspectives, for example, Africanisation and the African Renaissance, call for research that has an agenda to regain communities' knowledge systems and cultural identities in order to allow continuous creativity in the processing and production of new knowledge. Adults as active research participants have a lot to contribute because of their indigenous literacies, accumulation of experiences that is a function of age, and expectations that research should improve their lives. In this context, the role of the adult educator is to listen, learn more and create space for African communities' indigenous knowledge systems.

The diversity of African communities requires the researcher's sensitivity to cultures, localities, language, ethnicities, gender, social class and age. These factors have a bearing on the type of research that should be carried out, how it should be carried out, the methodology of the study and the interpretation of the data. The context-laden socio-cultural realities of the researched compete with the researcher's own socio-cultural experiences, worldviews and perceptions. The researcher's worldviews and personal experiences, for instance, influence the choice of the problem to be researched, what to know and what counts as knowledge. For an illustration of how worldviews and personal experiences influence the choice of problems and how they are researched, refer to the three studies by

Omolewa et al. (1998), Mabongo (2000) and Central Statistics Office (1997) that are summarised in Chapter 2.

Identifying a research problem for the adult education researcher should thus begin with a conscious *definition of the self* in relation to the researched, in this case the majority of the adults in rural areas with low literacy levels. Crucial to this self-definition are:

- The relationship of the researcher to the researched
- Perceptions of reality
- What counts as knowledge
- The values that inform the process of knowledge production (refer to Chapters 2 and 3).

Much as the researcher's self-definition is desirable, it also needs to be pointed out that the researcher works within a complex global system where Eurocentric epistemologies are the recognised universal norm, and where Western multinational corporations and donor agencies exercise power in the construction of the researcher's experiences and preferences. In this context, adult education researchers need to consciously negotiate their position to ensure that the research is acceptable to the researched while at the same time finding a place in the global knowledge system. The position of the researcher and the type of problem to be researched should inform the methodology that is adopted for the study. The choice lies in one of three possible approaches, namely the positivist, interpretive or participatory research approaches. See Chapter 2 for research approaches. It is important to note that, for both the researcher and the researched, the choice of a methodology is essential; it is a definition of the researcher in relation to the researched and the position of the researcher with regard to Western epistemologies and the influence of global perspectives. For instance, a researcher who adopts Africanisation, Afrocentricism and African Renaissance perspectives would probably use research approaches anchored in worldviews that emphasise belongingness, connectedness, community participation and people-centredness. Such Africa-centred approaches would include creating space for indigenous researchers or intellectuals that include chiefs, poets, social critics, diviners and story-tellers in the production of knowledge, as well as community-centred techniques of gathering data that are informed by democratic ways of knowing in African communities; it would also employ stories as a framework for knowing and poetic frameworks as a way of perceiving social reality. Refer to Chapter 3 for a discussion of these frameworks.

⊞ ACTIVITY

Discuss the usefulness of the following questions as a guide to a definition of self in relation to the researched:

1 What is my relationship to the researched? Is it involved or detached? Is it that of a person who knows more than the researched?
2 Which worldviews inform my perception of reality? Where do I place Africanisation, Afrocentricism and the African Renaissance in the production of knowledge?
3 What counts as knowledge? Where do I place indigenous knowledge systems? How do I access this knowledge? What is its place in the produced knowledge? How do I use global science and technology to further develop indigenous knowledge systems?
4 What community value systems guide

my interaction with the researched and my treatment of the data?

KNOWING THE DISCIPLINE

The adult education researcher also operates within the boundaries of the discipline of adult education. Identifying a research problem thus entails locating it within its discipline. The adult education field is broad, multidisciplinary and its boundaries almost elusive. Researchers in adult education, for instance, include nurses, doctors, literacy teachers, social workers, trade union activists, and extension workers, such as agricultural demonstrators, to mention a few. Each one of these would identify a problem related to their work experiences. A nurse and a doctor, for instance, may be interested in the health-related issues while a literacy teacher may be interested in curriculum and pedagogical issues. Although research problems may be work or profession related, there still remain some common, agreed-upon strands that define the discipline. These include the way the discipline is conceptualised, methodological approaches used in problem solving in the field, and common theories that inform and are informed by practice. The following are examples:

- *Conceptions of adult education*: lifelong learning; informal learning; non-formal learning; workplace learning; and literacy
- *Adult education methodological approaches*: anti-oppression; feminist; participatory and action research
- *Theoretical frameworks*: liberalism, Marxism, feminism, postmodernism, post-colonial theory and critical theory. See Chapters 3, 11 and 12 for a discussion of some of these theories.

An adult education researcher, whether a teacher or a nurse, has to conceptualise the specific disciplinary context within which the problem is investigated. For example, is a teacher investigating curriculum issues within the context of workplace learning, literacy or non-formal education? One also has to be conversant with the theoretical frameworks and concepts that are the tools of analysis in a research study. In investigating curriculum issues, for instance, is the marginalisation and exclusion of indigenous knowledge systems (post-colonial perspectives) the main tool of analysis? Or is it Marxism, with its emphasis on education and the reproduction of inequalities that is the tool of analysis? Methodological approaches that inform practice in the discipline are also useful in informing the researcher about methods to be employed in the study. Participatory rural appraisal is, for instance, a common methodological approach used in research among indigenous communities.

⌗ ACTIVITY

Summarise the issues to be taken into account when preparing to do research in the field of adult education in Africa.

IDENTIFYING A RESEARCH PROBLEM

An understanding of the researched, of the researcher's personal, ideological, theoretical and methodological biases, and knowledge of the discipline thus precede identifying a research problem. With this knowledge base, the researcher can begin the process of selecting a research problem. The first step is to select a general problem that is related to one's area of expertise. The problem should also be of interest to the

researcher. The general problem should then be narrowed to a specific researchable area. A problem that is too broad has too many variables or issues to investigate and may produce results that are difficult to interpret, while a problem that is too narrow may not contribute sufficiently to new knowledge. A well-written research problem raises an issue that becomes the subject of inquiry. Within this issue, a problem is identified and further clarified by raising research questions and research objectives or by stating a research hypothesis that point to the most important aspects of the research problem. The following example from the summary of the study by Omolewa et al. (1998) helps to illustrate this.

EXAMPLE 5.1 (Drawn from Chapter 2 of Omolewa et al., 1998)

Research issue

Enrolment and retention of adults in literacy programmes in Nigeria.

Problem

Non-expansion or growth of literacy programmes in the rural areas in Nigeria.

Research objectives

- Identify alternative strategies for the promotion of literacy in Nigeria, especially in rural settings.
- Provide a solution to the intractable problem of non-growth.
- Improve the replicability of literacy programmes.
- Reduce the pattern of wastage and learner apathy.
- Promote learner empowerment as literacy's ultimate goal.

One important criterion for a research problem is that it should contribute to new knowledge and better practice or address concerns. The process of identifying a research problem thus requires familiarity with the literature in the area of interest. The community of adult education researchers is diverse. Some would have work experience while others would not. Consequently, the process of identifying a research problem will be diverse. There are various ways of identifying a research problem.

Researcher experience: A research issue might arise from experiences in the workplace. In the example of the study on literacy, for instance, the researchers might be coordinators of national literacy programmes in Nigeria. It is clear from the objectives of the study that findings will hopefully inform practice and influence policy in literacy programmes.

Theory-based: A theory might form the basis for a research problem. Myths, taboos, superstitions and community stories in African societies could also form part of the theory base for a research problem. Think about the myths, rituals and practices and their implications for research that you may want to conduct. These beliefs, rituals and practices raise issues that could form the basis for research problems. The common practice has been for researchers to mention some of these practices as symbols of barbarism that still go on in African societies and rarely as practices that should be investigated to find solutions to social problems. These myths, rituals and practices could be used to create a platform for a research-based dialogue with the community and a space for developmental change informed by people's experiences and ways of life.

Replication of research studies: From the literature, one might come across a study of interest done in a different context or country. For instance, one might want to replicate in Africa a study done in Asia such as the 'Ethnographic study of functional literacy in marginal Philippine communities' by Canieso-Doronilla (1996). The advantage of a replicated study is that the issue, research problem, research questions, methodologies and related literature and data analysis procedures are already defined and can easily be adapted to the study context.

Learning from previous studies: Most research studies recommend further areas of investigation. A novice researcher can identify a research problem from the recommendations made by others. For example, one might locate in a university library a postgraduate dissertation in the field of adult education and consider the research recommendation made in the final chapter.

Action research: Adult education researchers who combine work with learning may wish to find a solution to a problem in the workplace. They may thus research a problem that is action oriented. The research could lead to intervention strategies that bring about change. (See Chapter 11 for examples.)

Contemporary issues: National or community concerns such as HIV/AIDS may create a platform for the identification of a problem. The advantage of such contemporary issues is that there is urgency in accumulating knowledge to inform practice or bring about change. The researcher is therefore assured of an audience.

New area: One might want to research a new area previously marginalised in the discipline of adult education. For instance, part of the theme of this book is that researchers have marginalised indigenous knowledge systems. Health care delivery systems that include bone setters, herbalists and diviners in African contexts might be a challenging area of research for the health educator.

ACTIVITY

Discuss strategies of coming up with a research problem and generate research problems in adult education based on these strategies.

WRITING A RESEARCH PROPOSAL

Once a research problem has been identified, a research proposal is written. A research proposal is a plan of how a research study will be executed, and an estimate of the time and costs involved during the study. The purpose of a research proposal is to convince the reader that there is a problem that is worth addressing. The reader should also be convinced that the researcher has the expertise, skill and knowledge to execute the task. For example, adult education practitioners write research project proposals to seek funding from donors. Different donors have their own research project proposal formats and it is important that, before writing proposals, the practitioners familiarise themselves with the donor requirements. Students write research proposals to write dissertations, theses, projects and essays to satisfy the requirements of their programmes. In an academic setting, students' dissertations and projects that accommodate African perspectives should demonstrate whether the student is able to:

- Identify a researchable and worthwhile problem grounded in African contexts and communities' ways of life
- Review conventional and oral literature related to the problem of the study
- Choose research methodologies that create space for the review and development of indigenous knowledge systems while at the same time ensuring continuity with global knowledge systems

- Identify analysis procedures that place African views at the centre of knowledge production.

In some academic settings, there are guidelines on the format and types of research projects that can be carried out. The University of Botswana Faculty of Education has, for instance, outlined the types of research projects that students can do. These are categorised according to the source of data for the study. The faculty's main concern was cost and time available to Master's graduate students who are expected to complete their programmes in a maximum of two years. The objective was thus to outline research project types which could minimise data collection time and the costs of carrying out the study, while at the same time ensuring that students demonstrate the acquisition of basic research skills. The following are examples of identified research project types.

State of the art review/library study

A library study research proposal focuses primarily on a review of literature. A library study will have the following elements (grouped into problem formulation stage, methodology and analysis procedure):

Problem formulation stage

- A background to the review and justification of the review
- Operational definitions of the issues or variables that are part of the study, in such a way that the reviewer is able to distinguish relevant from irrelevant studies.

Methodology

- Definition of the population of studies, e.g. studies on literacy in Botswana conducted between 1975 and 2000
- Characteristics of the population of studies, e.g. by methodological inclination, such as studies on literacy that employ the conventional survey methodology, participatory rural appraisal methodology or ethnographic methodology
- Estimation of the total population from which the sample of studies is drawn
- Criteria for sampling studies to be reviewed
- Procedures used to identify the studies.

Analysis procedure

- Explanation of the way the studies will be analysed.

Analysis of data set research proposal

This project proposal type requires students to formulate a research problem from existing data sets and to choose the appropriate methodology and analysis procedure for the data set. The steps in the proposal design are as follows:

- Formulating and identifying a research problem
- Conducting a literature review
- Developing criteria for identifying and developing a data set to address the research questions
- Choosing appropriate analysis procedures.

Programme or curriculum development research proposal

This involves designing and introducing an entirely new programme or replacing an old

one. For instance, one might wish to write a proposal to design a training programme for HIV/AIDS caregivers. The typical steps in project design proposals are:

- Problem formulation and identification
- Literature review
- Needs assessment
- Programme design
- Programme implementation
- Programme evaluation.

The last three steps are discussed in detail in another book in this series: *Developing Programmes for Adult Learners in Africa* by Gboku and Lekoko (2006).

Empirical research study and field studies

This is a procedure for investigating a problem and for data collection from the field. An empirical research proposal will contain the following elements:

- Formulated and identified research problem
- Literature review
- Methodology
- Analysis procedures.

⊞ ACTIVITY

Discuss the possible limitations of the above research project types.

ELEMENTS OF A RESEARCH PROPOSAL

Although the types of research proposal may be many, there are typical elements that ensure clarity of the proposal and demonstrate the knowledge, skills and expertise of the researcher. The following elements are typical in a research proposal:

- Introduction and background to the problem
- Conceptual framework
- Statement of the problem
- Research questions
- Significance of the study
- Literature review
- Research design.

The following is a discussion of what each one entails, as well as the writing approach for each.

Introduction and background to the problem

The background to the study is a summary in which one argues that there is a problem and that one is aware of the literature related to the problem. A common weakness in formulating the problem is the absence of a framework. The suggestion here is that the researcher begin with a general overview of the problem. The overview should demonstrate the magnitude of the problem internationally and/or locally. The information should build a solid foundation for the statement of the problem. The discussion can be expanded by focusing on all or any one of the following: the conceptual/theoretical framework, the historical background to the problem, and the context of the problem.

The guiding principle in writing the background to the problem is to include only those details that will be relevant to the understanding of the problem, and the analysis and interpretation of the research findings.

Conceptual framework

This should be very brief and should be a summary of what is discussed in the literature review later in the proposal. A conceptual framework explains the concepts and the principles from which the knowledge of the problem is derived. The relevant theories to utilise in approaching the problem are briefly explained. These concepts, theories and principles are integrated into the statement of the problem. Theories and concepts are interwoven to indicate the scope and boundaries of the study, as well as the rationale and context of the study. Concepts are defined in multiple ways to ensure that issues and variables of interest are not left out. It is important that these multiple definitions include meanings based on the research participants' life experiences and perceptions of reality. The multiple definitions and descriptions of concepts and constructs also enable the researcher to distinguish relevant from irrelevant studies during the literature review.

Statement of the problem

Following the theoretical framework is the statement of the problem. The statement of the problem should be placed as close to the introduction as possible so that the reader is made aware of the purpose of the study right from the beginning. The statement of the problem should indicate variables/issues of interest to the researcher and the type of subjects involved. The variables should be defined either directly or operationally and their relationship also discussed. Delineating the variables in the study serves to show what the researcher hopes to achieve. In a qualitative study the meanings attached to the variables/issues of concern may be elaborated elsewhere in the study. One major weakness of most proposals is that variables are not operationally defined and the relationship between the variables is not made clear.

Research questions

Research questions or a hypothesis are written to further clarify the purpose of the study and to indicate the type of information that is required to fulfil the purpose of the study, and how it will be investigated. Hypotheses are common in quantitative studies, especially with topics where there is a lot known about the problem or where the purpose of the study is to test a theory. A hypothesis is formulated following a review of the literature to show the researcher's expectations of the relationship between the variables. The hypothesis will thus affect the design, the instruments, analysis techniques and conclusions. In the experimental research on the nutrient value of leafy vegetables by Monageng (1999), for instance, it is clear that the design will involve an experiment and that instruments will be needed to cook and dry the vegetables and to measure their nutrient content. Refer to Chapter 6 for a more elaborate discussion of the study.

Research questions serve the same purpose as a hypothesis. Research questions are broad and are common in qualitative research and studies that are exploratory. They help to clarify the purpose of the study. The general weakness in studies that utilise research questions is their failure to distinguish between questionnaire items or interview questions and research questions. In some studies, the research questions are too specific and too numerous and therefore would serve better as interview questions or questionnaire items. Questionnaire items or interview guides are different in that they further clarify and operationalise each research question to indicate the type of data that are needed to address research questions.

Significance of the study

A research proposal also includes a statement on how the study will contribute to theory, knowledge or practice in the discipline. The assumption in mainstream research has always been that theory, knowledge and practice are value neutral. There is a need to question this perspective and to think of significance in the context of multiple epistemologies, realities and value systems. In the adult education discipline, the significance of a study should be judged in terms of the usefulness of the knowledge produced in empowering the research participants to improve their quality of life. Significance should also be judged in relation to the impact of the knowledge produced in advancing the development of indigenous literacies and knowledge systems in such a way that they find a place in global science and technology. This is a challenge for researchers who wish to integrate indigenous knowledge systems with dominant knowledge systems.

How to review the literature

In Chapter 4 you learnt about the general purpose of the literature review. In this chapter the focus will be on how to write a literature review as part of a research proposal. The basic principle is to start with the general literature related to the problem. This could take the form of theories and concepts and the varying ways in which they have been addressed over a period of time. From this review will also emerge the rationale and significance of the study. The general literature can be followed by a review and discussion of empirical studies related to the study. One way to review the studies is to organise the review by variables identified in the statement of the problem. In the review the researcher should report consistencies as well as inconsistencies in

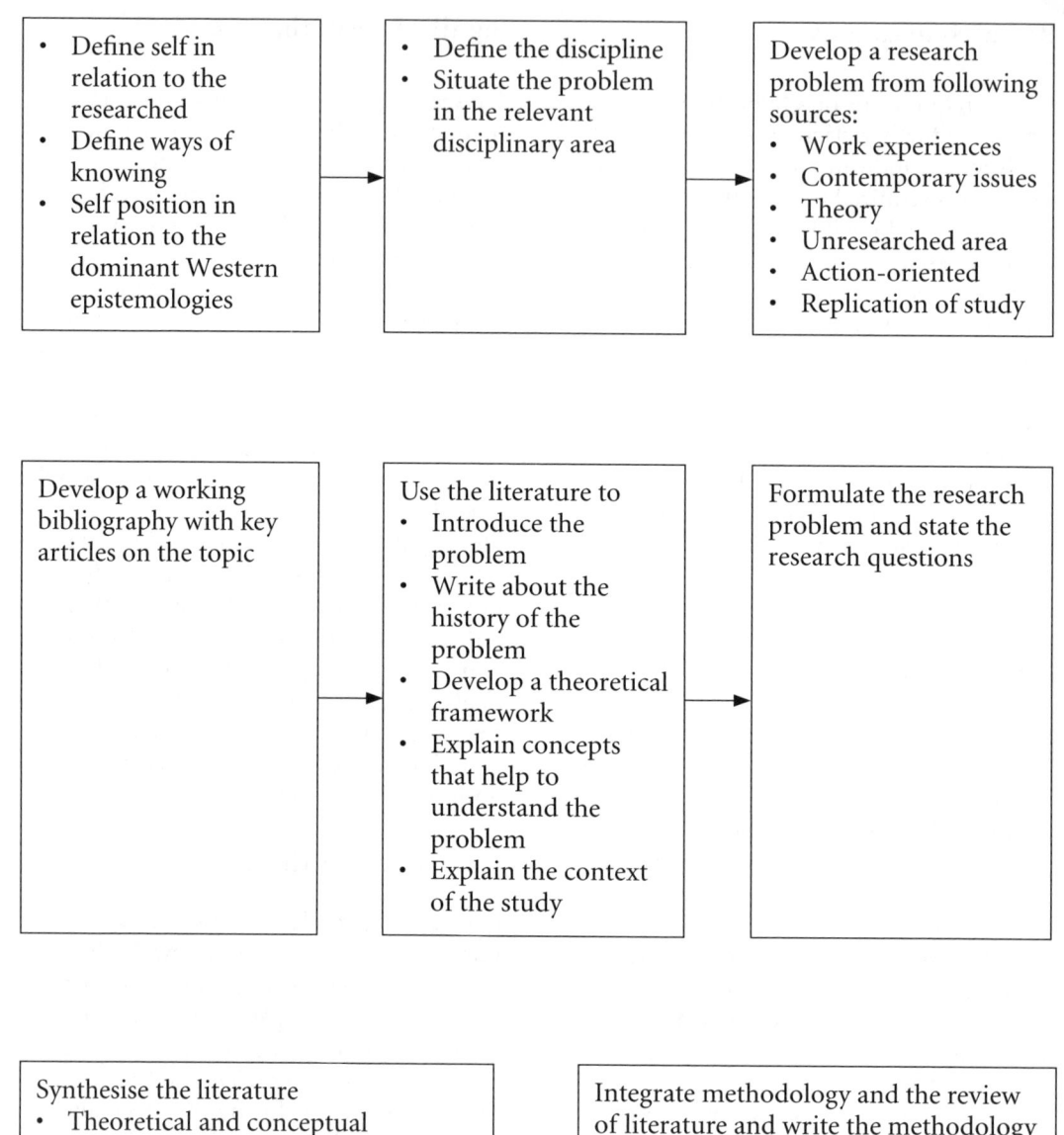

Figure 5.1 Getting started with a research proposal

the findings of comparable studies. The review should also point to omissions in the literature. The exclusion and marginalisation of African voices is an example of omissions in studies informed by Western epistemologies. It is in the literature review that knowledge which privileges Western ways of knowing can be critiqued. Such a critique would create a rationale for the inclusion of other sources of knowledge and ways of knowing. Chapter 4 discusses ways in which to guard against Eurocentric bias and to draw on African knowledge sources in the literature review. Inconsistencies in the findings may again serve as a rationale for the significance of the study. Another important aspect is to review the methodology used in the studies. A review of the methodology gives researchers a basis for the method they choose for their study.

The review should conclude with a brief summary of the literature and its implications for the problem investigated. The implications discussed should also serve as a rationale for the problem studied. There should be a clear link between what is discussed and the problem under investigation throughout the review. This link should be consistently brought to the reader by discussing implications of the review on the study.

Methodology

Another important element in the research proposal is the methodology. This section of the proposal discusses the design adopted for the study, a description of the target population, the sampling techniques, instruments for gathering data and the procedure used to carry out the study. These elements in the methodology section will vary depending on whether the research is quantitative or qualitative. For a detailed description of methodological procedures, see Chapters 6 and 7 for quantitative research methodology and Chapters 8 and 9 for qualitative research methodologies. The methodology should end with a research design framework to illustrate how each research question will be addressed.

SUMMARY

Conceptualising and writing a research proposal involve a number of steps as described in this chapter. Figure 5.1 on page 82 summarises steps for preparing and writing a research proposal.

KEY POINTS

- Researchers have to define themselves in relation to the researched so that they make an effort to incorporate in the research proposal ways of recognising knowledge from the perspective of the researched.
- It is important to recognise a variety of sources from which problems can be identified.
- Indigenous knowledge systems should be included in the planning and writing of research proposals.

⊞ ACTIVITY

1 Read the research proposal in Example 5.2 and discuss the following:

- The issue
- The problem
- The theoretical framework
- The significance of the study
- The target population
- Sampling techniques
- Data-gathering instruments
- Literature review.

2 When you have done this, do the extension activity under 'Further questions' after Example 5.2.

EXAMPLE 5.2 (This is the research proposal for the study undertaken by Kaye, 2002.)

Title: Women in the urban informal sector: Effective financial training in Botswana.

There is an often and openly voiced belief that, since women are not supposed to be good at mathematics, they do not and should not pursue careers in which mathematics plays an important role (Leder 1990). Ample evidence indicates that in Botswana, women are not well represented in occupations requiring mathematical competence, such as computers, finances, and engineering. The Botswana government's Central Statistics Office (2002) reported that, of the 265 378 people in formal employment in 2000, 155 378 were men and 109 904 were women. Women are in the majority in the health and education sections of both government and private industry. It is argued that a bias against women learning financial, technical and mathematical fields is problematic because women are increasingly owners of micro-businesses in the informal sector. Recent Botswana statistics indicate that women own 75% of the estimated 50 000 micro businesses in the country (Botswana Institute for Development Management, 1999).

Adequate training is one solution to providing better skills and knowledge, but a recent report of the Botswana government's training policy for the informal sector conducted by PEER Consultants (1997) has noted that quality, access and relevance of training are major areas of concern.

Training is a significant consideration when taken in conjunction with the government of Botswana's policies regarding the importance of encouraging sustainable small businesses. It has actively supported their formation since independence from the United Kingdom in 1966. There are several reasons for such support: these businesses can help create employment for its citizens because of their flexibility, ability to specialise and their local nature, thus providing more work, notably for women and other disadvantaged groups. They also promote the economic diversity needed for a healthy economy.

It appears that there may be contradictory and confusing attitudes towards the value of a small business and the social status of an entrepreneur in spite of the government's encouragement of their formation. Until very recently, the education system had not offered specific and relevant entrepreneurial training. At the core of the interlocking issues of appropriate training is the issue of how women learn the skills necessary for running businesses. Given that women do learn in spite of little or no formal training, and do run businesses – however marginal their profits may be – the question of how these business owners learn is a key to understanding how to provide effective training. Learning theories such as constructivism suggest that individuals construct their own understanding according to their particular cultures, personalities and life circumstances. It is therefore suggested that this is a necessary avenue of research to see how women learn given the particular cultural and educational attitudes and practices in Botswana. The PEER Consultants study, quoting from Daniel and Fissehe (1992: 37) reports that poor knowledge of finances represents 53% of the perceived problems of micro enterprises. The next highest concern is regarding markets: 17.3%

perceive problems at start-up and the concern increases to 24.5% as the business progresses. Given these previous studies, further study of how women learn is considered relevant.

This research aims to suggest financial training programmes for women owners of informal sector businesses that take into account their learning needs and styles, with the intention of helping to ensure a higher rate of success than is currently being experienced. Present statistics indicate that 80% of small and micro-enterprises cease trading within five years (Republic of Botswana, Small, Medium and Micro-Enterprises Task Force Report 1998: 11). There are an estimated 50 000 micro-enterprises in Botswana, of which 75% are women owned (Republic of Botswana, Small, Medium and Micro-Enterprises Task Force Report 1998, 9). Although records are too poorly kept to know definitely whether they fail or not, other factors, such as levels of income for women, indicate that at best the businesses function on a subsistence level.

Theoretical framework

The study is informed by theories on ethnomathematics. The term 'ethnomathematics' has been defined as 'the study of mathematics which takes into consideration the culture in which mathematics arises' (Case 2002). Given the above definition, the concept of ethnomathematics is relevant to this study since one of the major questions being investigated is how women in Botswana acquire the financial knowledge and skills needed to run a business. The premise is that learning mathematics, or learning in general, is interwoven with cultural influences and cultural ways of learning. The connections of culture and learning are inseparable; it is argued that one cannot discuss learning mathematics

without understanding the cultural knowledge, applications of mathematics and how one learns. One of the research questions being examined in this study is to understand why many small women-owned businesses fail, and a possible cause may be in the education and training received. For this reason, theories propounded in ethnomathematics are examined in some detail to see whether they substantiate the view that the way mathematics is taught may in itself be a contributing factor to the failure of businesses. Ignoring the influence of culture on learning – in this instance, mathematics – implies that a student's learning may be separated from their culture and can create a feeling of dissonance or discontinuity between formal learning and what is learned within one's culture.

Statement of the problem

The aims of this research are to investigate women micro-business owners, training programmes and underpinning theories related to women and mathematics, and to:

■ Discover how they acquire financial knowledge and mathematical skills
■ Identify their financial and mathematical training needs and the barriers they face in acquiring this knowledge
■ Appraise selected existing training programmes.

The research questions to be used in this study are:

■ How do women micro-business owners in Botswana learn the mathematics and financial management skills necessary to run their businesses? What financial knowledge is needed in this context? Does it vary among types of businesses? What approaches are successful? What barriers are there to learning, whether cultural, access to training, bias, self-perception, lack of formal education, rural and urban influences, or knowledge and abilities of the trainers?

■ What are the most effective training approaches, given the above? What changes would be most useful in training the trainers, writing training materials, and reconsidering the location, cost, and length of training?

Significance of the study

If research can help to provide better training for women, improve their ability to earn a reasonable income and give them the necessary tools to have the businesses grow to a higher level, this should significantly improve quality of life, not only for them individually, but for the families they are supporting. The research can assist all organisations involved in SMME training in designing more effective training programmes that also help towards the goal of diversification of businesses. Finally, as women become more equal partners in all aspects of the society, the society as a whole can improve as women add diversity to the understanding of what constitutes effective training.

Limitations and assumptions of the study

Given that the sample is relatively small, and fewer than 30 businesses are to be included, it is possible that the attitudes identified are not reflective of a broader range of women. Therefore a limitation of the study is that it will be difficult to generalise findings to all women business owners. Making recommendations for changes in training programmes may be difficult for this reason. Further, it is very likely that different needs are manifested in different

kinds of businesses. Another important limitation is that of language, and that attitudes are very difficult to identify and articulate. Cultural nuances are often known but may not be stated. Although most of the research will be conducted in Setswana instead of English, it limits the researcher from following up on threads of thought or practice that may come out only later in translation; the research assistants may not be aware the point needs clarification or further discussion, and it may be hard to come back to re-discuss the concept.

Description of the research method and scope of the study

This study is to be qualitative. Small samples of businesses in three urban locations, with each business meeting specific criteria, are to be used to address the research questions. The criteria have been partially determined by the definition of a micro-business in the informal sector as stated above and also to be as representative as possible of the major types of women-owned businesses in Botswana: the owner is a woman, the number of employees should be fewer than ten, the business should be in one of the three locations, there should be businesses from the manufacturing, service and retail sectors, and the business should have existed for at least one year. Because the problems of a large urban village, small urban village, and an urban town are perceived to be different, it was thought that it might be informative to examine businesses in each type of location to see if varying conditions produce varying results. Selected training programmes, training providers and trainers are to be interviewed to provide relevant information about attitudes of trainers, course materials, and methodology.

Literature review

At the core of finance and marketing are the mathematical activities that include quantities to be determined and the units to be used in the selling and buying of various commodities in market places, streets and shops. The amounts must either be measured by some device, or estimated. Many people have highly developed estimation skills. Values are often combined when different commodities are sold simultaneously. In many African markets, values and prices are negotiated. Prices may be reduced in order to keep customers, while at the same time avoiding selling at a loss. According to Zaslavsky (1979) systems have developed in many African markets to indicate numbers by elaborate hand and finger symbols. Mathematical skills thus have a cultural context that is highly dependent on the purpose for which they are to be used. D'Ambrosio claims that attempting to remove mathematics from a cultural perspective may well result in students, ignoring their own values, habits or beliefs and keep them from constructing their own conceptualisations. This leads to the need for learners to memorise rather than understand the deeper application in ways that are relevant to the student. When learners are taught formal mathematics and its history, the Eurocentric view is stressed. Mathematical discoveries from non-European groups are infrequently mentioned.

There are many universally expressed examples of activities that require mathematics, according to Casey, such as weaving, sewing, agriculture, kinship relations, ornamentation and spiritual and religious practices. In the Botswana context, there are many examples of the above mathematical activities. For example, the Batswana were constructing traditional housing and walled courtyards long before mathematics was taught in schools. The attractive wall decorations have required knowledge of shapes and patterns. Their weaving, the most well-known of which has been the traditional patterned baskets, has been used for a wide variety of purposes. Making them involves symmetry of design, well-balanced forms, and a variety of sizes and shapes. To make clay pottery, they had to form two halves, join the pieces and fire the pot in an open wood fire.

The most well-known beadwork still remaining in the culture is the ostrich egg shell necklace. Making these necklaces involves breaking the ostrich shell, smoothing and rounding the sides into a flat, round bead with a hole drilled into the centre by a hand-tooled awl. Agriculture too, long an important part of life in Botswana, requires the knowledge of storage, fields, and planting. The large herds of cattle and other livestock requires accurate means of keeping track and counting. The above examples are given to confirm the view that mathematical knowledge has existed in Botswana for centuries and eons, long before the arrival of Europeans or Westerners, and that a system of teaching and learning was well established in the culture. Although traditional financial systems may have been lost to history, commerce and trade existed and systems of accounting had to have been practised.

Attempts to integrate culture into teaching mathematics have to first overcome pitfalls of what Eglash (2002) has characterised as a one-way bridge across the digital divide. Eglash notes that, when people talk about the digital divide, they characterise the people on one side as those with plenty of technology, and the people on the other side as those who lack it. In response to this perspective, a one-way bridge in which the haves can send computers and camcorders and other gadgets to the have-nots is constructed. Culture, in such a one-way transaction, is not considered. Eglash describes a student project in which designs, culture and stories were developed by the Shoshone Native American people in Idaho, United States of America. All the stories, games and crafts were written into the educational computer materials being developed for students. In one instance, the computer developers, 'the haves', had difficulty in creating a virtual model of bead making. The computer-model beads were uneven, whilst 'the bead-workers had algorithms in their heads that were better' (Eglash, 2002). Once the computer designers learned the complicated algorithms being used by the bead-workers, they were able to replicate them in the computer. Eglash concludes that we can create problems if we talk only about absence – that is, if we reduce one side to the have-nots.

According to Green (2000) there are academics who argue that moving away from European to non-European methods of working out maths problems may well be a waste of the learners' time. Weiger (2000) confirms that there are critics of ethnomathematics, who say there is a lack of data to support the claim that incorporating cultural ways of learning helps students learn mathematics. It is argued that, since this attitude prevails in the academic world and the technological world, both may deliberately or inadvertently disregard cultural ways of learning. This attitude may be problematic in cases, for example, where the training materials are produced in the 'West' but used by African learners who have their different ways of learning, and could contribute to the discontinuity between formal training and 'doing things the Setswana way'. The end result is a devaluation of one's cultural ways of learning, as noted above.

To conclude, the intimate link of learning to culture, in this case, in learning mathematics, has been elaborated in the theories of ethnomathematics, and it is argued that there is sufficient rationale and an increasing amount of data to validate that these theories can provide a framework for investigating mathematical related skills used by the businesswomen in the study.

References

Bishop, A. 2001. 'What values do you teach when you teach mathematics?' *Teaching Children Mathematics*, Vol. 7, Issue 6, p. 346.

Casey, N. 2002. Ethnomathematics. http://www.cs.uidaho.edu/~case931/seminar/ethno.html accessed August 2002.

D'Ambrosio, U. 2001. 'What is ethnomathematics, and how can it help children in schools?' *Teaching Children Mathematics*, Vol. 7, Issue 6, pp. 308–310.

Eglash, R. 2002. 'A two-way bridge across the digital divide.' *Chronicle of Higher Education*, Vol. 48, Issue 41, p. 12.

Green, E. 2000. 'Good-bye Pythagoras?' *Chronicle of Higher Education*, 10/6/2000, Vol. 47, Issue 6, p. 16

Weiger, P. R. 2000. 'Re-calculating math instruction.' *Black Issues in Higher Education*, 08/17/2000 Vol. 17, Issue 13, p. 58.

Zaslavsky, C. 1979. *Africa Counts: Number and Pattern in African Culture*. Brooklyn, NY: Lawrence Hill (Kaye, 2002).

FURTHER QUESTIONS

Use the checklist that follows to evaluate the adequacy of the above proposal. Justify the ratings you make.

Research proposal evaluation checklist

Introduction and background to the problem

1 Does the introduction adequately convince the reader of the global, national or local significance of the problem?
2 Does the background give sufficient information on the nature, history and context of the problem?
3 Are the theories and concepts that inform the framework of the study discussed?
4 Is there a framework for discussing the introduction and background to the study?
5 Does the discussion framework create space for including African voices, ways of experiencing realities and ways of knowing?

1	2	3	4	5	6	7	8	9	10

Discuss and give reasons for your rating.

Statement of the problem and research questions

1 Is the purpose of the study clear?
2 Are the variables/issues and their relationships adequately delineated?
3 Are the variables operationally defined or indirectly explained?
4 Do the research questions/hypotheses adequately clarify the problem?
5 Can one deduce from the research questions the nature of instruments to be used, the research design and how the analysis of the problem will be done?

1	2	3	4	5	6	7	8	9	10

Discuss and give reasons for your rating.

Significance and limitations of the study

1 Is the significance of the study discussed in terms of its contribution to the empowerment of the adult research participants?
2 Does the contribution to new knowledge discussed include the development of indigenous literacies and knowledge systems?

1	2	3	4	5

Discuss and give reasons for your rating.

_____

_____

Literature review

1 Is the place, and inclusion or exclusion, of African epistemologies and worldviews covered in the review?
2 Do the literature sources include materials that privilege African contexts, ways of perceiving realities and ways of knowing?
3 Are the implications of the review for the study discussed? Is there a clear and logical framework for the review?
4 Does the review conclude with a brief summary of the literature and its implications for the problem investigated?

| 1 | 2 | 3 | 4 | 5 | 6 | 7 | 8 | 9 | 10 |

Discuss and give reasons for your rating.

_____

_____

Methodology

1 Is the design sensitive to African contexts and appropriate for answering the research questions?
2 Are procedures described in sufficient detail to permit replicability in a quantitative research study?
3 Is the application of the qualitative method chosen described in detail?
4 Are the size and major characteristics of the targeted population described?
5 Are the target and accessible population described?
6 Is the sample selection appropriate for African contexts and is it clearly described?
7 Are the sample size and its characteristics described?
8 Does the sample size meet the minimum requirements?
9 Are data-gathering instruments inclusive of African community-centred techniques and are they appropriate for measuring the intended variables?

| 1 | 2 | 3 | 4 | 5 | 6 | 7 | 8 | 9 | 10 | 11 | 12 | 13 | 14 | 15 |

Discuss and give reasons for your rating.

_____

_____

SUGGESTED READINGS

Pallas, A. 2001. 'Preparing education doctoral students for epistemological diversity'. *Educational Researcher*, Vol. 30, No. 5, pp. 6–11.

Chapter 6

Carrying out a survey

OVERVIEW

In this chapter the following questions are addressed:

- How can researchers conduct survey research without producing distorted knowledge on the researched?
- How can researchers frame research problems in survey research so that participants give information that is relevant to their life experiences?
- How can researchers construct questionnaires in a language that does not limit or restrict the discussion of the research problem to Eurocentric definitions?

This chapter outlines the characteristics and types of survey research designs. Features of a survey design, namely types of surveys, steps in carrying out a survey and sampling selection procedures, are discussed. The chapter also covers the construction of questionnaires and suggests ways of constructing questionnaires that are culture sensitive as well as accommodative of African community worldviews and indigenous knowledge systems. Advantages and limitations of survey research in African contexts are discussed with particular focus on the populations of adults that are researched. The chapter also explores possible ways of designing surveys that are relevant and responsive to the needs of adults in the rural areas in Africa.

LEARNING OBJECTIVES

By the end of this chapter, you should be able to:

1 Describe and recognise different research designs in quantitative research.
2 Discuss types of surveys and their appropriateness in African contexts.
3 Describe conventional sampling procedures.
4 Describe how each of the sampling procedures might be used in diverse settings in adult education contexts.
5 Design survey questionnaires informed by communities' knowledge systems and (indigenous) worldviews.

bese saka

KEY TERMS

census survey Research that gathers data from each member of the population.

control group A group that either does not receive treatment, is treated as usual or receives a treatment different from the experimental group.

correlational studies Studies designed to find the degree and nature of association or relationship between two or more quantifiable variables.

cross-sectional survey Collection of data at a specific point in time from one or more populations.

longitudinal survey Collection of data at two or more points in time, separated by days, hours, weeks, months, or years.

one-shot survey Collection of data at one point in time.

quasi-experimental design Experimental research designs that do not have all the requirements of an experiment that takes place in a laboratory.

sample survey Research where a representative sample from a population is drawn to enable generalisation of findings from the sample to the population.

survey research Research that gathers information to describe a population with respect to identified variables.

⊞ BEFORE YOU START

In Chapter 2 you learnt that the emphasis in positivist/post-positivist research is mainly quantitative and emphasises the following:

- Logic
- Objectivity
- Establishing cause-and-effect relationships
- Establishing general principles and laws that govern the universe
- Quantifying social reality and being able to say with a certain amount of confidence that a phenomenon exists.

Discuss your understanding of these characteristics.

QUANTITATIVE DESIGNS

Research within the positivist/post-positivist paradigm is mainly quantitative. Common quantitative approaches within the paradigm are experimental research, correlational research and descriptive or *survey* research.

Experimental research

Experimental studies are those that attempt to establish a cause-and-effect relationship. A cause-effect relationship refers to the fact that a researcher is able to conclude that variable A caused variable B to occur. To demonstrate causality, all extraneous variables must be controlled so that the effect of the causal variable can be isolated. Extraneous variables are those which are not part of the study but could affect its outcome. Highly rigid and specific controls are only possible in laboratories. Take, for example, a study to determine the nutrient value of bean leaves called *Vigna unguiculata*. In this study Monageng (1999) carried out an experiment where the nutrient value of the uncooked green leafy vegetable was compared to the same vegetable when boiled and dried in an oven in a laboratory. If the bean leaves were dried in the open instead of the oven, it would be difficult to control for extraneous variables such as winds, temperatures and weather in general. Most experiments in adult education are, however, done in the field. It is not possible to place the same controls on field research as it is on laboratory research. It is for this reason that experimental field research is also referred to as quasi-experimental research.

Parts of an experiment

Experimental designs have specific components that are necessary for the quality of the research. Neuman (1997) divides an experiment into seven parts.

1 *Treatment or independent variables.* The term treatment comes from medical science where a patient is given treatment, which may be in the form of drugs. The treatment is commonly referred to as the independent variable. An independent variable is that variable in the study that causes, determines or makes a difference with respect to another variable called the dependent variable.
2 *Dependent variable,* also referred to as outcome or effect variable, refers to results after receiving treatment. It is a variable assumed to be caused by another.
3 *Pre-test* is also associated with the medical field, where a patient is tested to diagnose an illness.
4 *Post-test* is testing to see the progress after administration of treatment. Changes would be due to treatment if other plausible explanations were eliminated.
5 *Experimental group* refers to the group receiving treatment.
6 *Control group* is the group that does not receive treatment. A comparison of the control and experimental groups at the end of the experiment gives assurance that changes in the experimental group were due to treatment.
7 *Random assignment.* This means assigning participants either to the control or experimental group with the end result that the two groups are equivalent.

EXAMPLE 6.1
(Extracted from Monageng, 1999)

Title

Determining the nutrient content of morogo wa dinawa (*Vigna unguiculata*)

Research problem

To find out how much of the nutrient content of the *morogo wa dinawa*, leafy vegetables known as *Vigna unguiculata,* is lost in processing, and then come up with a nutrient composition table.

Hypothesis

The leafy vegetables (*Vigna unguiculata*) that have been dried before boiling have more nutrient value than those that have been boiled and then dried.

Dependent variable

Nutrient content of leafy vegetables.

Independent variables (which the researcher manipulated)

- Temperature for drying the *Vigna unguiculata*
- Time taken for drying the *Vigna unguiculata*.

Control of extraneous variables

Instruments for testing different nutrients were carefully checked and tested before carrying out the experiment. Good harvesting methods were followed to control for micro-organisms that could contaminate the vegetables.

Methods used for determining nutrients

Various methods were used: Determination of lipids by soxhlet method; determining the total energy value by bomb calorimeter and determination of mineral elements by atomic absorption spectrophotometry.

Conclusion

The leafy vegetables (*Vigna unguiculata*) that have been dried before boiling have more nutrient value than those that have been boiled and then dried.

Advantages of laboratory experiments

- The control procedures used in the laboratory enable the experimenter to establish a cause-effect relationship.
- The experimental approach enables the experimenter to manipulate one or two variables of their choosing. For instance, in Monageng's study, the experimenter manipulated the temperature and the time taken for drying the *Vigna unguiculata*.
- The experimental approach has produced results that have lasted over a period of time. It has also led to suggested studies to be carried out and suggested solutions to practical problems.

Disadvantages of laboratory experiments

- Research findings produced in laboratories cannot easily be generalised to real-life situations. Also, procedures used in the laboratory may not be easily accessible to the ordinary men and women whose lives are affected by the experiment. For instance, although Monageng concluded that the *Vigna unguiculata* that had been dried before boiling had more nutrient value than that which had been boiled and dried, it would be difficult for the majority of people to process the leafy vegetables under the conditions that the experimenter in the study observed.
- Experiments are generally time-consuming and expensive because of the equipment that is required.

- Experiments are not adequate for studying human behaviour because manipulating human beings would violate their human rights. Refer to Chapter 13 on ethics.

Quasi-experimental research

Quasi-experimental refers to the fact that the research design does not meet all the requirements of an experiment that takes place in a laboratory. Quasi-experimental designs represent an effort by researchers to carry out experiments in the real world. There are a variety of *quasi-experimental designs*. Example 6.2 shows a pre-test/post-test control group experimental design.

EXAMPLE 6.2

Title

Effect of group-based projects on the achievement of adult part-time graduate students taking a research methods course.

Participants

The sample of the study was drawn from a total population of 80 part-time M. Ed. students in their first year at Ibadan University in Nigeria. The population consisted of 95% Nigerian citizens with the rest classified as non-citizens. The ratio of women to men was 1 to 1. Fifty students were selected using a table of random numbers. They were then randomly assigned to two groups of 25 each. See Table 6.1.

Instruments

A test battery used to measure achievement on the research methods course for second-year students was used.

The battery, which consists of several parallel test forms measuring the same instructional objectives, has been used before. The content validity of the test is good. The test objectives and the instructional objectives of the research methods course were highly correlated. The test was therefore a good measure of achievement in the research methods course.

Group	Assignment	N	Pre-test	Treatment	Post-test
Control	Random	20	A test battery measuring achievement on research methods	Traditional lecture method	Parallel test form measuring achievement on research methods
Experimental	Random	20	A test battery measuring achievement on research methods	Group-based projects	Parallel test form measuring achievement on research methods

Table 6.1 Summary of study design

Experimental design

The design used was the pre-test/post-test control group design. The design was chosen because it controls for most sources of invalidity. In addition, random assignment of treatment to the group was possible. A pre-test was administered to help establish initial group equivalence and to help control for mortality. A parallel form of the test was used for the post-test to control for testing effects.

Procedure

At the beginning of the first semester of the 2002/2003 academic year, the Department of Adult Education randomly assigned adult education students to two groups of twenty-five each. One group was randomly chosen to receive group-based project instruction while the other group received the traditional lecture method instruction. The same teacher taught the two groups. Each group was taught for three hours, once every week, for 12 weeks. In the experimental group, the lecturer introduced the topic, provided the learning objectives and the group task to assist in achieving the instructional objectives. The role of the lecturer was that of a facilitator and a guide. Completed group tasks were assessed by the lecturer and feedback was given to the groups. In the control group, the lecturer used traditional methods of lecturing and open class discussions. Individual exercises were given to students, marked and feedback given. Throughout the study, the same subject matter was covered and the two groups used the same reference materials. A post-test was given at the end of 12 weeks and achievement scores of the two groups compared.

The value of quasi-experimental research

An adult educator would like to know what would have happened if they had not introduced an intervention programme. For instance, would incidences of child abuse in a community have been reduced without a three-month programme on child abuse? Would leadership skills among traditional leaders have improved without the six-week training programme on leadership skills? A family welfare educator might want to know whether the number of people using contraceptives increased after six weeks' training on the use of contraceptives.

Quasi-experimental research designs are useful in gauging the effectiveness of intervention programmes. The greatest challenge is to eliminate all other plausible explanations that could bring about a change, so that one can confidently associate the change with the intervention treatment. While this is easy in experiments conducted in laboratories, it is difficult in natural settings. To achieve experimental results close to those conducted in laboratories, the researcher has to control for factors that might impact on the internal and external validity of the study. Internal validity is the degree to which changes or results in a study can be attributed to the independent variable. External validity refers to the degree to which the findings in a study can be generalised to other populations, settings, groups and situations. Threats to internal and external validity identified by Campbell and Stanley (1963) and Cook and Campbell (1979) are discussed below.

Threats to internal validity

- *History:* This is a threat where events, public or private, occur during the experiment that have an effect on the outcome or dependent variable. Suppose, for example, a researcher is investigating the effect of a programme on leadership skills on traditional leaders' time management and leadership styles. The outcome or dependent variable is measured before introducing the treatment programme (the independent variable). Suppose that, during the course of the programme, the government broadcast a radio or television programme on leadership for a week. When time management and leadership are measured at the end of the programme, we can no longer conclude that the changes observed were due only to the educational programme on leadership skills. The history threat is most likely to occur in studies that take a long time.

- *Mortality:* This is when participants drop out or cease to participate in the experiment before the end of the study. The researcher has no way of knowing whether the results would have been different if they had stayed. The researcher cannot rule out the possibility that most of those who dropped out had the same characteristics. A researcher studies and reports the characteristics of those who drop out of the study to detect this threat to internal validity.
- *Differential selection of research participants:* Ideal experiments require random sampling from the population and further random assignment of treatment to groups so that the experimental group and the control group are equivalent. Selection bias occurs when participants in one of the groups have a characteristic that affects the outcome or dependent variable.
- *Statistical regression:* This occurs when the groups selected have characteristics of the outcome or dependent variable. Suppose adult learners in two equivalent groups are pre-tested on numeracy skills before a breakthrough programme to

teach numeracy. If 90% in both groups get perfect scores before the programme, then a post-test is not likely to detect any changes in the test scores.
- *Maturation:* This occurs when biological, psychological or emotional changes in the participants affect the dependent/outcome variable. This occurs in experiments that take a long time, especially when participants are children who are still growing. Responses to treatment may in some cases be due to maturity or cognitive development. Participants may also feel sleepy, bored, irritated – with the result that the dependent variable is affected.
- *Testing:* This may occur in a study where a pre-test and a post-test are administered. Participants may, for example, score high on a post-test on numeracy skills because they discussed the test after the pre-test and remember some items and answers because of these discussions.
- *Instrumentation:* The threats may occur where two different tests, for instance a post-test and a pre-test, are not of equal difficulty. If the pre-test is more difficult than the post-test, the experiment might indicate a gain or change that is not present.
- *Selection maturation:* This occurs when one of the groups in the experiment experiences an advantage over the other. This advantage could result from history or instrumentation.

Threats to external validity

The following threats might limit the generalisability of experimental results to study populations.

- *Pre-test treatment interaction:* The pre-test might sensitise participants to aspects of the treatment and thus influence post-test scores.

- *Selection-treatment interaction:* If participants are volunteers, and are not randomly selected or randomly assigned to treatment, the results may not be generalisable to the population of the study.
- *Reactive effects:* These threats occur when participants behave differently in a study because of the knowledge that they are being studied.
- *Experimenter effects:* These occur when actions of the researcher affect participants' performance or responses.

Control of extraneous variables

In experiments, participants are randomly selected from a population and then randomly assigned to treatment. Randomisation is effective in creating groups that are essentially the same on all relevant variables. Matching can also be used to create groups that are equivalent on one or more variables. Matching refers to the technique for equating groups with one or more variables such that each member of one group has a direct counterpart in another group. The researcher might want to match the groups on gender. If so, the groups must have the same gender ratio.

Correlational studies

Correlational studies are designed to determine the relationship or association between or among two or more variables. The degree of the relationship between two variables is measured by a correlation coefficient, which is a number between -1 and $+1$. A correlation coefficient close to 0 is an indication that two variables are not related while a correlation coefficient close to -1 or $+1$ indicates a high relationship.

A relationship can be negative, indicating that while one variable increases the other decreases. Take, for example, an extension worker who wants to establish the relation-

ship between the nutrient value of a leafy vegetable and the amount of cooking. The direction of the relationship is most likely to be negative (between 0 and -1), indicating that as the amount of cooking time increases the nutrient value decreases. A relationship can be positive (between 0 and $+1$), indicating that as one variable increases the other variable also increases. Take, for example, an agricultural extension worker who wants to find out the relationship between crop yields and the use of manure. The relationship is likely to be positive, indicating that an increase in the use of manure (up to a point) leads to an increase in crop yields. Correlational studies relate behaviour of subjects with similar characteristics to different variables measured at different levels. For instance, a study on the relationship between the use of manure and crop yields would require that farmers with the same size plot, and planting the same crop, be identified. The sample would consist of farmers who have used different amounts of manure.

EXAMPLE 6.3

Respondent	X (manure)	Y (crop yield)
1	1 bag	50 bags
2	1½ bags	75 bags
3	0	20 bags
4	½ bag	10 bags
5	2 bags	100 bags

Also note that correlational studies require large sample sizes. Stable correlation coefficients can be established with a sample of at least 50 respondents. It is also important to note that, while this may be true, the appropriateness of the sample sizes will differ depending on the type of study and the number of variables for which the relationship is sought.

The following are examples of correlation research studies:

- A study to determine whether there is a significant relationship between adult attendance of the numeracy skill classes and scores on the numeracy test.
- A study to determine whether there is a relationship between the amount of water used for irrigation and the yield of maize per acre.

⊞ ACTIVITY

Study Example 6.2.
1 Identify the independent and dependent variables.
2 Discuss how the researcher eliminated threats to the internal and external validity of the study.
3 Discuss settings to which the findings of the study could be generalised.

SURVEY RESEARCH

Survey research systematically gathers information about a situation, an area of interest, a series of events, or about people's attitudes, opinions, behaviour, interests or practices. Survey research is predominantly descriptive. It is for this reason that the terms descriptive and survey research are sometimes used interchangeably.

Types of surveys

We can distinguish survey types according to the number and composition of the participants involved in the study or the technique used to gather data for the survey. When the size and composition of the research participants is used to categorise surveys, we can distinguish between *census* surveys and *sample* surveys.

Census surveys

These involve the enumeration of all subjects covered by the area of the survey. Such surveys are usually required by governments for planning and decision-making purposes. Participation is usually compulsory. In Botswana, examples of surveys where everybody is required to participate are the population census, livestock census and agricultural census. The law states that a person who for no apparent reason refuses to participate in a survey 'shall be guilty of an offence and liable to a fine not exceeding P100, or to imprisonment for a term not exceeding three months, or to both.'

Sample survey

Sampling involves selecting a representative number of units from the population of study. The aim of a sample survey is to study the sampled population and be able to generalise the findings to the population from which the sample was drawn. The literacy survey (CSO, 1997) discussed in Chapter 2 is an example of a sample survey. Other examples are the literacy survey in South Africa (Aitchison, 1999) and the literacy survey in Uganda (Oxenham, 2000). There are two main advantages of a sample survey:

- It saves on costs and time because a limited number of units from the population of study are investigated.
- It can lead to greater accuracy compared to a census survey because close monitoring and supervision of the data collection, analysis and interpretation are much more feasible.

The main disadvantage of a sample survey is sampling bias. Sampling bias occurs where a sampling procedure leads to over-selection or under-selection of respondents of a particular kind. For instance, in a survey of people's attitudes towards government projects earmarked to alleviate poverty, those who are pro-government might be more willing to participate in the survey while those who are anti-government may be reluctant. Under the circumstances, the findings of the study are more likely to reflect the opinions of those who are generally satisfied with government rule, and by extension, the government projects. Alreck and Settle (1995) list the following biases:

- *Accessibility bias*: Fieldworkers are more likely to pick respondents who are accessible. A survey that is conducted during seasonal periods of planting and harvesting, for instance, might exclude the majority of adults who spend long hours in the fields.
- *Affinity bias*: Fieldworkers may select respondents they are attracted to and thus have an over-representation of these in the study. For instance, male fieldworkers may be attracted to male respondents. If the majority of fieldworkers are male, then there is a likelihood that there will be an over-representation of male respondents. A bias is introduced because these male respondents may not necessarily represent the views of female respondents.
- *Non-response bias*: This occurs when some sampled research respondents refuse to participate in the survey or to answer certain questions in the survey instrument. The bias occurs if the non-response can be associated with some groups of the sampled respondents.
- *Self-selection bias*: This occurs when respondents are allowed to volunteer to participate in a survey. The volunteers

may possess characteristics that are different from those who do not volunteer. If that happens, the sample can only be said to be representative of the population with characteristics similar to the volunteers.
- *Termination bias*: Respondents of a certain type might withdraw their participation in a survey before it is completed. For instance, the majority of women might withdraw from a literacy survey before it is completed because they have to attend to harvesting of crops.
- *Visibility bias*: Some respondents may be more recognised than others and therefore be more likely to participate in the survey. For instance, in a survey on adult literacy, older people may be more likely to be selected compared to the youth also participating in literacy classes.

ACTIVITY

Discuss ways to reduce or eliminate each of the different sampling biases.

SAMPLE SELECTION METHODS

Sample selection methods in a survey are used to minimise errors that occur when some respondents or subjects are over-represented or under-represented in a study. Quantitative surveys use probability sampling methods. In probability sampling, every member within a population of study has a known and equal chance of being selected for the sample. The procedure allows the researcher to conclude that the sample is representative of the population from which it is drawn.

The choice of a sampling method to be used in a study is determined by the characteristics of the population or unit of study, its size and the problem investigated. Selection of a sampling method thus always begins with a description of the unit or population of study and its size. Characteristics that distinguish members of the unit or population are of utmost importance. When people are the unit of study, age, ethnicity, location, gender and social class might be important characteristics to describe, depending on the purpose of the study. There are a variety of sampling strategies that researchers can choose from.

Simple random sampling

Simple random sampling is a procedure of selecting a sample out of a population in such a way that every member of the population has an equal and independent chance of being selected to form the sample. It is used when the assumption is that variations in the characteristics of the respondents will not affect their responses to the research questions in the study.

Simple random sampling begins with defining the population of study, identifying each member of the population and selecting individuals from the population. One way to select the individuals that form the sample is to write down the name of each individual on a piece of paper, place all the papers in a container and randomly pick the papers from the container until the desired sample size is achieved. During the process, each selected element must be returned to the container before the next selection is made. This is necessary to ensure that the probability of all selections remains the same throughout the selection process. This procedure might be cumbersome where large sample sizes are required. Another feasible strategy is to use a table of random numbers. A table of random numbers appears in most research books and is specifically used to draw samples.

Here are the steps and procedures for simple random sampling, using a table of random numbers:

1 Use when the population is homogenous.
2 Identify the population.
3 Determine the desired sample size.
4 List and number all members of the population starting with 1. If you have a target population of 200, for example, number all the members from 001 to 200.
5 Arbitrarily select members with a number between 001 and 200 using the table of random numbers. Continue to pick up numbers until you have the desired sample size, say 50.

Consider a hypothetical study to investigate the dropout rate of adults in a literacy programme in village X. Figure 6.1 illustrates simple random sampling. Ten adults who dropped out of the literacy programme are randomly selected from the population of 30 adults who dropped out of the literacy programme between 1995 and 2000.

Population

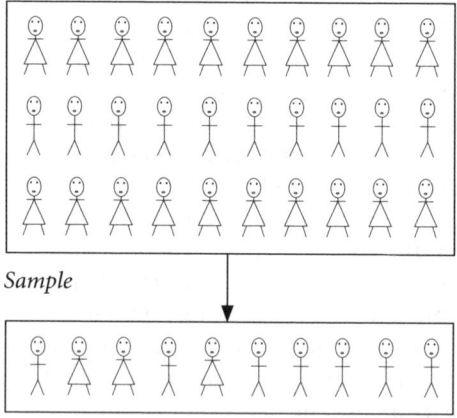

Sample

Figure 6.1 Simple random sampling

The method assumes that age, occupation, socio-economic status, gender, and location in the village will not affect the dropout or retention rate of the literacy participants. This assumption – that the population is homogenous – is not always true. The literature review will usually indicate the characteristics of respondents that affect their behaviour or responses to a problem under investigation. The characteristics identified allow the researcher to divide the population of the study into sub-groups so that members in each sub-group can be randomly selected. This introduces stratified random sampling.

Stratified random sampling

In stratified random sampling, respondents are divided into subgroups called strata. The size of each stratum is then determined. The size of each stratum should be proportional to and representative of the population from which it is drawn. When a sample is randomly drawn that is proportionally representative of each stratum, that is called proportional stratified random sampling. When members of a certain strata are small, it may not be feasible to draw a proportional sample large enough to give accurate estimates about the strata. In that case, the number drawn from the subgroups may be disproportionate to the subgroup. This is called disproportionate stratified random sampling.

The following points illustrate the steps and procedures in stratified random sampling:

1 Use when there are characteristics that distinguish the population that can affect responses to the research questions.
2 Identify and define the population.
3 Identify the characteristics or variables that you will use to classify the subgroups or strata.

4 Classify members of the population according to the identified strata or subgroups.
5 Determine if proportional representation of the subgroups will yield valid statistical estimates from all the subgroups. If not, use disproportional stratified random sampling instead of proportional random sampling.
6 Determine the number to be selected from each subgroup and, using a table of random numbers, randomly select members from the subgroups until you have the desired sample.

Using the example of a hypothetical study on the drop-out rate of adults in the literacy programme in village X again, suppose village X is divided into settlements called Lands (stratum 1), Cattle Posts (stratum 2) and Centre (stratum 3). The researcher has a hunch that the settlement patterns would explain some of the reasons for dropping out of the literacy programme. The researcher has to determine the population in each stratum and draw a proportional or disproportional random sample from each stratum. Assume that a sample of 12 is to be randomly drawn and that there are 10 dropouts in stratum 1, 20 in stratum 2, and 10 in stratum 3. Figure 6.2 illustrates the procedure.

Systematic random sampling

Sometimes researchers use systematic random sampling instead of using a table of random numbers to randomly select their sample. Systematic sampling selects subjects from the population in a systematic rather than random fashion. It involves selecting one unit or member of the sample on a random basis and choosing additional units or members at evenly spaced intervals until the desired sample size is achieved. Suppose there are 50 students in your class. You want

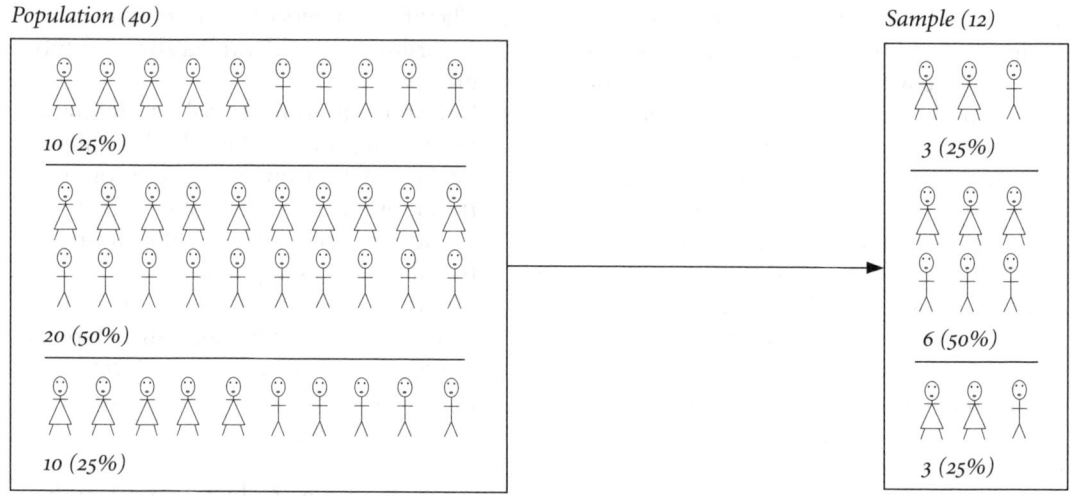

Population (40)

10 (25%)

20 (50%)

10 (25%)

Sample (12)

3 (25%)

6 (50%)

3 (25%)

Figure 6.2 *Proportional stratified random sampling*

a sample of 10. You have their names listed in alphabetical order. If you choose to use systematic random sampling, the procedure is as follows:

1 Number the units in the population from 1 to 50.
2 Decide on the sample size, which is 10 in this example.
3 Decide on an interval (obtained by dividing the population size by the sample size: 50 ÷ 10 = 5)
4 Randomly select an integer between 1 and 5. In this example, 4 was selected as the place to start the selection.
5 Take every 5th unit from 4 onwards. Figure 6.3 illustrates this.

1	2	3	**4**	5
6	7	8	**9**	10
11	12	13	**14**	15
16	17	18	**19**	20
21	22	23	**24**	25
26	27	28	**29**	30
31	32	33	**34**	35
36	37	38	**39**	40
41	42	43	**44**	45
46	47	48	**49**	50

4, 9, 14, 19, 24, 29, 34, 39, 44, 49

Figure 6.3 *Systematic random sampling (with a random start)*

Cluster sampling

Cluster sampling is a technique whereby the entire population is divided into groups or clusters and random or systematic selections of these groups are made. Cluster sampling is most appropriate in national studies when the populations of study are large and widely dispersed.

The following points illustrate the steps and procedures in cluster sampling:

1 Identify and define the population.
2 Determine the extent to which those within an area or cluster are more likely to be similar. For instance, reasons for dropping out in each area are likely to differ depending on the level of study (primer, 2, 3, or 4).
3 Define a cluster.
4 Using the definition, list all clusters that make up the population of clusters.
5 Estimate the average number of population members per cluster.
6 Specify the minimum number of clusters that will be large enough to sample the entire area, region or population adequately.
7 Divide the total sample size by the minimum number of clusters to obtain the number within each cluster.
8 Randomly sample clusters and study all units within each sampled cluster.

The main disadvantage of this sampling strategy is that the selected clusters may not be representative of the entire population from which the clusters are selected.

Multiple-stage sampling

Simple, stratified, systematic and cluster sampling are the simplest random sampling strategies. In most situations, a combination of these strategies is used. This is called multiple-stage sampling. For illustration

purposes, consider the sampling strategies in the Uganda literacy survey (Oxenham, 2000) in Example 6.4. First the researchers divided the country into the eight administrative regions of Uganda. Cluster sampling was used to select districts within each administrative region that had literacy programmes. They then used simple random sampling to select 100 graduates from a list of all the graduates in each district. It is possible that the researchers stratified the graduates according to some variable before they applied simple random sampling. You can see that multi-stage sampling indeed uses a variety of strategies. This is the sampling strategy that you are most likely to use in most situations.

EXAMPLE 6.4
(Taken from Oxenham, 2000)

Title

Signals from Uganda: what an evaluation suggests for adult educators

Method

To obtain a sound sample of people who had been successful in literacy courses, the evaluators first identified the 26 districts with literacy programmes. Then, under advice, they selected one district in each of the eight administrative regions of Uganda. Two regions were unfortunately closed for security reasons. However, the evaluators kept the number of districts at eight, but distributed them between the six remaining regions. Next, the evaluators asked each district for lists of all the people who had been successful in the literacy courses. From these lists, the evaluators took a random sample of 100 graduates from each district, yielding a total of 800 graduates.

⬚ ACTIVITY

One main disadvantage of systematic sampling is that some subgroups may be left out of the final sample. Think of a study that you wish to do. Use systematic random sampling to draw the sample. Use simple random sampling for the same study. Compare results.

SAMPLING IN AFRICAN CONTEXTS

Conventional sampling strategies rely on accurate descriptions of the population of study to determine the sampling strategy and the sample size appropriate for the study. The characteristics used to describe the populations are usually limited to categories of analysis in conventional research such as age, education, and occupation. These categories exclude other categories of analysis informed by communities' value systems and ways of perceiving reality. For instance, a sample survey to determine the income profile or wealth of a community might use indicators of wealth that are not compatible with the way a given community might categorise the wealthy and the poor. Stratifying and sampling on the basis of these indicators will automatically bias the sample towards the researcher's perception of what it is to be wealthy or poor. Some African communities are also more likely to recognise group categories rather than individual characteristics. For instance, in some communities in Botswana, adults remember their age regiments rather than their own specific ages. In some villages, wards are organised in hierarchical structures that signify social status as well as wealth.

These local variations are important if the researcher is to draw a sample that is representative of the population. Knowing the size of the population from which to draw the sample is also essential. This is not always possible in most contexts because of poor record keeping.

Participatory sampling methods

Participatory rural appraisal (PRA) approaches have been used to complement and improve conventional sampling procedures. PRA strategies such as village and social mapping can bring out characteristics of people in the community that can inform decisions on the sampling strategies to be used. Social maps might show, for instance, characteristics or indicators that distinguish individuals from one another, and how people might be grouped according to their social status. Chapter 11 discusses and illustrates the use of some of these techniques.

Village mapping

A village map involves participants drawing their village and incorporating all the features that are important in understanding a problem of study. The following is an example where a village map is used to determine the size of a population so that representative samples can be drawn. Suppose that a researcher wants to draw a proportional representative sample of adults participating in a literacy programme in a village made up of five wards. The researcher does not know the size of the population in each ward and is therefore unable to estimate the sample size from each ward. Here are some of the steps that the researcher could follow:

- Hold discussions with the community to explain the problem and identify community members from each ward who are interested in participating in the study.
- Make plans for map drawing in each ward.

- Make a list of what should be shown in the map that can assist in sample selection.

The following can be indicated on the map:

- Each household
- The names of each household's head.
- The number of family members in each household who attend literacy classes
- Separate symbols for recording females and males.

The main advantage of this procedure of determining population size is that ward members know each other and are able to give accurate information on current situations in each household. The village map could be re-checked through discussions with different ward members. In most cases researchers have used population projections made during a census. These projections may often overestimate or underestimate the populations of study because they are not sensitive to disasters such as HIV/AIDS. For instance, more people might have died of HIV/AIDS than was projected by the census. Table 6.2 summarises the sampling strategies, when they are used, advantages and disadvantages of each strategy and how conventional sampling procedures can be complemented with PRA methods.

▩ ACTIVITY

Imagine that an agricultural demonstrator wants to find out about farmers' views on the use of fertilisers in village X. In groups, discuss the most appropriate sampling strategy to use. Compare answers and discuss what the best strategy would be.

SURVEYS AND DESIGN STRUCTURES

A survey can assume different design structures. It can involve a *one-shot survey* study, *cross-sectional survey* study or a *longitudinal survey* study.

One-shot survey

This involves the collection of data at one point in time. The main disadvantage of the design is that the data collected is not sensitive to seasonal changes. For instance, data collected on fuel in winter may communicate different information from that collected during the rainy season.

Cross-sectional survey

This involves the collection of data at a specific point in time from one or more populations. For example, a researcher might wish to study the characteristics of students enrolled in an adult education programme. A cross-sectional survey will involve a study of first-, second-, third- and fourth-year students enrolled in adult education at the time of study. This design is also not sensitive to situational changes.

Longitudinal survey

This involves the collection of data at two or more periods separated by hours, days, weeks, months or years. A longitudinal survey study may use the trend analysis method, cohort method or panel method.

Technique	What it is	When to use	Advantages	Disadvantages	Use in adult education contexts in Africa
Simple random sampling	Simplest form of random sampling. Each case has an equal chance of being selected. Involves defining population, identifying case and selecting individuals by chance.	When the population is homogenous.	Simple. Each case has an equal and independent chance of being selected.	Selection depends on luck, thus not a good representation of the population.	Use with PRA technique, for example, village and social mapping, to determine population size.
Stratified random sampling	Process of selecting whereby identified subgroups in the population are represented. Involves dividing the population into homogenous subgroups and then taking a random sample from each.	When population is not homogenous, consists of subgroups/strata.	Ensures representations of population, subgroups, and minorities.	Might be tedious and time-consuming.	Use with PRA technique, for example, village and social mapping, to determine criteria for forming groups or strata and determining population size in each stratum.
Cluster sampling	Sampling in which groups and not individuals are randomly selected.	When population is large and widely dispersed.	Saves time and might be the only option when the population is large.	Not easy to select a sample that is a good representation of the entire population because groups differ. Available statistical methods are not appropriate for analysing such data and those available are less sensitive to differences that may exist in the groups.	Village mapping and social mapping can assist in identifying social groups or strata and population size.
Systematic random sampling	Sampling in which individuals are selected from a list in intervals. Members do not have an equal, independent chance of being selected.	When sampling from a large population.	It is easy and more accurate.	Certain subgroups may be excluded from the final sample.	
Multiple-stage sampling	A combination of sampling methods.	When none of the methods is effective on its own.	Efficient and effective method in some situations.	Time consuming.	Village mapping and social mapping might assist at each stage of sampling.

Table 6.2 Sampling strategies

Trend analysis method

Trend studies investigate how a population being studied changes over time. For instance, a literacy group leader might be interested in finding out about the characteristics of adults who enrol in the national literacy programme. The person would survey adults who enrol in that particular year. This would be followed by annual surveys of adults enrolling in the programme. The annual survey of beginners would continue until sufficient data is gathered to enable a discussion on trends in the characteristics of adults enrolling in the literacy programme.

Cohort method

In a cohort study, a group of people with the same characteristics is followed over a period of time. With the cohort procedure, the same population is involved, but a different sample is selected at different periods of the survey. For instance, a researcher might be interested in the career development of the adult education graduates of 2000. The researcher might choose to survey different samples every two years for a period of ten years. The main disadvantage of the cohort survey is that some members of the population of study or the sampled participants might terminate their participation before the study is completed, thus introducing some form of sample selection bias.

Panel method

With the panel method, the same sample is used at different times for a period of time. For instance, in the study on the career development of adult education graduates of 2000, the first sample of graduates that is drawn would be followed over a specified period of time. There is even greater loss of

respondents in the panel method compared to the cohort method because the same sample is used for each measurement.

ACTIVITY

Think about the different types of studies for which each of these design structures would be most appropriate.

QUESTIONNAIRE SURVEYS

So far we have distinguished surveys according to the size and composition of the sample population. Another way to distinguish surveys is according to the technique used to gather data. When technique is used to distinguish survey types, they may be categorised into questionnaire surveys, interview surveys and observation surveys. The discussion in this chapter will be limited to questionnaire surveys.

Questionnaire surveys involve the gathering of data from a population or sampled population through the use of a questionnaire. The major criticism of questionnaire surveys is that the questionnaires are designed by specialists informed by their own worldviews or perspectives and thus exclude the worldviews of the researched. Researchers are also informed by a literature review, in most cases written from perspectives informed by Western ways of knowing. The researched play mainly a passive role, answering questions thought by the researchers to be relevant and important. It was noted in Chapter 2, for example, that in the Botswana literacy survey (CSO, 1997) the definition of literacy used by UNESCO informed the construction of the questionnaire even though the researchers were aware of its limitations. In developing countries, the views of donors and international organisations funding development projects often take precedence over the views of the researchers and the researched. For a comprehensive discussion of this issue, refer back to Chapter 1 on adult education research in Africa. Gill cited in Mukherjee (1997: 96) argues that using a survey questionnaire in developing countries is like 'adopting inappropriate technology from a developed country'. The problems are summed up as follows:

- Participants are usually not familiar with the rationale behind surveys and are likely to give incorrect information. For example, in Botswana, farmers associate the cattle census with tax and are more likely to give smaller numbers in response to questions on the number of cattle they have.
- Questionnaires are written in another language and translated before or during the interview to the language that the participants understand. There is always a danger of distorting the information during translation.
- In most cases questionnaires are administered by enumerators who have a different socio-economic background from the participants. Under the circumstances, the participants are not likely to correct mistakes or misunderstandings in the questionnaires as the assumption is usually that the enumerators are more knowledgeable than them.
- Sensitive information may be difficult to collect, especially when participants are adults who are older than the enumerators. In some cultures, there are certain topics that adults cannot discuss with those younger than they.

One of the challenges facing adult education researchers in Africa is, therefore, how to construct questionnaires that are relevant to the purpose of the survey, sensitive to the culture, age and need of the participants, and inclusive of their worldviews.

Conducting a questionnaire survey

In Chapter 2, it was noted that post-positivist researchers encourage the use of multiple measures in order to reduce the amount of error in a study. Questionnaire surveys must be designed so that they serve the purpose of the survey and include the worldviews of the participants.

Defining objectives for the survey

The first step in survey research, irrespective of type, is to clearly define the objectives of the study, including the specific variables in the study. It is at the first step that adult education researchers can enhance the utility of survey reports. Researching adults, as discussed in Chapters 1 and 3, has many advantages. For instance, adults are keen to improve their lives and have a bank of knowledge that researchers can tap into so that research is relevant to the needs of the researched. The researcher can thus make use of adult knowledge by involving them at the preparatory stage of defining objectives and variables in the study. Strategies discussed in Chapter 3, namely community-centred ways of knowing, story-telling frameworks and language as a bank of knowledge, can be utilised to ensure that the voices of the respondents are included in the definition of the problem.

- *Community-centred ways of knowing:* The place where the consultation takes place is important for bringing together would-be participants and involving them in defining the problem.
- *Story-telling frameworks:* Communities' stories about the problem are important in determining the scope of the problem.

- *Language as a bank of knowledge:* Framing the problem using the people's language ensures that the problem is not limited to either the researcher's or Western ways of perceiving the problem.

Designing the questionnaire

An important step in questionnaire design is to minimise error so as to ensure the validity of the study. Error can be minimised by ensuring that the items in the questionnaire address the objectives of the study or provide information to answer the research questions raised in the study. It is always helpful, therefore, to match questionnaire items to the research questions which have been specified in the research proposal. Other important considerations include:

- *Layout of the questionnaire:* A questionnaire should have the following: cover letter, title and instructions on how to fill the questionnaire. It should also be attractive.
- *Cover letter:* Self-administered questionnaires should be accompanied by a cover letter. The cover letter should state the purpose of the survey and advance a convincing argument about the benefits of the study to the participants. It should be made clear to the participants who is conducting the study and why they are conducting the study. The expected date for completion of the questionnaire should be stated and procedures for returning the questionnaire explained. Participants should be reassured about issues of anonymity and confidentiality.
- *Title:* The questionnaire should be given a title. A questionnaire with a title may be perceived to be more important than one without. The title also helps to focus the reader on the purpose of the survey.
- *Directions:* The questionnaire should include clear and concise directions on how to complete the questionnaire.
- *Attraction:* For mail surveys, the envelope could be designed in a unique way to distinguish it from other mail. For instance, a commemorative stamp could be used to capture the research participant's attention.

Question sequence

Question order plays an important role in improving the response rate in a survey. The general recommendation is to start with easy, interesting and non-threatening questions and move to more difficult ones. For example, it is advisable to start with demographic information on the respondents and then move to questions about opinions and perspectives. The basis for this recommendation is the belief that, if the respondents are able to answer the first questions quickly, they will overcome the fear of attempting the questions that follow. For example, the first question in most household surveys in Botswana is: 'What are the names of all those persons who spent last night with this household?' This question causes a lot of anxiety among adults. Some have interpreted it as an intrusion into the private lives of family members while others fail to see its relevance to the surveys. Such a question, when placed at the beginning of the questionnaire, creates tension and could reduce response rates. In some cases respondents might refuse to participate in the survey.

Another important procedure is to place the most important questions halfway through the questionnaire rather than at the end. Questions should be in a logical sequence. For example, related items should be grouped together.

Question content

It is possible to distinguish between four different types of content, namely behaviour, attributes, beliefs and attitude (De Vaus, 1991). Formulating a questionnaire item should begin with a clear understanding of the type of content that is sought. If information sought is on behaviour, the questionnaire item should focus on what people do. If the interest of the researcher is on beliefs, the focus of the questionnaire should be on what people think is true rather than on the accuracy of their beliefs. Questionnaire items about attitudes should seek to find out what research participants think is desirable. Attribute questions focus on the characteristics of the respondents, such as their age, occupation, education, ethnicity, sex, and marital status. Failure to distinguish between these types of information can lead to the collection of the wrong type of data (De Vaus, 1991).

Question structure

A questionnaire can adopt a variety of item types. Suppose you wish to conduct a survey to identify areas of improvement in a literacy programme. Your areas of interest could include demographics of teachers who teach literacy classes and their perceptions of the quality of resources. You could construct demographic variables using the closed-ended item format, questionnaire items on resources using a checklist format, items on views on the curriculum using a Likert scale format or free response item format. See Example 6.5.

Wording of questionnaire items

Questions guide the respondent to the answer and also help to motivate the respondent to continue to cooperate and go through all the questions. It is important, therefore, that the questions be framed in simple language, be unambiguous, and be sensitive to culture, age of participants, gender, minority groups and people with disabilities.

In most instances, word usage makes a pronounced difference in creating a climate conducive to communication. Most surveys in developing countries import questionnaires designed elsewhere and adapt them for use in developing countries. In most cases these adapted questionnaires use language insensitive to adults in African contexts. Some issues, such as sexual attitudes and behaviour in a family planning survey, might be sensitive in some cultures.

Under the circumstances, knowledge of local terms that are respectful can ease the tension and anxiety of adults. There are in every African community topics that are not discussed because of their sensitivity. Knowledge of local terms that are polite could help to make the wording of the questions culture-relevant and -sensitive.

Length of questionnaire

Generally, long questionnaires get lower response rates. Low response rates introduce error in the survey because they affect the sample. There may be many participants who do not respond from a particular strata or group. In that way, their views might be under-represented. It is thus important to maximise response rate by shortening the questionnaire. One way to keep the questionnaire short is to specify how a question will be analysed and how the information will be used. If you cannot specify how you intend to analyse a question or use the information, it is advisable not to include it in the questionnaire.

EXAMPLE 6.5

Topic

Investigating areas of improvement in the literacy programme

Demographic information

Instructions: Please respond by placing a tick   in the spaces provided.

What is your sex?
1. Male   2. Female

What is your highest academic/professional training?
1. Junior Certificate
2. Cambridge certificate
3. Cambridge plus Primary Teacher certificate
4. Other

Checklist

The following is a list of educational materials. Put a check after each educational material that is available to you as a teacher of literacy classes.
1. English second language course book 1
2. English second language course book 2
3. English second language teachers guide level 1
4. English second language teachers guide level 2

Likert

The following are a number of statements describing the literacy curriculum. Indicate by making a cross [×] whether you strongly agree [SA], agree [A], are uncertain [U], disagree [D] or strongly disagree [SD].

The goals of the literacy curriculum are clear to most teachers	SA	A	U	D	SD
Teaching materials are available in most teaching centres	SA	A	U	D	SD
Most teachers follow the curriculum	SA	A	U	D	SD

Free response

Describe the quality of teaching in your centre.

⌗ ACTIVITY

List the issues that would be considered sensitive in your community. How can you word questions about these issues in an appropriate way?

ADMINISTERING A SURVEY

A questionnaire survey can be administered face-to-face, through the mail, the Internet or by telephone. The choice of which mode to use depends on a variety of factors. Among the factors to consider are:

- Level of education of the respondents
- Length of study
- Availability of resources
- Spread of respondents
- Topic and its sensitivity
- The language barrier
- Level of accuracy of information required.

Modes of administering questionnaires are discussed and their implication for use with adults in the context of African communities highlighted.

Face-to-face survey questionnaire

In a face-to-face questionnaire survey, the researcher interviews the participants using the questionnaire as a guide. This is the most common mode of administering surveys in contexts where literacy rates are low. It is also appropriate for adults who are visually or hearing impaired. Livestock surveys, census surveys and most literacy surveys in Africa have used face-to-face survey questionnaires. The main advantage is that the questionnaire can be adapted to the situation and data collected that will accommodate adult voices otherwise

excluded by the standardised questionnaires, for example, those administered through the mail. There is room to allow the respondents to express themselves using their own ways of knowing. The interviewer can explain unclear questions and probe to obtain meaningful information. The interviewer also gets to know the kind of person who declines to take part in the interview. This enables the researcher to explain possible selection biases that might arise. Face-to-face questionnaires also have the advantage of high response rates.

Face-to-face questionnaires are, however, not appropriate for sensitive topics. For instance, in a survey on sexual behaviour, adults may not feel comfortable to disclose their sexual behaviour. Confidentiality is also compromised in a face-to-face questionnaire, as anonymity of respondents is not possible. As such, information that is sensitive might be excluded from the questionnaire, as it may cause anxiety among respondents. The technique is also time consuming, resource intensive and expensive. Interviewers have to be well trained.

Mail survey

This is when questionnaires are sent through the mail. Mail surveys have advantages. They can be administered to a wide range of respondents. Respondents fill out the questionnaire at a time convenient to them. They are easy to administer and the costs are minimal. Issues of confidentiality are addressed, as respondents can be anonymous. They are therefore appropriate when personal and sensitive information is sought. Variations in the responses introduced by questions from the respondents and probing by the interviewer as in a face-to-face survey are avoided. Responses are therefore easy to analyse.

Mail surveys, however, have their disadvantages. The response rates are low. It is also not possible to explain difficult and unclear questions to respondents or probe for more answers. They are not appropriate to the majority of adults in the rural areas in Africa because of the low literacy rates. Mail might not reach respondents quickly enough for a variety of reasons. Some African communities have a variety of settlement patterns. In Botswana the majority of the people have three homes: the lands, the cattle post and the home. During the year people move between these three settlements. In some countries communication systems are slow because of poor infrastructure. It is also not appropriate for people with disabilities, such as those who are visually impaired. The medium of communication is also a problem. In some countries in Africa adults are literate in their mother tongue. Establishing the language of the respondents to whom the questionnaire is mailed might be a problem.

Telephone survey questionnaire

In this mode, the researcher interviews the respondent through the telephone using a questionnaire guide. Telephone interviews can produce very high response rates. It is easy to cover a large geographic area within a short time at reasonable cost. The interviewer can explain questions that are unclear. The interviewer can probe for more information. It is also easy to avoid unknown bias from refusals. This strategy is, however, less appropriate for communities of adults in African contexts for a variety of reasons. The majority of those residing in the rural areas in Africa do not have telephones. Another common problem is that

Mode	Advantage	Disadvantage	Appropriateness to adult education contexts in Africa
Face-to-face	■ High return rate ■ The researcher can probe and adapt questionnaire items to situations ■ Appropriate for illiterates, adults, visually or hearing impaired.	■ It is time consuming ■ Anonymity is not possible ■ There is possibility of interviewer bias ■ Its expensive ■ Complex scoring of unstructured items is required.	■ Most appropriate in adult education research contexts ■ People's voices can be accommodated.
Mail	■ Inexpensive ■ Easy to score most items because they are standardised ■ Research participants respond in their own time ■ Responses can be confidential and anonymous.	■ Associated with low response rates ■ Cannot probe to get further clarification ■ Can only be used with literate people ■ Mail might not reach respondents ■ Takes a long time ■ Has low return rate.	■ Not appropriate because of low literacy rates ■ Determining language of communication can pose problems.
Telephone	■ High response rate ■ Quick data collection ■ Can reach a wide range of respondents.	■ Requires phone numbers ■ Difficult to get in-depth data ■ Interview can be easily terminated.	■ The majority of the poor and those residing in the rural areas may not have telephones.
Internet	■ Costs are low ■ High response rate.	■ Accessible to a small percentage of the population.	■ Not accessible to the majority of adults.

Table 6.3 Modes of administering questionnaire surveys

the few who do have phones may not be listed in the telephone directories or the lists may be incomplete. Determining the size of the population thus becomes difficult and errors in sampling become inevitable. There is also the risk of the respondents' terminating the interview either because the interviewer has asked a sensitive question or because other people have interrupted the respondent. Telephone surveys, like face-to-face surveys, also need trained interviewers.

Internet surveys

Unlike mail surveys, these have high response rates. It is easy to guide respondents by using visual elements. They are also fast and generally cheap. Web surveys are not appropriate for adults in the majority of communities in Africa because they do not have access to e-mail and the Internet. Another disadvantage is that, even when audio-visual equipment is used with those who have access to email, it can be confusing. One needs technological expertise to administer surveys online.

Table 6.3 summarises modes of administering questionnaire surveys and their appropriateness to African contexts.

⊞ ACTIVITY

Write down ways in which you can ensure that mail surveys in African contexts produce adequate results.

IMPLEMENTING A SURVEY

Pilot testing questionnaires

Survey questionnaires should be pre-tested with a sample population identical to the population in which the survey will be

carried out. With self-administered instruments, for instance, a questionnaire sent through the mail or the Internet, the pilot test seeks to:

- Find out whether participants understand the rationale for the survey and are willing to participate.
- Establish whether there were unclear or ambiguous terms; cultural, gender or ethnic bias or offensive language used in the questionnaire.
- Find out whether directions in the questionnaire are clear and easy to follow.
- Find out whether the questionnaire format is acceptable.
- Ask the participants for suggestions that can help to improve the instrument.

Sending out self-administered questionnaires

The following is a checklist for preparing to send out a mail or Internet questionnaire survey:

- Write a covering letter.
- Prepare postage envelopes and decide on a method of returning responses to questionnaires only.
- Select a date for mailing and deadlines for returning responses.
- Decide on follow-up of non-responses.

Follow-up to increase response rates

It is important to note that no matter how much effort the researcher takes to construct an appropriate questionnaire, there will always be participants who do not respond to the self-administered questionnaires. Response rates of about 60% raise concern about the representativeness of the sample (Gay and Airasan, 1997). For instance, the characteristics of those who responded to the questionnaire may be different from those who did not respond. Where the non-respondents are known and can be contacted, the researcher can randomly sample and interview them to obtain their demographic information so that they can be compared with those who responded. If the two groups are similar, it can be assumed that the sample, even though smaller, does not differ from the initial sample and is therefore representative of the population from which it is drawn. If the two groups are different, then findings can no longer be generalised to the population from which it is drawn. These should be discussed in the report.

Researchers should aim to raise response rates to at least 80%. The initial step in increasing response rates should entail sending reminder letters to those who did not return the questionnaires, provided the researcher is able to identify them. Where it is not possible to determine who returned questionnaires, reminder letters should be sent to all.

Table 6.4 summarises steps and decisions to be considered in carrying out surveys.

SUMMARY

Designing a quantitative study involves making decisions on a lot of factors. In almost all cases, decisions are made in order to help reduce the amount of error in the study so that the study can be considered to be objective, valid and reliable. You have seen in this chapter that, in improving the objectivity, validity and reliability of studies in adult education in African contexts, researchers need to:

- Involve adults in the formulation of research problems so they can understand the problems from their perspectives

- Adopt a variety of participatory methods when constructing questionnaires
- Observe all procedures that improve objectivity, validity and reliability in quantitative research.

KEY POINTS

- Quantitative studies assume that knowledge is objective and findings can be generalised to the population from which the sample is drawn.
- Errors in sampling may introduce bias in the research findings.
- In questionnaire construction, the researcher's perceived view of the problem may marginalise the voices of those who are researched.
- PRA methods can be used to complement sample selection procedures, to define and focus the research questions and to inform the construction of relevant gender- and culture-sensitive data-gathering instruments.

▦ ACTIVITY

Find a journal on adult education in your library and select two studies that used a particular survey method. For each:

1 Describe the type of survey used.
2 Describe the sampling procedure used.
3 Identify the size of the sample and discuss whether it was representative of the population from which it was drawn.
4 Discuss the possible sampling biases that could have arisen and how the researcher would have controlled for them.
5 Identify the instrument used to collect the data and its appropriateness to the research problem and the research participants.

Steps in questionnaire surveys	Issues to consider
1 Decide on topic and formulate the research problem.	Involve the researched communities in formulation of the research problem.
2 Decide on type of survey. Is it a census survey or a sample survey?	Consider the size of the population and implications for costs and time required to complete the survey.
3 Decide on design: Is it a ■ One-shot survey ■ Longitudinal survey ■ Cross-sectional survey?	Consider the sensitivity of problem to situational changes.
4 Describe the population of study.	Consider availability of records for estimating the size of the population to be studied. Identify other ways of establishing the size of the population.
5 Select the sampling procedures from the following: ■ Simple random sampling ■ Stratified simple random sampling ■ Cluster sampling ■ Systematic sampling ■ Multiple-stage sampling.	Involve researched communities in identifying indigenous ways of complementing conventional sampling methods.
6 Design the data-gathering instruments.	Involve communities in the design of the data-gathering instruments to ensure gender, ethnic and cultural sensitivity.
7 Select a mode of administering questionnaire from the following: ■ Face-to-face interview ■ Mail ■ Telephone ■ The web.	Consider duration of study, resources and characteristics of the research participants.
8 Pilot test the instrument.	The population on which the instrument is pilot tested should be identical to that on which the survey will be carried out.
9 Implement the survey.	Decide on procedures for follow-ups.

Table 6.4 Steps and decisions in carrying out a survey

FURTHER QUESTIONS

Discuss ways in which indigenous knowledge systems could be used to inform the formulation of a research problem and complement sample selection procedures and conventional questionnaire instruments.

SUGGESTED READINGS

Aitchison, J. 1999. 'Literacy and adult basic education and training in South Africa: A quick survey'. *Adult Education and Development*, Vol. 53, pp. 99–120.

Alreck, P. and Settle, R. 1995. *The survey research handbook*. Chicago: Irwin.

Gay, L. R. and Airasian, P. 2000. *Educational research: Competencies for analysis and applications*. Upper Saddle River, NJ: Prentice Hall.

Murkherjee, N. 1997. *Participatory rural appraisal and questionnaire survey*. New Delhi: Concept Publishing Company.

Merriam, S. B. and Simpson, E. L. 2000. *A guide to research for educators and trainers of adults*. Malabar: Krieger.

Oxenham, J. 2000. 'Signals from Uganda: What an evaluation suggests for adult educators'. *Adult Education and Development*, Vol. 55, pp. 228–260.

Chapter 7

Working with survey data

OVERVIEW

This chapter introduces approaches to organising, summarising, analysing and interpreting quantitative data. It focuses on how quantitative data is organised and the importance of using appropriate statistical tests to analyse different types of quantitative data. The chapter further demonstrates how tables, graphs and charts can be used to communicate research findings.

LEARNING OBJECTIVES

By the end of this chapter, you should be able to:

1. Summarise survey data using graphs, charts and tables.
2. Code data and use the SPSS computer package to analyse survey data.
3. Interpret t-tests and chi-squares.

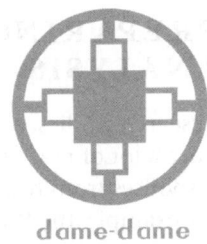

dame-dame

KEY TERMS

coding Translating responses from research participants into a form that can be read by a computer.

descriptive statistics Data analysis techniques that allow the researcher to summarise and compare sets of data.

inferential statistics Data analysis techniques that allow the researcher to determine whether the results obtained from a sample are the same results that would be obtained from the entire population.

interval scale Measures a specific amount so that differences in the measures can be determined.

nominal scale When persons or objects are classified, categorised or named without implying that one category is better that the other.

ordinal scale Ranks according to degree to which a participant possesses a characteristic of interest.

ratio scale A measurement based upon predetermined equal intervals and which has a time zero point.

⊞ BEFORE YOU START

You have probably read some research reports. Most of them will illustrate findings with numerical figures; some with illustrative devices such as graphs and charts. Some will refer to statistical tests and significance of results. Think of the statistics that you are already familiar with and how they could help you to summarise data from a survey. Imagine that you carried out a survey to describe the characteristics of all students taking a research methods course of your choice. You will probably use *descriptive statistics* such as percentages to report the findings. Suppose that you wanted to carry out a sample survey to describe the characteristics of first-year students in your university. You would want to generalise the findings to the population of first year students. Descriptive statistics will no longer be sufficient. In addition to descriptive statistics you would need *inferential statistics*. This chapter introduces you to the use of descriptive and inferential statistics to summarise and report findings from survey data.

PREPARING DATA FOR ANALYSIS

Research studies, especially surveys, produce a lot of raw data in the form of responses from research participants. Take, for example, the Botswana Literacy Survey questionnaire and the Setswana Reading and Writing Test administered to research participants included as Appendix 1 at the end of this chapter. The reading and writing tests have to be scored and each participant assigned a score. Similarly, responses on the questionnaire must be assigned labels called codes so that they can be systematically organised and summarised.

The coding process

Coding begins with identifying variables in the study and assigning them names. In the Botswana Literacy Survey questionnaire, for example, all the numbered items from 1 to 7 represent a variable. Variables thus include the participants' identity, age, sex, school and grade-level. In the example above, every questionnaire item is a single variable. This, however, is not always the case. Sometimes a questionnaire item can assume different variable names.

Naming variables

Once variables have been given names, responses for each variable are assigned codes.

Codes can assume numerical values (numbers) or legend values (letters). The Botswana Literacy Questionnaire shows how each variable was coded using numerical values. Table 7.1 illustrates data

entered into a computer using the Statistical Package for the Social Sciences (SPSS), which is the most frequently used software package for computer analysis of survey data. The variable names are **ID, Gen** (for gender), **Age, Grade, Rea** (which stands for reasons for not attending school), **Reads** (which stands for score in reading Setswana) and **Writset** (which stands for score in writing Setswana). Fifty participants responded to the questionnaire, and also wrote the Setswana reading and writing tests. You can see that there are variations in the way participants responded to questions on each variable. In some cases numerical values were assigned to the responses while in others the response was recorded as provided by the respondents. For instance, the actual score and age for each respondent were recorded. Sex and reasons for not going to school were assigned numerical codes. Gender was coded as 1 for male and 2 for female.

Characteristics of variables

Once the data are entered into the computer, the next stage is determining the appropriate statistical procedure to use. The first step in determining the procedure is to identify the types of scale used to measure each variable. Variables have two basic characteristics. They can be described as continuous or discrete. A continuous variable is one that can take a variety of values, including decimals and fractions. A discrete variable is one that is only whole numbers, where the numbers represent ranking or classification. There

Id	Gen	Age	Grade	Rea	Reads (max score 50)	Writset (max score 50)
1	2	12	1	1	18	20
2	1	45	1	1	18	18
3	1	40	1	1	23	20
4	1	35	1	2	19	19
5	2	20	1	1	21	21
6	2	21	1	3	18	18
7	2	15	1	4	17	15
8	2	15	1	1	16	16
9	1	30	1	3	24	24
10	1	35	1	3	26	23
11	2	16	2	3	25	25
12	2	14	2	3	23	23
13	1	30	2	4	26	23
14	1	31	2	4	28	28
15	1	35	2	4	26	25
16	1	30	2	4	25	25
17	1	30	2	3	27	20
18	1	31	2	3	24	23
19	1	32	2	3	25	25
20	1	35	2	1	31	28
21	2	36	3	4	29	29
22	2	35	3	3	32	30
23	2	35	3	1	34	34
24	2	28	3	3	36	30
25	1	28	3	3	36	28
26	1	27	3	4	28	28
27	1	25	3	4	27	27
28	1	30	3	4	31	29
29	2	20	3	1	25	25
30	2	22	3	3	22	22
31	2	35	4	3	28	28
32	1	18	4	3	26	26
33	2	18	4	2	31	31
34	2	40	4	2	35	30
35	1	41	4	2	36	36
36	1	30	4	1	20	20
37	1	25	4	2	25	25
38	1	26	4	2	26	26
39	2	27	4	2	30	30
40	2	30	4	2	31	26
41	2	30	5	2	34	34
42	2	15	5	1	35	32
43	1	16	5	1	36	32
44	1	17	5	4	18	18
45	2	17	5	4	22	22
46	1	18	5	4	23	30
47	2	19	5	2	24	24
48	1	20	5	2	25	28
49	2	24	5	3	27	27
50	2	34	5	2	33	33

Table 7.1 SPSS data layout

are four scales of measurement: nominal, ordinal, interval and ratio. All variables are represented in at least one of these four measurement scales.

1 *Nominal:* This is when variables can be classified as categorical. A *nominal scale* labels, classifies or categorises variables without implying that one variable or category is better than the other. In the Botswana Literacy Questionnaire, variables with a nominal scale or measurement are **ID**, **Gender**, and **Rea**. Data at this level is less useful compared to that in other measurement scales because the amount of difference between variables cannot be determined.

2 *Ordinal:* This is when variables can be classified and also ordered according to the characteristic of interest. An example of data in an *ordinal scale* of measurement is grading student assignments on a scale that orders the work from excellent to poor. An assignment that is classified as 'excellent' is the best, while 'good' is better than 'poor'. The disadvantage of this measurement scale is that it is not possible to measure the amount of difference between the ranks. For instance, assignments given a grade of poor can have marks ranging between 0 and 4 out of a 10 point scale. When poor is given as a grade or score, it is not possible to determine the extent to which it is poor.

3 *Interval:* These variables have all the characteristics of nominal and ordinal variables and in addition have equal intervals of a specific amount. The points can be located along the scale and the difference between each point determined. Examples of the variables with data measured at the interval level are the Setswana Reading and Writing Test scores. When variables have equal intervals, it is assumed that the difference between a score of 18 and a score

24 is the same as the difference between a score of 30 and a score of 36. *Interval scales*, however, do not have a true zero point. Thus when Chipo scores 36 and Mugabe scores 18 in a reading test, it does not mean that Chipo knows double what Mugabe knows. The advantage of data at the interval level of measurement is that it can be converted into ordinal and nominal data. For instance, scores on reading and writing Setswana can be regrouped such that scores of 10–20 are awarded a C grade, 21–30 a B grade, and those with 31 or more an A grade. The flexibility to change the data to lower scales makes it possible to choose from a wide variety of statistical analysis procedures.

4 *Ratio*: This is a measure of a specific amount with an absolute zero. *Ratio scale* represents the highest, most precise level of measurement and has all the characteristics of nominal, ordinal and interval scales. For example, the difference between a person weighing forty kilograms and one weighing eighty kilograms is the same as that of a person weighing sixty kilograms and a person weighing twenty kilograms. However, the person weighing eighty kilograms is twice as heavy as the person weighing forty kilograms.

ACTIVITY

Read the literacy questionnaire at the end of the chapter and identify variables at the nominal, ordinal and interval level.

DESCRIPTIVE STATISTICS

Once data is organised in a manner that is retrievable, the next step is to describe the data by presenting it in a readable and interpretable form. Statistics refers to the collection, organisation, analysis and presentation of data which is numerical. The results of the analysis, which are presented in numbers, are used to answer questions about the situation that relate to the data. *Descriptive statistics* are used when the purpose of the research is to describe the data in the study. In a survey study, one of the first steps is to describe the sample size and its characteristics. In the Botswana Literacy Survey, for example, there were 26 female and 24 male respondents. The description allows the researcher to compare the sample to the original (or planned) sample size. Descriptive statistics are also used when data is obtained from a whole population. Take, for example, annual educational statistics on enrolment, retention dropouts, school resources and teachers in formal and non-formal education. The education statistics yearbooks present massive numbers indicating the occurrence or frequency of these variables for both formal and non-formal education.

Large numbers are difficult to remember and their implications difficult to understand. Researchers thus usually summarise responses using graphs, charts, figures, pictures and tables. These illustrative devices provide some idea of the occurrence of variables at a brief glance. Illustrations communicate quickly and have a more forceful impact and a more lasting impression than written material. They are more revealing than written materials and may even be more convincing than a discussion. The description of data is illustrated using bar graphs, histograms and line graphs as shown in Figures 7.1, 7.2 and 7.3.

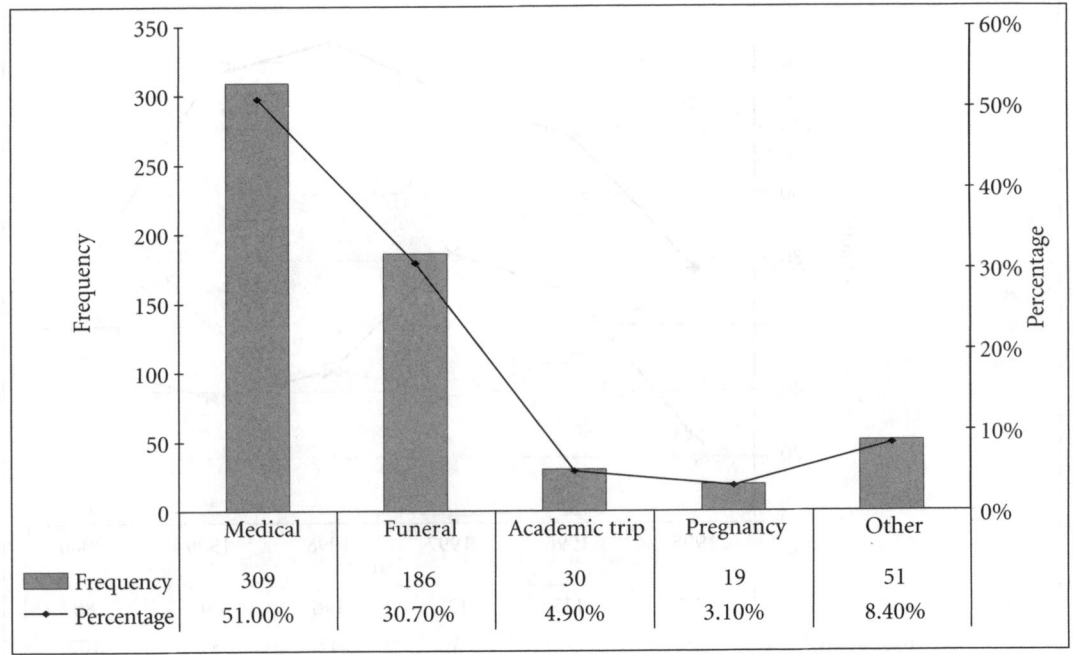

Figure 7.1 Reasons for students' absence (bar graph)

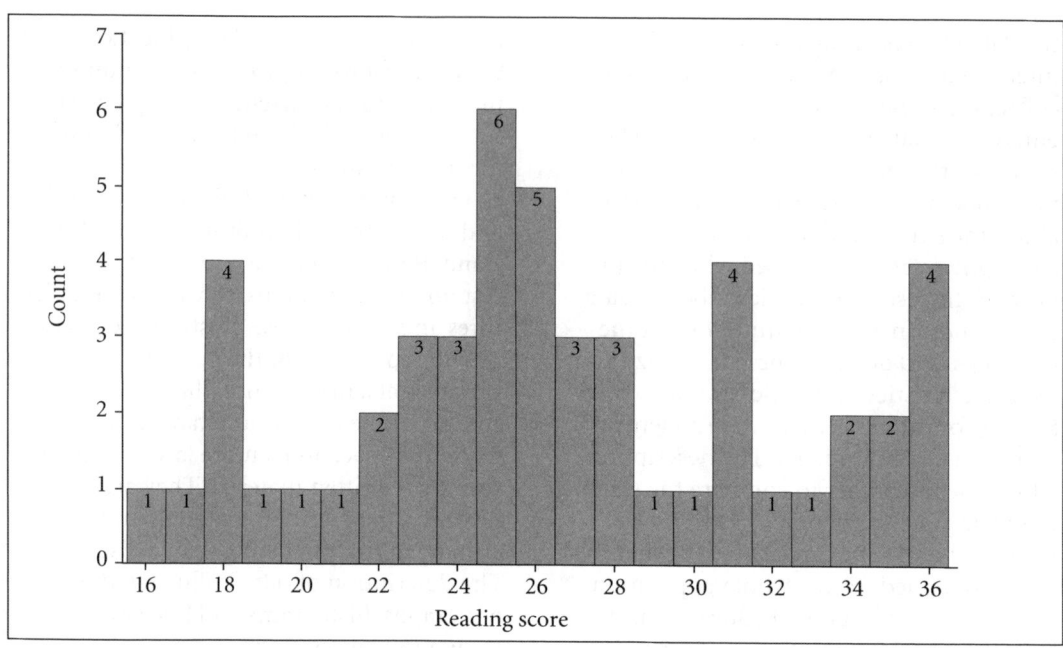

Figure 7.2 Setswana reading score histogram

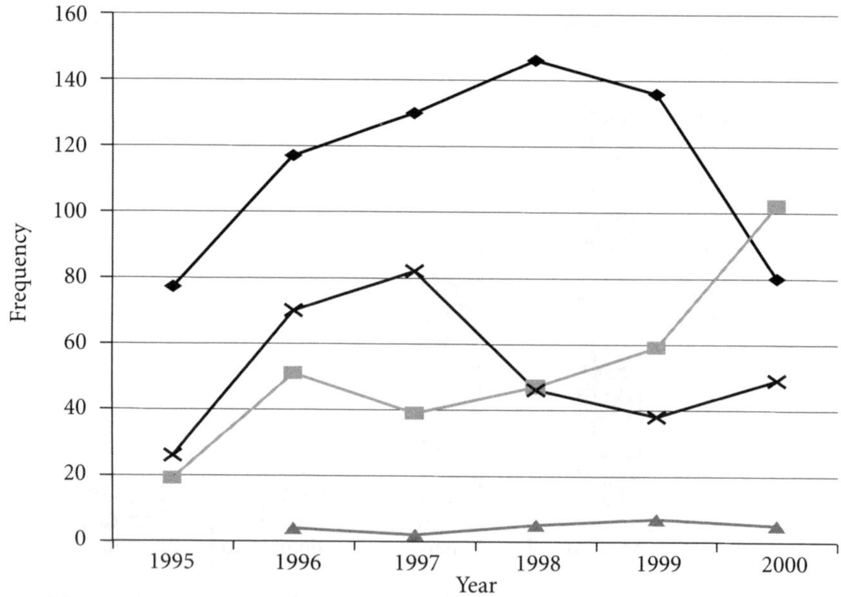

	1995	1996	1997	1998	1999	2000
Sick leave	77	117	130	146	136	80
Compassionate leave	19	51	39	47	59	102
Leave without pay		4	2	5	7	5
Maternity leave	26	70	82	46	38	49

Figure 7.3 Trends in four types of leave: University of Botswana, 1995–2000 (line graph)

Bar graphs

Bar graphs can be used to illustrate the frequency of a response where the data for a given variable is at nominal or ordinal levels of measurement. The bars are placed in the graph with space between each bar to illustrate the discreteness of each category. Figure 7.1 illustrates the use of a bar graph to summarise reasons for which students were absent from school. From the bar graph you quickly see that, most of the time, students were absent from classes for medical reasons. Percentages and figures are also given to provide facts on the visual graph.

Histograms

Histograms illustrate numerical data at either interval or ratio level. They basically illustrate continuous variables. In a histogram, the bars show the frequency of occurrence of responses to a questionnaire item or a variable. In a histogram, each bar touches the one adjacent to it. This is to illustrate that the data or variable is continuous. Figure 7.2 is a histogram describing the distribution of the Setswana reading scores.

Line graphs and polygons

Polygons illustrate interval or ratio level data for continuous variables. A polygon is a line form of a histogram. Other types of line graphs that can replace bar graphs are generally used with nominal or ordinal data where the variables tend to be discrete. Figure 7.3 shows a line graph illustrating types of leave taken by employees of the University of Botswana. You can see that the frequency of sick leave increased from 1995 until 2000, when it declined. The graph also allows you to make a quick comparison of the trends in the four types of leave, namely sick leave, compassionate leave, leave without pay and maternity leave.

ACTIVITY

Use the data from the Botswana Literacy Survey provided in Table 7.1 to illustrate the use of bar graphs, histograms, and line graphs and polygons.

MEASURES OF CENTRAL TENDENCY

Survey data can be summarised by using a point in a given distribution around which responses tend to centre. This point can therefore be used as the most representative value for a particular distribution. These points are called measures of central tendency, of which the mode, median and mean are the most common.

Mode

The mode is a measure of central tendency that is used most appropriately with nominal data. The mode is the most common value, answer or response in a given distribution. In a frequency distribution table, the mode is the value with the highest frequency. In a histogram, it is the value with the highest bar. In Figure 7.2, for instance, the score of 25 is the mode. It allows the researcher to draw conclusions about the distribution of scores. The mode is a very crude measure of central tendency, as it does not consider other values in a distribution. For instance, it is silent on the highest and the lowest scores.

Median

The median is a measure of central tendency that is most appropriately used with ordinal data. The median is the middle point in a distribution. This is the point below which or above which 50% of the values fall. To identify this point, values are ordered. When there is an odd number of values in the distribution, then there will be a value left at the center when the values are ordered: this would be the median. If there is an even number of values, then the two values in the middle (when the values are ordered) will be averaged to give the median.

In the Botswana Literacy Survey, for example, the age of participants was recorded. Age can be ordered and therefore age is an ordinal variable. In ordering age, the lowest age is 12 and the highest age is 45. In the ordered list of age of the 50 participants, the 25th and 26th age will be in the middle. The 25th age is 28 and the 26th age is 28. The median therefore will be the average of the two $(28 + 28) \div 2$, which is 28.

The median is also a crude measure of central tendency as it only considers one value in the distribution. Suppose you were assisting an income generation project that makes shoes, and that you helped the members to conduct a market survey in which you wanted to find out about the demand for a specific shoe brand. You calculated the median shoe size for the brand from the data and found that it was size five for women and seven for men. Using the median as an indicator of the shoe sizes to buy will be less useful than using the mode. The mode would, for instance, tell you the shoe size most people are likely to buy.

Mean or average

The mean is a measure of central tendency that is used most appropriately with interval and ratio data. The mean is the average of the values for any given variable. The mean is calculated by dividing the sum of all values by their number. In the Botswana Literacy Survey, for example, the Setswana reading scores of participants were recorded. Scores represent interval data. The mean will be the sum of all 50 scores divided by 5. Most measures in educational research use interval or ratio data. This makes the mean the most frequently used measure of central tendency. The mean is one measure that accounts for all the values in a distribution and this makes it a more precise measure of central tendency than the mode and median. It is sensitive to extreme values because it considers all values in a distribution. Extreme values are values that are either very low or very high in a given distribution. For instance, zero scores or perfect scores in a distribution are most likely to lower or inflate the mean.

▦ ACTIVITY

Use the data from the Botswana Literacy Survey provided in Table 7.1 and calculate the mode, median and mean for both the reads and the writset variables. Discuss what each measure of central tendency is able to convey about the data.

MEASURES OF DISPERSION

A measure of central tendency does not indicate how spread out the values are. It is always useful to report a typical measure with another measure that shows the spread of values. Measures that show the spread of numerical data are called measures of dispersion or variability. Commonly used measures of dispersion are the range, variance and the standard deviation.

Range

The range indicates the distance separating the lowest and highest values in a distribution. For the reading score in the Botswana Literacy Survey, the lowest score is 14 and the highest score is 36.

EXAMPLE 7.1

Variance $(s^2) = \dfrac{(X - \overline{X})^2}{N}$

Standard deviation $(s) = \sqrt{\dfrac{(X - \overline{X})^2}{N}}$

Primer five example using Setswana reading scores

ID	X	$(X - \overline{X})$	$(X - \overline{X})^2$
41	34	6.3	39.69
42	35	7.3	53.29
43	36	8.3	68.89
44	18	−9.7	94.09
45	22	−5.7	32.49
46	23	−4.7	22.09
47	24	−3.7	13.69
48	25	−2.7	7.29
49	27	−.7	.49
50	33	5.3	28.09

$\Sigma(X - \overline{X})^2 = 36.10$

Mean of scores $(\overline{X}) = 27.7$

N = 10

$s^2 = \dfrac{360}{10}$

$= 36.01$

$s = \sqrt{36.10}$

$= 6.00$

The range is 36 − 17 = 19. If the range is a small value, it means that the values in the distribution are close together and if it is large, it means that the values are spread out. The range is not a dependable measure as it only considers two values in the distribution. It can be used to give an approximation of the spread of scores.

Variance and standard deviation

Variance is another measure of the spread of values. The square root of the variance is called the standard deviation. The standard deviation indicates the extent to which values cluster around the mean or the extent to which they spread away from the mean. Again, as with the range, a large value indicates that values are spread out and a small value indicates that values are close together.

Example 7.1 illustrates how to calculate a standard deviation using Setswana reading scores for primer five respondents. Scores from ten respondents are used. The calculated mean score is 27.7 and the standard deviation is 6.0.

✳ ACTIVITY

Calculate the variance and standard deviation of the writset (write Setswana) scores provided in Table 7.1 (the Botswana Literacy Study). What can you deduce about the scores from the standard deviation?

SIGNIFICANCE TESTING

In Chapter 6, it was shown that researchers limit data collection to a randomly selected population. Also shown was that samples are randomly selected to enable the researcher to generalise findings to the population from which the sample was drawn. When a researcher wants to use samples to draw conclusions that are generalised to the population from which the sample was drawn, *inferential statistics* are used. Inferential statistics are therefore statistics that allow one to draw conclusions about the population by using a sample. This is why it is important that the sample be:

- Randomly selected
- Representative of the population from which it is drawn
- Large enough to enable correct estimates of the population.

In using inferential statistics there are two tests that can be used: parametric and non-parametric tests. An example of a parametric test is a t-test and that of a non-parametric test is a chi-square. Non-parametric tests are useful with nominal and ordinal data while parametric are useful with interval and ratio data. Inferential statistics shall be considered using a t-test and a chi-square.

Suppose that, in the Botswana Literacy Survey, the researcher is interested in knowing whether there are any differences in Setswana reading mean scores for females and males. The mean score for females is 26.92 and for males is 26.12. The mean scores look different. But are these real differences? Could these be differences that are due to sampling error or chance? Are these differences the same as those in the population from which the sample was drawn? For instance, the differences could be due to an error in sampling. The mean for females in the sample could be higher only because higher achievers are over-represented in the sample. A researcher can carry out a statistical test to determine or to compare the means in the above example, relative to the degree of variation among scores for males and females, to determine the probability that the means of the two groups are real differences and not chance occurrences or differences due largely to error.

Which test to use depends on the research questions and research design.

✳ ACTIVITY

Determine the type of statistical tests to use to answer the following research questions.
1   Are there significant differences in the Setswana reading mean scores for females and males?
2   Are there any significant differences in the reasons that males and females give for not attending literacy classes?

Before a statistical test is carried out, researchers hypothesise about relationships between variables of interest. A statement about such relationships is called a research hypothesis. The research hypothesis is best written as a null hypothesis. A null hypothesis is a statistical hypothesis that proposes no relationship between variables. This allows the researcher to compare groups to determine whether the observed differences are based on chance or if they are a reflection of true differences. The probability of the differences is used to make the decision. The size of this probability is used to decide whether the null hypothesis is rejected or retained. Rejecting the null hypothesis implies that the observed differences probably represent true differences. When the null hypothesis is retained, it implies that the observed differences are probably due to chance.

At the beginning of the research, a researcher decides on a level of risk he or she is willing to take in making a wrong decision should the null hypothesis be rejected. This is called a level of significance, or alpha (α). When a true null hypothesis is rejected, it is said that the researcher has committed a Type I error. The null hypothesis is rejected when the probability of the observed differences is smaller than the set level of significance and it is retained if the observed probability is larger that the set value. The researcher determines this level of significance. In social sciences, this is usually set at 5%. That is, a researcher is willing to take the risk of rejecting a true null hypothesis 5% of the time. Consider the statistical test for the first research question.

Independent sample t-test

Researchers use t-tests to test whether differences are true or simply due to error. T-tests are used to compare two means. There are different types of t-tests. If you want to find out whether the mean of females is significantly different from that of males in the reading score using data from the Botswana Literacy Survey, an inde-

pendent t-test would be appropriate. This test can only be carried out if the following assumptions are met.

- Values or scores when plotted form a bell-like shape indicating a normal distribution.
- When there are two samples, the variances of the observations in each sample must be equal. If the scores are not normally distributed, then the t-test will not be appropriate.
- The dependent variable is at the interval measurement of scale.

The procedures in the analysis and interpretation of the findings on the research question are displayed in Example 7.2. An SPSS output of the analysis is shown in Table 7.2. From the output you need to extract the following:

- *Critical value*: An absolute value that a test statistic must exceed for the null hypothesis to be rejected.
- *Degrees of freedom*: The extent of possible variations that one can make with the variables of concern.
- *Level of significance or alpha* (α): The level of risk of rejecting a true null hypothesis.

EXAMPLE 7.2

Research question 1: Are there significant differences in the Setswana reading mean scores for males and females?

Null hypothesis (H_0): There is no significant difference in the mean reading scores of males and females.
H_0: $\mu_1 = \mu_2$ (where μ_1 is the mean of males and μ_2 is the mean of females)

Level of significance: $\alpha = .05$

		Levene's test for equality of variances		t-test for equality of means						
		F	Sig.	t	df	Sig. (2-tailed)	Mean difference	Std. error difference	95% Confidence interval of the difference	
									Lower	Upper
READ-ING	Equal variances assumed	4.612	.037	-.503	48	.617	-.80	1.59	-4.00	2.40
	Equal variances not assumed			-.498	43.415	.621	-.80	1.61	-4.04	2.44

Table 7.2 SPSS output

	Mean	Standard deviation	Number of participants	t-value	P
Male	26.12	4.91	26		
Female	26.92	6.31	24		
T_{48}				-.503	.617

Table 7.3 T-test on male and female mean differences in reading

Decision rule: Reject H_0 if the observed t-value is greater than the central t or if the probability of obtaining that t-value is less than the set level of significance. Retain H_0 if the probability is greater than the set level of significance.

From Table 7.2, t_{48} = -.503 p = .617

Decision: Retain H_0 because .617 > .05

Statistical conclusion: The mean reading score for male research participants is not significantly different from the mean reading score for females.

Researcher conclusion: The researcher goes further to interpret the statistical conclusion in relation to the data and the literature review. For instance, does the statistical conclusion concur with the literature? If not, what possible contextual variables explain the differences? What can one therefore conclude about male and female Setswana reading scores?

When the findings are reported, a table is drawn up showing the means, standard deviation, the critical t value and the degrees of freedom. The t-test SPSS output does not show the means or standard deviations. These should be requested separately. Table 7.3 displays the summary table that is reported with the findings.

⊞ ACTIVITY

Discuss why it is important to calculate the significance of your data.

CHI-SQUARE TEST

When data is nominal a t-test is no longer appropriate for testing statistical significance. In such cases an appropriate test would be a chi-square test. A chi-square is a test that makes use of cross-tabulation to assess categorical or count data. A chi-square test compares the observed proportions in a study to the expected proportions to see if they are significantly different.

The chi-square distribution is the most commonly used method to compare categorical or count data. Example 7.3 illustrates the use of a chi-square distribution to address a research question. The analysis and interpretation of the research question is as shown in Example 7.3. The findings are

	Value	df	Asymp. sig. (2-sided)
Pearson chi-square	3.416	3	.332
Likelihood ratio	3.552	3	.314
Linear-by-linear association	1.992	1	.158
N of valid cases	50		
0 cells (.0%) have expected count less than 5. The minimum expected count is 5.28.			

Table 7.4 SPSS output

Reason	Male	Female	χ^2	p
Distance	5(19.2%)	6(25.0%)		
High Fees	5(19.2%)	7(29.2%)		
Limb disability	7(26.9%)	8(33.3%)		
Poor sight	9(34.6%)	3(12.5%)		
χ^2 (4, N= 50)			3.416	.332

Table 7.5 Chi-square tests

drawn from the SPSS output in Table 7.4. In reporting findings Table 7.5 is displayed. Note that the researcher has to interpret the statistical findings and draw a research conclusion.

EXAMPLE 7.3

Research question: Are there any significant differences in the reasons that males and females give for not attending literacy classes?

Null hypothesis: There are no significant differences in the reasons that males and females give for not attending literacy classes.

Decision rule: The null hypothesis will be rejected if the obtained chi-square is larger than the critical value, that is, if its probability is less than the set level of significance ($\alpha = .05$). The null hypothesis will be retained if the probability for the obtained chi-squares is greater than the set significance level.

In Table 7.5, the probability of the observed chi-square ($\chi^2 = 3.416$) is .332. In a research report, this information is reported as: $\chi^2 (3, N= 50) = 3.416, p = .332$

The 4 represents degrees of freedom, 50 is the sample size, followed by the chi-square value and the probability for that value.

Decision: Since .332 > .05 the decision is to not reject the null hyphothesis.

Statistical conclusion: There are no significant differences in the reasons that males and females give for not attending literacy classes.

The Pearson chi-square is the value of the chi-square that is of interest. Under the table, it is reported that there are no cells with an expected count of less than 5. In calculating a chi-square, one is dividing by expected cell frequencies and the value can be inflated if the expected cell frequencies are very small (< 5). The computer programme therefore gives a report of how many expected cell frequencies were less than the minimum expected. Note that the SPSS output gives more information than you really want.

SUMMARY

There are many statistical tests that you can use to analyse survey data. Which statistical tests to use depends on the research design and the measurement scale used with the variables in the study. What is important to note is that readers of quantitative studies will ask the question: 'Is the analysis statistically valid?' The question seeks to find out whether:

- Assumptions about statistical tests were met
- Samples were not too large to enable the rejection of a null hypothesis when it should have been retained, or too small to retain the null hypothesis when it should be rejected
- Random sampling was used in the design
- An acceptable level of significance (not more than .05) was set for the study.

KEY POINTS

- Illustrative devices such as graphs and tables can help you to communicate effectively.
- Quantitative data is sensitive to misrepresentation.

- Statistical tests of significance have an implication for a researcher's conclusions.

◈ ACTIVITY

Enter the data in Table 7.1 using an SPSS statistical package. Repeat the analysis for the two questions and see if you arrive at the same conclusions. Discuss the researcher's conclusion for each question.

FURTHER QUESTIONS

1 Make a list of the different ways in which data can be represented. For each, say what data can best be presented in this way.

2 Summarise what you know about the t-test and the chi-square test. Describe when you would use each of them.

SUGGESTED READINGS

Fink, A. 1995. *How to analyze survey data*. Thousand Oaks, CA: Sage.

Thomas, S. J. 1999. *Designing surveys that work: A step by step guide*. Thousand Oaks, CA: Corwin Press.

APPENDIX 1
BOTSWANA LITERACY SURVEY QUESTIONNAIRE
(Central Statistics Office, 1993)

1.	How old are you?	
	If younger than 12 or older than 65 end interview	
2.	What is the country of your citizenship?	
	Botswana	= 1
	Other	= 2 (End interview)
3.	Sex	
	Male	= 1
	Female	= 2
4.	Have you ever attended formal school?	
	Yes. Attending	= 1 (End interview)
	Yes. Left	= 2 → 5
	Never	= 3 → 8
5.	What level did you complete?	
	Standard 4 and below	= 1
	Above Standard 4	= 2 (End interview)
6.	What is the main reason you left school?	
	Goal achieved	= 01
	Lack of money	= 02
	Lost interest	= 03
	Helping at home	= 04
	Parents not interested	= 05
	Ill health	= 06
	Distance	= 07
	Pregnancy	= 08
	Could not cope	= 09
	Too young to understand	= 10
	Looking after cattle	= 11
	Other _____	Specify
7.	How many years is it since you left school?	
	If 1 yr enter 00	→ 9
8.	What is the main reason you never attended school?	
	Distance	= 01
	High fees	= 02

Leg(s), arm(s). finger(s) disability	= 03
Blindness/poor sight	= 04
Deafness/poor hearing	= 05
No school in area	= 06
Ill health	= 07
Religious beliefs	= 08
Parents unwilling	= 09
Helping at home	= 10
Looking after cattle	= 11
Not interested	= 12
Other _____	Specify
9. Have you ever attended any literacy classes?	
Yes, attending	= 01 → 10
Yes, left	= 02 → 12
No, never	= 03 → 14
10. Which literacy classes?	
National literacy	= 01
Other _____ Specify	= 02 → 15
11. What prima are you doing?	→ 15
12. Which literacy classes did you attend?	
National literacy	= 01
Other _____ Specify	→ 15
13 What prima did you complete?	
(If none enter 0)	→ 15
14. What is the main reason you never attended literacy classes?	
Already literate	= 01
Too old	= 02
Lack of time	= 03
No facilities	= 04
Didn't know existed	= 05
Parents not interested	= 06
Distance	= 07
Job demands	= 08
Physical disability	= 09

	Ill health	= 10
	Not interested	= 11
	Other _____	Specify
15.	Can you read (in any language)	
	Yes	= 01
	No	= 02 (End interview)
16.	Where did you learn how to read?	
	At formal school	= 1
	At night school	= 2
	I learnt on my own	= 3
	National literacy programme	= 4
	Other (Specify) _____	
17.	Can you read Setswana?	
	Yes, fairly well	= 1
	Yes, just a bit	= 2
	No, not at all	= 3 → 19
18.	Can you write Setswana?	
	Yes, fairly well	= 1
	Yes, just a bit	= 2
	No, not at all	= 3
19.	Can you read English?	
	Yes, fairly well	= 1
	Yes, just a bit	= 2
	No, not at all	= 3 →
20.	Can you write English?	
	Yes, fairly well	= 1
	Yes, just a bit	= 2
	No, not at all	= 3
21.	If Question 17 = 1 or 2, administer the Setswana reading test	
	Has test been administered? Yes	= 1
	No	= 2 26
22.	If Questions 18 = 1 or 2, administer the Setswana writing test	
	Has test been administered? Yes	= 1
	No	= 2 27

Chapter 8

Qualitative research

OVERVIEW

This chapter describes the basic character-istics of mainstream qualitative research, approaches in qualitative research and tech-niques in gathering evidence. In Chapter 2 and Chapter 3 it was noted that researchers who favour the interpretivist and emanci-patory paradigms use qualitative research methods. It was noted that qualitative research methods, by their nature, create space for marginalised voices because research is carried out about peoples' expe-riences in the natural settings in which these experiences occur. The visibility of margin-alised voices in a research study depends partly on the techniques that are used to gather the data from research participants and partly on the skill of the researcher in the use of these techniques. The chapter describes some of the techniques and pro-cedures and their uses. The appropriateness of some of these techniques for inquiring into adult education in African contexts is explored.

LEARNING OBJECTIVES

By the end of this chapter you should be able to:

1 Distinguish between different qualitative approaches.
2 Comment on conventional qualitative methods of gathering data.
3 Construct interview and observation instruments.

dwennimmen

KEY TERMS

biography   A study that focuses on an individual and her or his experiences.

case study   A detailed study of a single phenomenon or unit of analysis.

ethnography   Studies that describe a group of people's way of life in their natural setting.

ethnomethodology   Study of how common-sense knowledge is created and used in social interactions.

focus group interview   A discussion-based interview in which multiple research participants simultaneously produce data on a specified issue.

grounded theory   A qualitative approach in which a theory is derived from data collected over an estimated period of time in real-world settings.

holistic perspective   An investigation that takes into account complex and multiple contexts in which an investigation occurs.

individual interview   A conversation between a researcher and a research participant.

▦ BEFORE YOU START

Imagine that you wanted to carry out a study to understand the role of the village council or village assembly in community development. If it is a qualitative study you will have to show evidence that you actually visited a village council and talked with the people. But how do you collect evidence that will be informative, believable and convincing? List the activities. Here are a few examples of what you might do.

- Take photographs of a village council.
- Videotape a village council meeting.
- Interview people in the village council.
- Make observations of what happens at the village council.

Each one of the techniques requires skill. In this chapter you will learn about techniques of gathering qualitative data that are informative, believable and convincing.

QUALITATIVE RESEARCH

Qualitative research refers to the type of inquiry in which the researcher carries out research about people's experiences, in natural settings, using a variety of techniques such as interviews and observations, and reports findings mainly in words rather than statistics. Some of the characteristics of qualitative research emerge from the way the research problem and research questions are conceived, the steps in designing the study and the analysis. The following are some of the characteristics discussed by Patton (1980).

Naturalistic inquiry: Research is a naturalistic enquiry because it takes place in settings where the experiences of the research participants occur. The research problem and research questions emerge from the setting and the data that is collected; They can only be finalised during the final analysis of the data, after the researcher has been in the field for some time.

Inductive analysis: Inductive analysis refers to the fact that analysis begins with the description and meaning making of individual experiences of the researched people in the field. The hypothesis emerges from the people's reported experiences. Analysis thus begins from the time the researcher enters the field and continues throughout the study. It is this analysis that informs the revision and final formulation of the research problem and questions.

Holistic perspective: Qualitative research assumes a holistic perspective. A holistic perspective refers to the fact that the research problem is investigated and reported taking into account the complex and multiple contexts in which it occurs. For instance, people's perspectives, experiences and insights are studied in the setting, contexts and value systems within which

they occur. Qualitative research is thus value laden and context dependent.

Qualitative data: Qualitative data refers to the detailed descriptions of what was observed, voices of participants and the researcher's reflections. The data can also be captured in pictures, photographs and diagrams.

Personal contact and insight: The researcher is the main data-gathering instrument and has to interact with the research participants. The researcher's experiences, prejudices and value system informs the research process. It is for this reason that researchers are expected to inform the reader about their position with regard to the topic of research and the people researched.

Context sensitivity: This refers to the fact that the purpose of research in qualitative research is not to generalise findings, but to describe each setting in its uniqueness; leaving the reader to decide whether what is described is transferable to other settings.

Design flexibility: The design is open to revision throughout the process of carrying out the study. One cannot always decide on the size of the sample prior to the study. Sampling continues until there is no more new information from participants.

While these characteristics are common to qualitative research in general, there are differences that hinge on what is to be researched, how it is researched and methods of analysis. Creswell (1994) distinguished five qualitative research approaches, namely *phenomenology, ethnography, grounded theory, case study* and *biography*.

Phenomenology

Phenomenological studies subscribe to the view that it is important to study people's experiences to know about their social lives. Within this category are differences of emphasis on how these experiences are to be studied. Some phenomenologists favour the hermeneutic approach, while others prefer the ethnomethodological approach. Researchers who prefer the hermeneutic approach emphasise detailed reading or examination of texts. Texts could include written words, pictures, artefacts and so on.

Ethnomethodology is the study of how common sense knowledge is created and used in social interactions in natural settings. It is the study of how ordinary people in everyday settings apply tacit rules to make sense of social life (Neumann, 1997: 347).

Ethnomethodologists thus analyse language, conversation and the context of speech to identify rules that govern the construction of reality. A researcher who uses the ethnomethodological approach would, for instance, carefully transcribe a taped interview, making sure that pauses, emotional tones, words that are emphasised and interruptions during discussions are noted. Ethnomethodologists attempt to uncover cultural rules that govern the process of human interactions. Silence, a pause, or an emotional tone may be cultural codes that are part of a set of rules that govern human interactions. Most phenomenological studies use a combination of ethnomethodology and hermeneutics. The study by Mabongo (2000) of caregivers, which is summarised in Chapter 2, is an example of a phenomenological study. The following typical characteristics of phenomenological studies emerge:

- A brief discussion of the basic characteristics of phenomenological studies is given to inform the reader of the guiding principles in the study.
- The study focuses on the experiences of ten caregivers of terminally ill people as they interact with the patients.

Ethnography

'Ethno' means people or folk and 'graph' means to describe (Neumann, 2000: 346). Ethnographers seek to understand and describe a group of people's ways of life, their cultural patterns and perspectives, in their natural settings. In adult education, an ethnographic study might consist of a holistic study of an entire cultural scene, such as a learning centre and its community and classrooms in the learning centre. In the study of a learning centre, for example, you could include a description of the buildings, classrooms within the buildings, resources, trainers, adults and out-of-school youths enrolled at the learning centre, the community where the learning centre is situated, training and administration practices and so on. The study by Kaye (2003) on effective financial training for women in Botswana's entrepreneurial sector, which is described in Chapter 5, is an example of an ethnographic study. In this study, the following typical characteristics of ethnographic studies emerge:

- The influence of culture on the way the women learn business-related mathematics and conduct their business is discussed.
- Detailed descriptions of the lives of the women participating in the study and their businesses are given.
- Each community setting where the business is located is described.
- There is a case description, analysis and interpretation of each business.

Grounded theory

In this approach the researcher attempts to derive a theory by using multiple data collection in such a way that the theory that emerges is grounded in the data. Seloilwe

(1997) used a grounded theory design to investigate family caregiving of psychiatric patients in Botswana. Example 8.1 contains an extract from the study that illustrate the features of a grounded theory design.

EXAMPLE 8.1
(Summarised from Seloilwe, 1997)

Statement of the problem

The purpose of this study was twofold. The first was to understand and describe the caregiving situation of families of relatives with mental illness in Botswana from the perspective of the families themselves. It is believed that this information will guide clinical practice and assist health providers in the development of appropriate and relevant interventions for the families of the mentally ill. The second purpose was to contribute to theory development about caregiving of the mentally ill in Botswana grounded in the ways families conceptualise their own caregiving situations.

Research questions

- What were the perceptions of families in Botswana about giving care to mentally ill relatives?
- What were the experiences of the families in the care of a mentally ill relative at home?
- What were the support networks and support interventions?
- Have these support interventions been appropriate and relevant in addressing the family caregivers' needs?

Method

The study used a grounded theory design. Data collection procedures included indi-

vidual interviews, group interviews and field observations.

Sampling

Caregivers included in the individual interviews were those who had lived with and cared for the mentally ill for at least a year. The family caregivers were recruited through psychiatric outpatient clinics which served as focal points of contact with the families The mentally ill were asked to identify a family member who they considered to be taking care of them. When a relative was identified, the person was contacted by the investigator and recruited to participate in the study. The procedure resulted in an individual sample composed of thirty individual caregivers. For the group interviews, members of the group may not have resided with the ill person, but were involved in the care by making certain decisions pertaining to care. The sample was composed of four groups.

Results and conclusions

Interviews revealed myriad experiences and problems that family caregivers encountered in providing care for their mentally ill relatives. The complexity of caregiving is captured through a conceptual model called 'the spider web metaphor of the caregiving situation of the mentally ill'. The web depicts the extent, magnitude, and intensity of the caregiving demands. A second theoretical model derived from the data shows how the caregivers negotiate the caregiving situation again and again. It is concluded that these two models need further refinement through further research.

The following typical characteristics of grounded theory emerge from the study:

- The author mentions from the beginning

that the purpose of the study is to generate a theory.

■ A conceptual model and a theoretical model that emerge from the data are systematically discussed and illustrated through the use of diagrams.

Case study

This involves a detailed study of single phenomena or units of analysis with the aim of making a holistic description of those particular phenomena. The unit of analysis or phenomenon may be a person or persons, for example a study on out-of-school orphans. Here the unit of analysis and the persons being studied are out-of-school orphans. The unit of analysis may be an object, for example, an institution such as a learning centre, or an event. In adult education an event can be a specific programme in specific sites such as a national literacy programme, the Breakthrough to Literacy pilot project in Uganda or an interactive radio instruction project for out-of-school children and youth in Zambia. Data is collected and conclusions drawn on this unit of analysis. An important characteristic of a case study approach is that it uses multiple data-gathering techniques to study a single phenomenon. For an example of a case study, see Example 4 in Chapter 14.

Biography

A biography is a study that focuses on an individual and his or her experiences. The experiences or story of the individual could be found in documents, archival materials, or be told to the researcher by the individual if still alive. In adult education, you may wish to study the life history of a scholar or a prominent figure in society who you believe has played a leading role in the development of adult education in Africa. You may report on the individual's life and show how it influenced agendas in adult educational research, how it led to the development of adult education learning centres, books and materials on adult education or how it resulted in an understanding of the meaning of adult education in Africa. Biographical studies are done on individuals who are alive and those who may have died. An example of such a study is the article by Taussig (1978) on the important role of Milton Margai in the development of adult education in Sierra Leone.

You will note that phenomenologists focus on the experiences of people but differ on how these experiences are to be studied. Researchers who use the ethnographic approach focus on culture, whereas those who use the case study approach are more oriented towards the number of units of study. The grounded theory approach is more concerned with deriving theory from data, whereas the biography approach focuses on life histories of people. Although there are differences in these approaches, most approaches will use similar techniques for gathering data.

▦ ACTIVITY

Choose someone involved in adult education who you know or might have heard of, or even read about. Imagine you are going to write a biography of that person. Draft a list of the questions you would want to ask that person. List any other sources you would consult, such as research papers, newspaper articles, as well as friends or associates of the person.

DATA-GATHERING TECHNIQUES

Data-gathering techniques in qualitative research include interviews, observations, audiovisual materials and documents. Additional techniques include African context-specific procedures embedded in community-centred ways of knowing, such as the story-telling framework and language as a bank of knowledge. Procedures of gathering data based on these frameworks are discussed in Chapter 3. The discussion in this chapter will be limited to how to conduct interviews and make observations, as well as the use of audiovisual materials and documents in collecting data.

Interviews

Interviews can be divided into *individual* and *focus group interviews*. An *individual interview* is a conversation or interaction between the researcher and a research participant. In this conversation the researcher focuses on getting information by asking the research participants questions relating to a specified topic. In conventional qualitative research the researcher plays a dominant role when asking questions of research participants. They in turn answer the questions passively. The researcher prepares an interview guide, which contains the questions to be asked.

The sample interview guide provided in Example 8.2 was taken from a study on Botswana rural women's transition to urban business success (Ntseane, 1999). The purpose of this study was to understand how women in Botswana learnt how to move from unemployment in the rural areas to owning successful small businesses within the formal sector of the economy in an urban setting. The interview guide sought to find out:

- What contextual and personal factors are associated with the success of women's business in the informal sector (including factors that facilitate or impede the transition)
- How women negotiate social and contextual barriers so that their business can succeed. The unnumbered questions are open-ended questions. The numbered questions are follow-up questions to enable the researcher to probe further.

EXAMPLE 8.2
(Taken from Ntseane, 1999)

To begin our interview, please tell me the story behind your business.
(Ask any questions below that have not been covered.)

1 When and how did the business start? What made you think of a business idea?
2 What triggered your interest in becoming a businesswoman?
3 Did you start the business in the village or did you come to the city for a job and couldn't find work and then decided to start your own business? Or you just came to the city to start a business?
4 When and what happened to make it what it is today?
5 When did you decide to register your business with the government small business department?
6 Why was it important for your unregulated small business to be registered?

Now that I have a better understanding of your business history, I would like you to talk about the business environment in your culture or situation.
(Ask any questions below that have not been covered.)

7 What support was crucial for the development of your business? What worked and what did not work?

8 How do the following factors play out in your business life: personal, family, cultural, economic and political relations? How did this help in starting your business and how did it hinder the process?

9 How do you feel as a woman business owner working in this business environment? Do you think that your experience is different because you are a woman?

The following important aspects of an interview emerge from the example above:

■ Each main open-ended question focuses on a particular research question.
■ There are sub-questions under each main question that assist the researcher to probe for more information.
■ There is a close relationship between the interview guide questions and the research questions.
■ The interview guide questions solicit information that addresses the initial research questions.

Interviews can be divided into three types:

■ The unstructured or non-standardised interview
■ The semi-structured interview
■ The structured or standardised interview.

The unstructured or non-standardised interview

Unstructured interviews start with a general question in the broad area of study. This is usually accompanied by a list of topics which will be covered in the interview. This type of interviewing allows for flexibility and makes it possible for researchers to follow the interests and thoughts of the informants. Interviewers freely ask ques-

tions in any order, depending on the answers.

The semi-structured interviews

These are focused interviews which have questions contained in an interview guide. They focus on the issues to be covered. The sequencing of questions is not the same for every participant as it depends on the process of the interview and answers from each individual participant. The interview guide ensures that the researcher collects similar types of data from all informants. The interview guide in Example 8.2 is an example of a semi-structured interview.

The structured or standardised interview

In this type of interview the interview schedule contains a number of pre-planned questions. Each informant is asked the same questions in the same order. The advantage of standardised interviews is that they are time saving and reduce interviewer effect, and that analysis of the data is easier. The disadvantage is that they direct the informants' responses and therefore are not appropriate for qualitative research (Holloway and Wheeler, 1996). Qualitative researchers, however, use structured interviews to elicit socio-demographic data as background information.

Interview guidelines

Conducting an interview needs careful planning and skill in asking questions and interacting with research participants. Pattman (2002) suggests the following guidelines for preparing and conducting interviews:

■ It is important to have some background information (e.g. age, socio-economic status, ethnicity, religion or marital status, etc.) about the subjects. This could be done during the sampling, familiarisation procedures and initial informal discussions using a structured interview.

■ Try to deal efficiently with the practicalities of interviews, e.g. ensure the tape recorder, batteries and microphone are in good working order and properly set.

■ Be careful about where the respondent and interviewer sit so that they are not so close as to cause cultural discomfort and not so far apart as to create a sense of power boundary. Also take care of the effects of direct sunlight, noise, and other forms of interruption.

■ It is important at the start of the interview to allow the respondent to relax by conducting introductions in a manner that encourages dialogue. For example, ask whether there is something they wish to know about the interview procedure before you start.

■ Help the subjects to position themselves within the discourse of the study by asking them questions that allow them freedom to express their perspectives.

■ Always try to ask simple (not loaded) questions, one at a time.

■ Be an attentive listener (avoid conducting interviews when you are tired).

■ Be careful not to pursue issues that appear to be complicated or sensitive too early in the interview.

■ Take note of answers that need follow-up later in the interview.

■ Give the subject time to reply. Do not attempt to 'cover' a silence with another question (unless you want to clarify the initial question).

■ Probe the answer until you are sure that the respondent has replied as fully as possible.

■ Keep reassuring the respondents about the importance of their replies. Indicate that what they are saying is interesting to you by making comments such as 'that is quite interesting' or 'that is a very interesting way of describing ...'.

■ Watch for non-verbal signs of boredom, lack of understanding, embarrassment and then respond appropriately. You can respond by changing the line of interviewing.

■ Try to end interviews on a positive note, for example, by giving the subjects an opportunity to ask questions and give their opinion about their experience of the process.

■ Summarise the main points raised and ask participants whether your summary is a correct interpretation of their views.

■ At the end of an interview, remember to thank the interviewee and reaffirm confidentiality if need be.

Advantages and limitations of the individual interview technique

There are several problems with the individual interview approach. The problems hinge on the power relationship between the interviewer and the interviewee. Questions being raised are: Whose knowledge is constructed during the interview, using whose language and whose vocabulary?

As early as the 1930s researchers started critiquing the interview technique, arguing that the researcher played a dominant role, whereas the researched played a passive role, with the result that data obtained from the interviews were most likely to embody preconceived ideas of the interviewers and their attitude towards the researched (Tyrell, 1998). The dominance of the researcher occurs in two ways. Firstly, interviewers construct their interview guides using topics and concepts established in the discipline (De Vault, 1999). For example, take HIV/AIDS research. Researchers invariably use terms such as 'a virus' and 'immune deficiency syndrome' that are located in the medical science discipline. The researched are then expected to talk of their experiences in terms of the dominant language and meanings. This practice limits the discussion to what the researchers know and thus excludes the voices of the researched, which are grounded in their experiences and spoken in their vocabulary (Chilisa, 2005).

Secondly, researchers derive power from their position as the ones who decide on the agenda for the interview and the place for the interview; who ask questions, control the discussion and decide when to stop the interview. During reporting the researcher pulls together the voices of the interviewees to create generalisations, patterns or sameness (Scheurich, 1997). The voices of the researched as individuals cease to exist except when cited to illustrate a theme or a pattern. Scheurich further notes that the power position of the researcher has met with some resistance from the researched, which should serve as a base to begin to chart other ways of conducting interviews. This point can be illustrated by looking at African resistance to the conventional individual interview method.

Resistance to the conventional individual interview method

There is evidence that some research participants are not comfortable with the conventional interview approach. Ntseane (1999), in her study on rural women's transition to urban business success, reflects on how an interview with a key informant ended up in a dialogue with three people. According to Ntseane (1999) the key informant, who was the owner of a business, wanted one of her employees to join in the discussion because she had more authoritative knowledge on some aspects of the business. Ntseane notes that during the interview, the employer and the employee

helped each other to elaborate on different aspects of the business. At times they asked each other questions and at times they directed the questions to the researcher. She notes that the procedure she was compelled to adopt by the researched was different from the typical interview procedure. The procedure adopted is similar to the community-centred way of producing knowledge with its emphasis on dialogue and community production of knowledge, that was discussed in Chapter 3.

Another concern about the individual interview method has been the visibility of the researched in the finished research report. Conventional educational research methods require that data from the researched be treated with confidentiality, which in most cases is ensured by not revealing the researched people's names. But what if the researched person wants to be visible in the scripts? Why should the names of the informants remain anonymous when they want them revealed? The researched women in Ntseane's study wanted readers to associate the stories in the study with their names and businesses. They argued that since they did not have the writing skills to document their stories, telling them to Ntseane was the only way to tell their communities and the generations to come about their knowledge contribution to women's business in Botswana. Unfortunately Ntseane could not reveal the names because it was against the stipulated research ethics of her university. These experiences in the field reveal an African orientation towards individual and community production of knowledge and an appeal for visibility where the position of the researched as a producer of knowledge is clearly marked.

It has been observed throughout the book that adults have an enormous amount of experience and knowledge about their environments. It has also been observed that they are experts or authorities in a variety of knowledge systems, just as researchers are experts in a variety of disciplines. Shouldn't researchers recognise adult experts or authorities in defined knowledge systems by giving full citation to their knowledge or innovative ideas? A study by Grant and Grant (1995) on housing demonstrates how adults' ownership of knowledge can be recognised. In their study Grant and Grant map out patterns of housing in Botswana. They illustrate each pattern with a photo of a house. With each photo are the details of the owner or the house designer and their biography. Figure 8.1 illustrates the use of indigenous paint and house design by Nani Mabechu in Tutume.

Most books, starting with those written in the nineteenth century by European trav-

Figure 8.1 (Grant and Grant, 1995)

Figure 8.2

ellers, missionaries and explorers, do not give recognition to the expert knowledge of indigenous communities. An example of the marginalisation of indigenous knowledge experts is that of four designs attributed to the Bakwena people of southern Africa (see figure 8.2). According to Grant and Grant (1995), these designs appear without authorship in Stowe's 1905 book titled *The Native Races of South Africa*. The names of the designers are not mentioned; instead, the designs are attributed to the Bakwena people in general. Such documentation ignores the existence of experts in crafts and in various skills, such as traditional medicines, music, story-telling and so on. It denies researchers opportunities to trace the evolution of trends in knowledge to community-recognised experts in specified knowledge systems.

Adult educators, for example agricultural extension workers and health workers, interact with farmers and herbalists with knowledge on plants or herbs that cure certain ailments in domestic animals and people. They know a lot about types of soil and vegetation and about the life cycles of plants and animals. It should be the duty of every adult education researcher to bring the erosion of these indigenous knowledge systems to a halt by adopting research protocols that recognise and document the names and particulars of community experts and their knowledge. This is an urgent agenda because as Hoppers (2003: 7) notes, 'the erosion of people's knowledge associated with natural resources is under greater threat than the erosion of the natural resources themselves'.

The individual interview method remains an important data-gathering strategy in qualitative research. The quality of the data gathered through this technique depends on the researcher's success in identifying knowledgeable informants or research participants, referred to as key informants. Chapter 3 discussed the role of wise men and wise women or indigenous intellectuals with various forms of expert knowledge, such as arts, medicine, community law and order, community value systems, beliefs, stories, songs and proverbs. They can serve as key informants depending on the nature of the research study. When such key informants are involved in a study they provide in-depth information that enhances the credibility of the study. Interviews of key informants can be flexible, allowing the researcher to pursue unanticipated topics. However, selection of key informants is susceptible to selection biases. For instance, in most traditional communities knowledge is a monopoly of the old (Kaphagawani and Malherbe, 1998), those up the social ladder, for instance, chiefs and their advisors, and mostly men. The researcher has to be aware of these limitations when selecting informants from the sages and sage philosophers.

Focus group interviews

The focus group interview technique was developed in the 1930s because of dissatisfaction with the individual interview. It is a discussion-based interview in which multiple research participants simultaneously produce data on a specified issue. The researcher takes a less directive and dominant role. A focus group interview allows the researcher to understand, determine the range of responses and gain insight into how people perceive a situation. Steps in the focus group process include deciding on the purpose of the focus group interview, the stimulus used for the discussion, the composition of the group and the place for the interview as well as the time and duration of the interview. The first step is to decide on the purpose for which one needs to use the focus group interview data.

Questionnaire development

Focus group interviews can be used to develop questionnaires. The researcher can use focus group interviews to identify the vocabulary, local terms, content and thinking patterns of the researched so that the questionnaire is made relevant to the needs of the researched, is sensitive to their culture and suits the purpose of the study. Refer to Chapter 6 for more information about questionnaire construction.

Creating new ideas

Focus group interviews can also be used to stimulate new ideas and create new concepts. They can be used as follow-up to data gathered through individual interviews, observations or questionnaires. When used

in this way, they help to clarify issues and to check interpretation by the researcher.

Focus group stimulus

In focus group interviews the researcher can use open-ended questions as is done for individual interviews (see Example 8.2). Pictures, photographs and cartoons can also be used to stimulate a discussion. The use of these materials allows the group to define a topic using their own frame of reference, and to define the scope and depth of the topic or issue. The groups discuss and describe their experiences in their own vocabulary and local terms, grounded in their lived experiences and ways of perceiving reality. In a study on youth, gender, sexuality and HIV/AIDS (Chilisa et al., 2003), pictures were used to stimulate dis-

Figure 8.3 Gender violence

cussions. One of the pictures (Figure 8.3), was on gender violence.

Participants were asked to discuss what they saw in the picture. In one of the groups, a participant had this to say:

This is a picture on rape. It happens at home, at night at the bars, and with stepfathers at home. Uncles abuse girls a lot. Sometimes you can tell your mother and she says, 'I will talk to him,' but by that time its too late or she simply does not. Sometimes the girls keep it a secret (Chilisa et al., 2005).

You can imagine the range of responses that can be generated through the picture. Pictures and photographs are useful when the research is exploring sensitive topics. They help to break the ice and allow entry to the topic from the participants' frame of reference and zone of comfort.

Another procedure is to use statements as a stimulus. In a study on the impact of HIV/AIDS on the University of Botswana (Chilisa et al., 2002), participants were asked to write on a piece of paper whether they agreed with, disagreed with or felt neutral about given statements. A discussion of the statements then followed. Table 8.1 shows the statements that were used and a summary of participants' responses. The procedure ensures that each participant starts the discussion from a position that is independent of the influence of the group. The discussion generates information to substantiate participants' positions on the statements.

Preparing for a focus group interview

Most of the preparation required for a focus group interview is similar to that for individual interviews (see the interview guidelines in Example 8.2). In addition to guidelines for individual interviews, there is a need to create ground rules. Ground rules are guidelines that bind all group members during the discussion. The researcher, with the help of group members, creates ground

	Agree			Disagree			Not sure		
STATEMENT	M	F	TOTAL	M	F	TOTAL	M	F	TOTAL
Cultural beliefs and practices expose those affected by HIV/-AIDS to discrimination.	1 (5 %)	2 (10 %)	3 (15 %)	4 (20 %)	4 (20 %)	8 (40 %)	4 (20 %)	5 (25 %)	9 (45 %)
Students affected by HIV/AIDS are discriminated against by the university community.	0 (0 %)	0 (0 %)	0 (0 %)	7 (35 %)	9 (45 %)	16 (80 %)	2 (10 %)	2 (10 %)	4 (20 %)
Orphans at this university should receive special help.	1 (5 %)	2 (10 %)	3 (15 %)	7 (35 %)	9 (45 %)	16 (80 %)	1 (5 %)	0 (0 %)	1 (5 %)

Table 8.1 (Chilisa et al., 2001)

rules that are embedded in the community value system. For instance, it was shown in Chapter 3 that some communities emphasise the importance of democracy, specifically the importance of giving every person space to share their views. It was, however, noted that women were often not expected to make contributions to discussions. In creating ground rules, the researcher should make use of positive values and discuss negative values that could discourage participation from some members of the group. Every member of the group could be given the responsibility of ensuring that everyone gets involved in the discussion.

Other logistics include composing the focus group. Most focus groups consist of between six and twelve people. The basic principle is to not allow the group to be so big that participation by all is impossible, or so small that it is not possible to cover a large number of issues. Members of a group should have a common background. For instance, a study on leadership in non-government organisations (NGOs) that utilises focus group interviews could form groups stratified according to leadership roles, gender, location of the NGO, or educational background of the leaders. In this way, several separate groups that represent different viewpoints are formed. The number of focus groups to be convened will thus depend on the variety of viewpoints expected. The more numerous the distinguishing characteristics in the population of study, the more likely it is that more separate groups will be convened.

Focus group interviews in African contexts

Focus group interviews are similar to group discussions that many communities in Africa employ when there are issues to be addressed. One can think of commu-

nity interviews where selected members of a community are invited for a discussion by a chief, headperson of a ward, a village leader or a wise person such as a sage. At times when researchers follow informants to their homes, most of the family members invite themselves to the discussion. In African contexts, it may be appropriate to distinguish formal focus group interviews where the facilitator determines the group membership. There is also the informal focus group interview where the identified key informant is joined by others; either because of invitation by the key informant or because of community or family values. For instance, the home is a space marked for family togetherness. When researchers visit homes to interview key informants, they should be aware that the overriding value is family togetherness, sharing and doing things together. Focus group interviews thus embrace community production of knowledge and are therefore easily adaptable to African contexts. Researchers should start thinking of acknowledging and systematising the variety of informal and formal focus group interviews, such as community focus group interviews, family focus group interviews and others.

Advantages and limitations of focus group interview techniques

One of the advantages of the focus group interview is that it is compatible with real communication systems in natural settings. Most of the time when people want to address problems, they meet in groups of more than two people and hold a dialogue. The group interaction in focus group interviews allows more realistic perceptions of issues. For instance, other members of the group can challenge participants with extreme views and thus more realistic information is obtained on the issues. Information is also checked for accuracy as members question, complement and corroborate what others say. The researcher can cover a wide range of issues in a short period. However, the focus group method has disadvantages. It requires a skilled researcher/moderator to facilitate the discussion. Even when the researcher is a skilled moderator, a few assertive individuals may dominate the discussion. The technique is also not appropriate for discussing participants' personal experiences or opinions on sensitive topics such as abortion. The group environment means that confidentiality of information cannot be ensured and a participant's opinion may be easily be judged by others as moral indecency.

ACTIVITY

1   Think of research on adult education that you might want to carry out in communities. Is there expert knowledge that you could source from the communities? How will you address selection bias in obtaining this knowledge? How can you recognise the experts so that others can follow them up?
2   Discuss Grant and Grant's presentation of Nani Mabechu's design. What are the advantages of the presentation? Discuss any disadvantages.

OBSERVATION

Qualitative research, as already noted, requires the presence of the researcher in the setting. Often, researchers do not only hear what the participants say, but also see, smell and touch as they interact with the participants. Observation is therefore another important procedure of gathering data.

Researchers conduct observations to enable an elaborate discussion of a specific issue, to corroborate findings, and to triangulate or complement data gathered through focus group interviews and individual interviews. Observations differ depending on the degree of involvement of the observer. Gold (in Holloway and Wheeler, 1996) lists four types of observer involvement, namely: the complete participant; the participant as observer; the observer as participant; and the complete observer.

The complete participant

When researchers are complete participants they become part of the setting and take an insider role, which involves covert observation, where they disguise their identity from participants. One of the advantages of this is that the observer can gain some insight and develop very close relationships with the participants. Covert observation may be problematic, depending on the nature of the research. Imagine that you were to be a complete participant in a study in which you wanted to study the experiences of sex workers. At some point complete participation might pose a moral dilemma for you. A number of researchers have attempted covert observations: at times with success, and at other times without success. For example, a British sociologist who carried out a study on a violent juvenile gang in Glasgow in the 1960s using the covert observation method abandoned the study when the gang wanted to involve him in gang violence (Nyamanjoh, 2003). Another American sociologist who successfully carried out a covert participant observation study of homosexuals nearly had his doctoral degree revoked by his university on grounds that the method he employed was unethical (Nyamanjoh, 2003). Chapter 13 discusses ethics in detail. In adult education, family welfare educators, agricultural extension workers and trainers in literacy programmes can be complete observers when they engage in action-oriented research, that is, research aimed at improving the work they are involved in. Hopfer's (1997) study on empowering adult education in Namibia and South Africa is an example where the researcher was a complete participant. Hopfer was one of the staff members working for Elm, a home for mentally retarded and disabled children run by a church in Namibia. The biggest problem for the Elm home she observed was that the staff did not want to work. The focus of her action research was thus to bring about changes in the attitudes of the staff towards work. As one of the staff members, she participated in all the activities that the other staff members did, thus she was a complete participant.

The participant as observer

This is when researchers negotiate a way into the setting. Researchers become part of the group under study. The advantage of this is that they can move around in the setting or location and observe in more detail and depth. Researchers participate in activities that are not part of their job description. While they spend most of the time at the setting, they do not participate in all the activities of the research participants. Their participation is therefore moderate compared to that of the complete participant.

The observer as participant

The observer as participant is marginally involved in the situation. The advantage of this type of observation is that the observer can develop rapport with research participants and can be accepted as a colleague and researcher who is free to ask questions. The disadvantage is that the observer is prevented from playing a real role in the setting and the restraint from involvement is not easy. Imagine that you are a health worker and carrying out a study on patients with life-threatening ailments. It would be difficult not to join caregivers in assisting a patient who suddenly suffers an attack during an interview. Mabongo's study (2002) used the observer as participant technique discussed in Chapter 2. She notes that she participated in caregiving where it was necessary. She also notes that caregivers declined her offer to assist when providing care like bathing their patients.

The complete observer

This is when the researcher as an observer does not take part in the setting. In this type of observation, the observer is not noticed and has no impact on the situation. Take, for example, a study on teaching methods in a rural training centre for farmers. A researcher who has permission to carry out the study may make observations on gender dynamics by sitting at the back of the classroom during the various activities that the trainees may be doing.

Informal or purposeful observation

Before an observation is made, the researcher should decide for what purpose the observation data would be used. Qualitative researchers make informal observations that allow them to acquire a holistic impression about the setting of the study. Under the circumstances the researcher records whatever they see that enables them to provide a detailed description of the study setting. Researchers also conduct observations to enable an elaborate discussion of specific issues. When there is a specified issue, it is useful to:

- Determine the focus and list specific features, issues, objects or events that you need to observe
- Develop direct observation forms, guides or instruments
- Select site and time for the observation.

Observation instruments can take the form of open-ended questions, checklists or rating scales. The study by Kaye (2003) referred to earlier used an observation instrument with open-ended questions.

Example 8.3 is an extract from her observation instrument.

An evaluation research study on the Breakthrough to Literacy programme for out-of-school youths in Uganda used a combination of rating scale, checklist and open-ended questions. Example 8.4 is an extract from that instrument.

EXAMPLE 8.3 (Extract from Kaye, 2003)

Date:
Time of day:
Location:
Name of business:
Type of business:
Address of owner:
Number of employees:
Observation points to note:

Business

General cleanliness and neatness of business

Description of physical building

What equipment is there?
What stock is there?
How is it stocked?

Workers

Physical appearance of the workers, clothing, cleanliness
Interaction of business owner and workers

Finances

Where is the money put after purchase of the items or service?
Who receives the money?
How is the money recorded?

▓ ACTIVITY

1 Individually conduct a participant observation during the same classroom session for thirty minutes. Record what you observed and discuss it. Did you observe the same things? Why?
2 As a class, construct an observation instrument that you could use to observe the session.

MATERIALS

Audiovisual materials

Audiovisual materials can also be used to collect qualitative data. The most common are photographs, videotapes and films. Unlike words, they capture reality as it appears, giving the viewers the opportunity to construct what they see. They provide an opportunity for participants to directly share their realities. Such data can be creative and captures attention visually. When used by the same researcher for triangulation purposes, audiovisuals give authority to voice or words. For those researchers for whom the histories of people form an important part of analysis and interpretation, descriptions of Africa by European missionaries and travellers can be contrasted with realities captured through photographs and pictures taken by the same missionaries and travellers. Take, for example, the general description of Africans in the 18th and 19th century.

Figure 8.4 (Grant and Grant, 1995) would contradict a description of people who lived simplistic lives of no value. The engraving, based on the observations of Reverend John Campbell in 1820, shows the interior of the house of Chief Sinosee of the Batlhaping.

Pictures and photographs allow for multiple constructions of the realities of the African peoples. Those taken in the colonial period provide evidence for repairing distorted African identities. Audiovisual materials such as videos, photographs and films in research provide evidence that can be used to dispute words or to reconstruct meanings. The main disadvantage of audiovisual materials is that confidentiality and the anonymity of the participants is not possible when the audiovisual materials are used as illustrations. See Chapter 13 for a discussion on ethics.

Documents

Public documents such as minutes of meetings, newspapers, dairies, letters, official documents and reports are also sources of data. They enable the researcher to access the language and words of the informants. Furthermore, as evidence, they save the researcher the time and expense of writing notes or transcribing tapes (as is the case with interviews). Documents are also used to support evidence from other sources, such as interviews. The study by Ntseane and Youngman (2002) on leadership, discussed in Chapter 9, shows how evidence from documents was used to support information from interviews.

Figure 8.4

SUMMARY

Table 8.2 is a summary of the data-gathering techniques discussed: their features, advantages, limitations and application in African adult education research contexts. In Chapter 14 you will learn how data from these sources are used to write reports.

You can see that there are various ways of collecting qualitative data. Every data collection technique, however, requires careful planning and skill in implementing it. It is also clear that, before you choose a technique for collecting data, you should first of all decide the purpose for which the collected data would be used. Some data-gathering techniques, such as visual

	Main features	Advantages	Limitations	Appropriateness to the study of adult education in African contexts
Individual interview	One person interviewed at a time	Provides in-depth data. Unanticipated topics can be explored	Interviewer plays a dominant role. Susceptible to selection bias	Indigenous intellectuals can provide insightful and in-depth information
Focus group interviews	Involves discussion with groups of five people or more	Information can be checked for accuracy. A wide range of issues can be covered in a short time. Resembles a more natural communication system	Can be dominated by a few individuals. Not appropriate for exploring personal and sensitive topics. Confidentiality not attainable	Community interviews, family interviews and informal focus groups informed by African value systems can be accommodated
Observations	Events are observed in their natural settings	May reveal information that informant-provided data does not	Observer bias a threat to the credibility of the data	Provides a wide scope for witnessing people's realities
Audiovisuals	Information is collected through videos, photographs, pictures and films	Viewers can construct their own realities and meanings. Provide evidence to contrast with the written word	Susceptible to researcher selection bias. Confidentiality is compromised	Can provide evidence for reconstructing African identities
Documents	Consist of personal diaries, letters, official documents and reports	Less time-consuming and inexpensive	Documents may not be authentic	Can provide evidence for reconstructing African identities

Table 8.2 Data-gathering techniques

aids, capture reality as it appears and can be used to give authority to voice when the researcher observed and used interviews, documents and visual aids at the same time. Others, such as interviews, simply capture the realities and experiences in words. All of these can, however, be used simultaneously – provided the researcher is clear about how the data will be used.

KEY POINTS

- Conventional data-gathering techniques are not always compatible with communication systems in African contexts.
- There are indigenous people who have expertise and knowledge that need to be recognised in research.
- Some photographs taken in the nineteenth and twentieth centuries can be used in research to dispute distorted African identities that continue to be reproduced.
- Gathering data requires careful planning and sensitivity to reproducing the research participants' voices.

⊞ ACTIVITY

Think of a study to conduct.

1 Write down the purpose of the study.
2 Write down the research questions.
3 Prepare an interview guide for a focus group and an individual interview.

4 Identify people who will act as individual key informants for individual interviews and focus group participants.
5 Simulate individual and focus group interviews in class.
6 Videotape the interviews and later use the video to evaluate interviewing skills.
7 To evaluate the videos, first create a checklist for use in the evaluation.

FURTHER QUESTIONS

1 What are the most appropriate techniques for gathering data in a village community?
2 What additional techniques, not mentioned in this book, can be used to collect data among adults in village communities?

SUGGESTED READINGS

Hopfer C. 1997. 'Empowering adult education in Namibia and South Africa during and after Apartheid'. *International Review of Education*, Vol. 43, pp. 43–59.

Mertens, D. B. 1998. *Research methods in education and psychology: Integrating diversity with quantitative and qualitative approaches.* Thousand Oaks: Sage Publications.

Taussig, L. 1978. 'Milton Margai and adult education in Sierra Leone'. *African Research Bulletin*, Vol. 8, Nos. 2 and 3.

Chapter 9

Doing a qualitative study

OVERVIEW

This chapter explains procedures for carrying out a qualitative study. Particular attention is given to ways of gaining entry that are informed by African value systems. Ways of triangulating and validating data gathered through mainstream techniques of gathering evidence are explored. The chapter also illustrates ways of storing data, coding, and reporting and presenting findings.

LEARNING OBJECTIVES

By the end of this chapter, you should be able to:

1 Carry out a qualitative study in an adult education context in Africa.
2 Analyse the data with careful attention to interpretation, presentation and credibility.
3 Analyse data based on interviews, focus group interviews, diaries and observations.
4 Triangulate data across mainstream and community-based ways of gathering evidence and reporting findings.
5 Demonstrate ways of storing data, coding, and reporting and presenting findings.

KEY TERMS

credibility   When participants in a qualitative study can recognise descriptions and interpretations of their human experience as true (equivalent to internal validity in quantitative research).

confirmability   When data delivered from respondents can be traced back to the respondents and settings and is not a result of the researcher's biases (equivalent to objectivity in quantitative research).

dependability   Consistency of research results with data collected (equivalent to reliability in quantitative research).

transferability   When results in a qualitative study can be found to apply in situations similar to those in which the study was conducted (equivalent to external validity in quantitative research).

⌗ BEFORE YOU START

Example 9.1 is a story about Somali Bantus who are going to resettle in the United States. After you have read it, you may have questions such as: who wrote the story? Is the information accurate? What are the sources of information in the story? You may make observations about how the writer illustrates some of the points. Still, you will have questions such as: Why did the writer choose these illustrations as evidence? Are the illustrations convincing? How does the writer portray those whom they write about and how do these fit with African concerns about always portraying other people as ignorant or lacking in some aspect? These are some of the questions that will be asked by people reading any research study, especially Africans concerned with their distorted identities. It is for this reason that qualitative researchers have put together guidelines on how to carry out studies that are credible. By the time you finish reading this chapter, you will be able to assess qualitative research studies for *credibility* and will also be able to carry out qualitative studies that are credible.

EXAMPLE 9.1

(Botswana Guardian, 23 May 2003: 16)

The first group of Somali Bantus are set to leave for the United States after years in refugee camps in northern Kenya. Some 74 left Tuesday and Wednesday with an additional 150 set to travel next month. They are the first of 12 000 refugees identified for resettlement by the US government because of persecution back home in Somalia – mainly because of their darker skin colour and hair. Many are illiterate, and for the last ten days have been attending special orientation courses at a transit centre in the Kenyan capital, Nairobi, to prepare them for their new life. 'We have been training them how to use toilets, how to use a shower, how to switch on lights and how to read time' says cultural trainer Lily Sonya of the International Migration Organisation.

... Seventeen-year-old Mokena Jamal says he is excited about life in America. 'I am ready for whatever awaits me. I plan to get a part-time job and complete my studies,' Jamal says.

Ethnically distinct from Somalis, the Somali Bantu have always been social outcasts. The lighter-skinned local people rejected and persecuted them because of their slave origins, their dark skins and wide features.

QUALITATIVE RESEARCH STEPS

Qualitative researchers study people's experiences as they occur in natural settings, the meaning that people attach to these experiences, and the multiple contexts within which these experiences occur.

Contexts have many dimensions. It could be in terms of time, space or value systems. For instance, a study on adult or out-of-school youth experiences with HIV/AIDS

could take into consideration the fact that HIV/AIDS is occuring during the globalisation era. The compression of time and space in this era could mean that information on how to deal with HIV/AIDS is easily accessible across nations. It could also mean that the virus spreads quickly within and across nations. The space could take many forms, for example, people's experiences at the workplace, hospital, school, home or community gatherings. The value system would include the way in which traditions and myths regulate people's behaviour in dealing with HIV/AIDS. For instance, some caregivers in home settings are reluctant to use gloves to protect themselves from infections because the practice violates some of the communities' values of showing tolerance and compassion to relatives and neighbours (Mabongo, 2002). It is because of the multiplicity of factors involved that researchers do not finalise what they want to study before they get to the setting of the study. A researcher does not begin with a well-defined problem, theoretical framework or set of well-structured research questions or hypotheses to be tested as in quantitative research (Neumann, 2000). The research begins with a loosely structured guiding question with the major focus of the study emerging only after the researcher has been in the field for some time. For instance, a researcher might start with a broad statement about people's experiences with HIV/AIDS. After spending some time in the field the researcher might find that stigmatisation of families and people affected by HIV/AIDS is the main area of concern. When that happens, the researcher refocuses the purpose of the study and the research questions.

Articulating the research design

It is important that researchers choose the qualitative research approach to be used in the study before they go to the field. This is an essential step because, as demonstrated in Chapter 8, each approach has unique assumptions about the type of data-gathering instruments to be used, sampling procedures, data analysis and presentation. For example, an ethnographic study emphasises multiplicity of methods for gathering data and triangulation across methods, data sources, time and space. A biographical study would use life histories, diaries and documentary analysis as important data sources and methods for gathering data. Research procedures, irrespective of approach, require flexibility and tolerance to adjustments as the research progresses. The emphasis is on the openness of the research to varied research procedures, which would include changes or adjustments in data gathering instruments used, sampling procedures, research problem and research questions.

Gaining entry

The next step in qualitative research involves gaining entry to the research setting and building rapport with the researched. One of the protocols includes acquiring permission to do the research from the institution or community involved. Once the permission is obtained, the researcher has to obtain the permission of those to be involved in the research. In most African communities the procedure involves reporting to community leaders, for instance, the chief of a village, headperson of a ward, or chairperson of an organisation. It is during these meetings with the community leaders that researchers should take every opportunity to familiarise themselves with the setting and take note of the cultural codes that govern day-to-day interactions, for example, greeting, showing respect, gratitude and paying attention. In Chapter 3 it was observed that the value

system of most African societies is built on respect for others and oneself, empowerment of oneself and the interdependence of self and other, because the welfare and existence of self is dependent on the other. These value systems require the researcher to consistently reflect on the following questions:

- Whose side am I on and where do I stand in relation to the researched? Who is the knower and who is the ignorant? Do I have personal biases or misconceptions about the researched that I need to put aside to ensure an open mind?
- Whose values inform the research process?
- What are the concerns of the researched with regard to my position as a researcher, and how do I address these concerns?

Take the concerns about visibility raised by participants in the study on women in business by Ntseane (1997) which is discussed in Chapter 8. How do you as a researcher intervene to challenge conventional qualitative research methods that reduce participants' voices to nameless group voices, even where participants want to be recognised as individuals in their own right?

Paying attention to the issues raised by these questions can help researchers to define more clearly their relationship with the researched, and to work out strategies to build and sustain rapport with them. The questions also raise general concerns about research ethics in African contexts. Chapter 13 discusses ethics at length.

Answer the questions on p. 165 with regard to a study you have participated in, a study you are planning or a study you have read about.

RIGOUR IN QUALITATIVE RESEARCH

One major concern in qualitative research, just like in quantitative research, has to do with the confidence that researchers and consumers of research studies can place in the procedures used in gathering data, the data collected, its analysis and interpretation, and its findings and conclusions. The researcher has to be aware of the possible threats to the credibility of the research study. For instance, quantitative researchers frequently describe qualitative research as 'subjective' and therefore inherently unreliable and invalid. They also maintain that participants may lie, distort the truth or withhold information. When that happens the researcher is misled by incomplete, inaccurate or biased data. There is thus a need to build into the research design procedures for ensuring validity and reliability of qualitative research studies. Lincoln and Guba (1985) have proposed that the validity and reliability of qualitative research studies should be judged according to criteria different from those used in quantitative research. They have suggested the following terms in qualitative research: credibility for internal validity, *transferability* for external validity, *dependability* for reliability and *confirmability* for objectivity. Procedures and strategies for establishing rigour and ensuring the credibility, transferability, dependability and confirmability of qualitative research studies are discussed.

Credibility

Credibility is the equivalent of internal validity in quantitative research. Qualitative research is characterised by multiple realities and therefore multiple truths. Research evidence is therefore credible if it represents as adequately as possible the multiple realities revealed by the participants. The participants should also be able to recognise the descriptions and interpretations of their human experience as accurate and true. The following are some of the common strategies for enhancing the credibility of qualitative research studies.

Prolonged and substantial engagement

The credibility of a study may be threatened by errors which occur when research participants respond with what they think is the desired social response (Krefting, 1991). Prolonged time in the field and engagement with participants is important in enhancing the credibility of a study. The assumption is that as more time is spent in the field, rapport with participants will increase and they will volunteer different and more sensitive information than they do at the beginning of a research study. The researcher should also observe long enough to identify salient issues. Researchers know they have spent enough time in the field when information, themes, patterns, trends and examples are repeated. When this happens the researcher may leave the field.

Peer debriefing

The researcher should engage in discussions with peers on the procedures for the study, findings, conclusions, analysis, and hypothesis. Peers should pose searching questions to help the researchers confront their own values and to guide the research process.

Negative case analysis

During the data analysis it should not be expected that all cases will fit the appropriate categories. It is important to document negative cases. Lincoln and Guba state that, when a 'reasonable' number of cases fit, negative case analysis provides confidence in the hypothesis that is being proposed (cited in Mertens, 1998). Working hypotheses can be revised based on the discovery of cases that do not fit.

Progressive subjectivity

Researchers should monitor their own developing constructions and document the process of change from the beginning of the study until it ends. The researcher can share this statement of beliefs with the peer debriefer so that the peer can challenge the researcher who has not kept an open mind but found only what was expected from the beginning.

Member checks

This is the most important criterion in establishing credibility. The researcher must verify with the research participants themes and patterns that are developing as data is collected and analysed. Member checks can be formal and informal. For example, at the end of an interview, the researcher can summarise what has been said and ask if the notes accurately reflect the person's position. Drafts of the research reports can be shared with members for comments. In a study on leadership in civil society organisations (Ntseane and Youngman, 2002) the interviewer checked with the research participant on main issues raised during the interview.

Triangulation

Triangulation is another strategy for enhancing the credibility of a study. It is based on the assumption that the use of multiple methods, data sources or investigators can eliminate biases in the study. There are various ways of triangulating data. Among them are methodological triangulation, investigator triangulations, triangulation of data sources and theoretical triangulation (Krefting, 1991).

- *Methodological triangulation*: This refers to the comparison of data collected by various means, such as data from structured interviews, observations, diaries, documents and oral traditions. Ntseane and Youngman (2002), in their study on leadership in civil society organisations, used observations, interviews and minutes of annual general meetings and other official documents as methods of collecting data. Qualitative research studies invariably use multiple methods. Refer to summaries of studies by Mabongo (2000) in Chapter 2 and Kaye (2003) in Chapter 5.
- *Triangulation of data sources*: This is based on the importance of varying the times during which events are observed, the spaces where they are observed and the participants in the study. For instance, in a study on gendered school experiences in community junior secondary schools (Chilisa et al., 2005), students were observed in the classrooms, in laboratories in the mornings, at the playgrounds during afternoon activities and during lunch time in dining halls. People interviewed included support staff such as cooks, cleaners, secretaries, librarians and school administrators. Trainers of out-of-school youths and adults who are interested in studying the

cultures of learning centres, for example, could also adopt a similar approach.

- *Triangulation of investigators*: Triangulation of investigators occurs when more than one researcher participates in the study. The assumption is that the team members bring a diversity of approaches that help to investigate the phenomena from multiple perspectives. Commonalities in their interpretations make a strong case for the credibility of the findings.
- *Theoretical triangulation*: This refers to the comparison of ideas from different theoretical perspectives. Take, for example, the social construction of gender. An adult education researcher who adopts a hermeneutic approach that is an interpretation of texts could analyse the language in the text to show how femininity and masculinity are constructed. Chilisa (2001) in her study on national policies on teenage pregnancy demonstrates the construction of femininity and masculinity through the analysis of language. She argues, for instance, that among the Tswana-speaking in Botswana the word for woman is 'mo-sadi', which means one who stays at home, while 'mo-nna', the word for man, means one who is up and about and therefore a provider. She concludes that language has a way of assigning roles to men and women. An adult education researcher might use folklore and legends to show values in these stories that inform the construction of femininity and masculinity. Refer to the folklore on Masilo, Masilonyana and Tsananapo in Chapter 3 for a discussion on the use of folklore and legends in the construction of masculinity and femininity.

Referential adequacy

The researcher in qualitative research is the measurement tool, therefore the trustworthiness of the human instrument has to be established. Miles and Huberman (1984) have suggested that the trustworthiness of the human instrument is enhanced if the following four conditions are met:

- The researcher is familiar with the setting and phenomenon under study.
- The researcher has a strong interest in conceptual or theoretical knowledge and has the ability to conceptualise the large amounts of qualitative data.
- The researcher has the ability to take a multidisciplinary approach.
- The researcher has good investigation skills.

Reflexivity

The truth value of a qualitative study is also affected by the closeness of the relationship which develops between the research participants and the researchers during the prolonged interaction considered necessary to establish credibility (Krefting, 1991). This closeness creates difficulties in separating the researchers' experiences from those of the participants. Reflexivity is a strategy to help ensure that the over-involvement of the researcher is not a threat to the credibility of the study. Reflexivity in this context refers to the assessment of the influence of the researcher's background ways of perceiving reality, perceptions, experiences, ideological biases and interests during the research.

The researcher is the main data collection instrument. The researcher also analyses, interprets and reports the findings. It is important, therefore, that the researcher's thoughts, feelings, frustrations, fears, concerns, problems and ideas are recorded throughout the study. Qualitative researchers keep a record of these observations in journals. A journal serves as a diary in which all events that affect the way the study is conducted are recorded, analysis made, interpretation reached and conclusions formed. There may be doubt about the exact nature of information recorded and how it is used in writing the research report. The following is a checklist for some of the information that may be useful to record after an interview session. The checklist is by no means exhaustive.

- Emotional tone: laughter, sadness, anger, etc. If so, when expressed (what was the interviewee(s) talking about)? Any sudden change in emotional tone? If so, when?
- Difficult or easy interview to conduct? In what sense?
- Your relationship with the interviewee(s)? How did you get on with them? How do you think they viewed you? Did they ask questions about you? If so, what?
- Any difficult moments, any embarrassing moments during the study (for you and/or the interviewees)? If so, what?
- Anything which surprised you in the data collected, e.g. unanticipated turns or raising of unfamiliar issues?
- Any ethical dilemmas for you?

The following excerpts are from three graduate students who had completed their PhDs. The thoughts they wrote down in their journals will also help you figure out what to write in a journal and how to use the information.

I also have a research journal (like a diary). I write this at the end of each day. Here I try to comment or reflect on what I am learning method wise, what I am learning substance wise, and perhaps see if I can

make connections with theory. I might also have a bright idea about the way to describe something that is going on in the research (Meloy, 2002: 134).

I believe that a journal is a must for qualitative research studies. The journal entries acted as catharsis, releasing my tension, renewing my spirit, and bringing to consciousness my thoughts, emotions, and fears. I wrote it during the data collection and analysis phases of my study. I went back to it during analysis to read various entries, which enabled me to draw some conclusions (Meloy, 2002: 135).

I did write all of these things into the text of my thesis, which is a running narrative of why decisions were made (logic, necessity, bureaucratic constraints) and of the trade-offs I made. For example, the choice of one participant for my study was very risky, for that person had an intense crush on me. I am fairly comfortable with such things, having experienced them myself, but that was one of the potential 'problems' I discussed with my advisor. It could have exploded in my face, and my degree with it. It could have been hard to be 'objective' (not quite the right word, I think, but you know what I mean). It could also have been an asset because of the nature of openness between us, and, in fact, that was what occurred (Meloy, 2002: 137).

Transferability

Transferability is the equivalent of external validity in quantitative research. Quantitative researchers randomly select representative samples from populations of study in order to be able to generalise findings to the target populations. Qualitative researchers focus on situationally unique cases, so generalisation of findings is not always necessary. A biographical study, for example, might represent one life perspective not transferable to any other life situation. In contrast, in an ethnographic study, the researcher might wish to generalise or transfer findings to similar situations. Transferability of research findings in qualitative research can be enhanced through sampling and dense description of the setting of the study. In qualitative research small samples are selected purposively. The researcher selects participants who are knowledgeable on the topic under study to build a sample that is specific to the needs of the study. Excerpts of studies by Seloilwe (1998) in Chapter 7, Mabongo (2000) in Chapter 2, and Kaye (2003) in Chapter 5 illustrate purposive sampling. There are nevertheless a variety of purposive sampling strategies that can be used. The following are examples.

Snowball sampling

In this approach, the researcher selects a few participants who have the information that is important for the study. These selected participants help identify others who they believe have knowledge or information on the phenomenon under study. Suppose you wished to sample youths and adults who graduated from a vocational training centre. You could use records to select your sample. If records are not available, you could get a few names from the trainers and then ask the few who were identified by the trainers to identify others. This is what is called snowball sampling.

Intensity sampling

Sites or individuals are selected in which the phenomenon of interest is strongly represented. Seloilwe's study (1997) used intensity sampling. In this study Seloilwe sampled only those participants who lived and cared for the mentally ill for at least a year.

Homogenous sampling

This is selecting participants who are very similar in experience, perspective or outlook. This approach is used when the intention of the researcher is to describe the experiences of subgroups of people who share similar characteristics. Kaye's study (2003) illustrates homogenous sampling. Kaye's criteria for sampling were that the owner should be a woman, the number of employees should be fewer than ten and the business should be in one of three identified locations. These were to be businesses from the manufacturing, service and retail sectors, and the business had to have existed for at least one year. A group of women from each of the sectors, it was presumed, would have common experiences.

Random purposive sampling

This involves randomly selecting from a group of participants who were selected in the first place because of their knowledge in the researcher's area of interest. This approach is used when participants selected purposively are too numerous for all of them to be included in the sample. For example, if the homogenous sample of women in each of the three business sectors in each location in Kaye's study was too big for all of them to be included in the sample, the researcher would randomly select the sample from the population of identified businesswomen in each sector.

Dense description

Sampling alone does not provide enough information for those who read the research study to decide whether findings are applicable to other settings. The researcher needs to provide dense background information about the research participants, research context and setting so that those reading the study can determine whether there are similar settings to which findings of the study could be applicable or transferable. For example, one needs to read the descriptions of the settings in Mabongo's study (2000), Kaye's study (2003) or Hopfer's (1997) study on the empowerment of adults in South Africa and Namibia to decide whether there are other settings to which findings of their studies apply.

Dependability

Dependability is the equivalent of reliability in quantitative research. In qualitative research the notion of reliability, where the emphasis is on replication or re-occurrence of the behaviour under observation, is problematic because human behaviour is never static. Moreover, qualitative research seeks to study the uniqueness of these human occurrences. Replication is not feasible or defensible in qualitative research. Rather, the important question is whether the results are consistent with the data collected. Variability is thus expected and consistency is defined in terms of dependability. Dependability may be enhanced by using a number of strategies such as dense description of methods used in conducting the study, and triangulation. These are described under credibility of the study. Other methods include the stepwise replication technique and the code-recode procedure.

- *Stepwise replication:* In this procedure two researchers or teams analyse the data separately and compare results.
- *Code-recode:* The researcher codes data, waits for a week or two, and recodes the data to see whether the results are the same.

Confirmability

Confirmability is the equivalent of objectivity in quantitative research. It refers to

the extent to which findings in a study can be traced to data derived from the informants and the research settings and not to the researcher's biases. Some of the strategies for enhancing confirmability, namely reflexivity and triangulation, are discussed under credibility. Another important strategy is auditing. This strategy involves an external auditor following through the steps in the progression of a research study to try to understand how and why decisions were made. Auditability also implies that another researcher could arrive at comparable conclusions given the same data and research context.

The table below summarises the strategies with which to establish trustworthiness in qualitative research and the criteria for each strategy.

Strategy	Criteria
Credibility	Prolonged and varied field experience Triangulation Member checking Peer examination Referential adequacy Reflexivity (field journal)
Transferability	Sampling Dense description
Dependability	Dependability audit Dense description of research methods Stepwise replication Triangulation Peer examination Code-recode procedure
Confirmability	Confirmability audit Triangulation Reflexivity

Table 9.1 Summary of strategies with which to establish trustworthiness (Krefting, 1991)

1 Discuss what the doctoral students
  wrote in their journals.
2 Discuss how notes from the journals
  were used.
3 Discuss your personal reactions to these
  excerpts. Would you be comfortable
  with revealing information such as that
  in the third exerpt? If not, what are the
  implications when you are a 'measurement tool'?
4 Create a checklist of what to include in a
  journal.

DATA ANALYSIS

As soon as the data collection process starts,
so must the analysis. One striking difference between quantitative and qualitative
research is that, unlike quantitative research,
where the analysis starts at the end of the
data collection, in qualitative research the
analysis is tied to the data collection and
occurs throughout the data collection, as
well at the end of the study. This is done
to make decisions concerning the purpose
of the study, namely the research questions and the setting of the study. Another
reason is to inform the researcher about
emerging themes, patterns and issues that
need probing, as well as questions that need
to be asked.

By the time the data collection has been
completed there will be volumes of field
notes, data transcribed from tape recorders,
notes from observations, information from
documents and a collection of artefacts. The
biggest challenge is organising this information in a way that it will be easy to retrieve
for use. There is no one way of organising
the data. Researchers create frameworks for
retrieval that are workable given the nature
of the study.

Organising data for easy retrieval starts
as soon as the data collection begins. It may
start with open coding. Open coding refers
to the process of 'breakdown of data' into
themes or patterns, to create a meaningful
story from the volumes of data. The patterns, themes or categories are codes that
are then identified and marked across all
the types of data generated. When similar
codes are identified across data generated
through different data-gathering techniques (such as individual focus group
interviews and observations), a strong case
for the credibility and confirmability of the
research findings can be made.

Figure 9.1 is a grid illustrating how
data was organised for easy retrieval. The
research focused on leadership in Emang
Basadi, a women's rights non-governmental
organisation. Data collected was based
on 13 one-hour interviews (which were
tape-recorded), analysis of documents, and
observation of the organisation's annual
general meeting. The researcher identified
seven themes on leadership which emerged
from the data gathered, namely: vision and
personal commitment; pragmatism; commitment to alliance building; non-partisan
politics; advocacy and organisational skills,
commitment to internal democracy; and
volunteerism.

The grid shows the themes, the interviewees who revealed information to which
the themes could be traced, and the frequency of the themes. On the basis of the
data analysis grid, the researcher was able to
take each theme separately during the write-
up stage and re-read those interviews that
have information on the theme under consideration. The use of a data analysis grid is
therefore a useful way of organising qualitative data in order to facilitate report writing.

ACTIVITY

Think about ways in which you can organise (or code) and keep track of your data while you are still busy with data collection – this may save time when you do the analysis later.

INTERPRETATION AND PRESENTATION

The coded data must be interpreted to construct a story that addresses the research questions. In qualitative research, data interpretation involves making connections and linkages between the categories and patterns identified during analysis. It involves identifying and abstracting important information from the detailed, complex data and identifying the important themes, patterns and trends in the data. It includes triangulating data across methods and sources, and across theoretical perspectives. It also involves making choices about the type of evidence that is used to illustrate findings and conclusions. Of concern to research in African contexts is the lack of recognition and use of evidence from community-based knowledge systems in making interpretations and drawing conclusions. In most cases, data derived from community-based knowledge systems is either ignored or used by researchers to portray the backwardness of the researched.

In interpreting the data, the researcher has to consistently revisit the questions raised at the beginning of the chapter about the nature of the relationship between the researcher and the researched, and the possible biases that might arise when researchers regard themselves as 'the

Theme	Interview no. 1	Interview no. 2	Interview no. 3	Interview no. 4	Interview no. 5	Interview no. 6	Interview no. 7	Interview no. 8	Interview no. 9	Interview no. 10	Interview no. 11	Interview no. 12	Interview no. 13
1 Vision and personal commitment		•		•				•					•
2 Pragmatism			•			•	•	•	•	•			
3 Commitment to alliance-building	•							•	•				
4 Non-partisan politics	•		•	•				•	•	•			
5 Advocacy and organisational skills	•	•						•	•				
6 Commitment to internal democracy	•	•	•	•	•	•		•	•	•	•	•	•
7 Volunteerism			•					•	•			•	•

Source: F. Youngman (personal communication, May 2003)

Figure 9.1 Data coding: emerging themes

DOING A QUALITATIVE STUDY

knowledgable' and the researched as ignorant and lacking. Additional questions to
ensure that the interpretation is embedded
in the experiences of the researched and
their ways of perceiving reality are listed:

- Was there any evidence to illustrate findings and conclusions derived from the
  story-telling framework explained in
  Chapter 3?
- Was the concept of language as a bank
  of knowledge, as illustrated in Chapter 3,
  used as part of the evidence?

In Chapter 5, steps in writing research proposals that are inclusive of community
knowledge systems are discussed. A checklist to assess representation and visibility of
community voices in research reports is also
provided. What is important to remember
is that the data interpretation should take
as its contextual framework African worldviews, cultures, histories of colonisation,
exploitation and distorted identities. This
is one of the ways that the researcher can
guard against dismissing all data embedded
in community ways of knowing as irrelevant or evidence of backwardness.

It is also important that the voices
of the researched are heard through the
use of direct quotes of what they actually said. Example 9.2 demonstrates how
the researcher extracted information from
interview transcripts and documents to
report on the theme of 'commitment to
alliance-building'. Key words and phrases
that informed the themes are underlined in
the report (Example 9.3). As you can see, in
writing about the theme the author used
the interviewer's words and quoted from
documentary sources.

EXAMPLE 9.2 (Taken from
transcription of interview by Youngman for
Ntseane and Youngman, 2002)

Researcher: Thank you very much for
agreeing to this interview. As you know,
I'm interested in understanding the nature
of the leadership in Emang Basadi since it
started. I am aware that you are one of the
pioneers and were for many years on the
executive committee. This is why I selected
you for interview, because of your long
experience with the organisation. I am
interviewing some other committee members, some employees, and relevant people
in government. The interview will take
about an hour. I have some key questions
I'd like to cover, but we can also explore
other things you think may be helpful. If
you don't mind, I'd like to record our conversation to make it easier for me to analyse
the information later.

Question: What has been the nature of the
leadership of Emang Basadi since it started?

Respondent: … We were a very small group.
We recognised early on we needed support of all women's organisations. The
YWCA was very supportive, it was our
mother when starting as a group. We had
a deliberate strategy to work with other
organisations because we were so small.

Researcher: But I thought you were seen as
very radical and …

Respondent: Some organisations took a
long time to come on board but we had
very little conflict. The Red Cross, for
example, was supportive of the case for
equality of citizenship for women. Yes, in
some circles we were seen as radical – there
was no support initially from Government. But we stressed to the Government's
Women's Affairs Unit that women's NGOs

should be stakeholders – for example, in running International Women's Day. We had a strategy to enter partnership with Government. We felt it important to sit in Government committees and influence the agenda ...

Researcher: Thank you very much for giving so much of your time. I think the main things I have heard you say are that ... Emang Basadi's leaders from the beginning saw the importance of working with other partners in order to achieve its own agenda on women's rights ... Do you agree these are the main points you have made? ...

EXAMPLE 9.3 (Extracted from Ntseane and Youngman, 2002)

Commitment to alliance-building

One dimension of the leadership's pragmatism was the commitment from the beginning to build alliances. Thus, even before the formal establishment of Emang Basadi, the pioneer group strategised to work with older established women's organisations, such as the YWCA. The key goal of giving a voice to women's concerns led the leadership of Emang Basadi to pursue a deliberate strategy of seeking alliances with women's non-governmental organisations, government, the private sector and individuals whenever possible. This strategy is clearly expressed in the annual report for 1996:

Women's development cannot be achieved through the activities of a single agent. Rather it requires concerted efforts of many agents. Emang Basadi recognises its role as that of a catalyst, which must work with other agents, like government departments, non-governmental organisations, the private sector and individuals.

Thus it a took a wider role in the NGO sector of civil society and devised strategies 'to enter partnerships with government'. Emang Basadi felt it 'important to sit in government committees and influence the agenda'. The commitment to build alliances and work with others has been a strong characteristic of the organisation's leadership style, and it has certainly enabled Emang Basadi to promote its agenda of women's demands more effectively than it could have done on its own.

Presentation of findings in qualitative research takes many forms. Findings can be illustrated with diagrams and pictures, or through drama, songs or poems. Commeyras and Montsi (2000), in a study of Botswana youths' perspectives on gender, presented themes from data in poetic form. The words in the poems were taken from the essays that the youths wrote about what it would feel like if they woke up as the other sex. Following are stanzas from the poem that illustrate themes of discontentment from boys waking up as girls and girls' disapproval of the type of life that boys lead.

If I woke up tomorrow as a girl ....
I would feel disturbed, frightened, shocked, and worried.
I would feel embarrassed, humiliated and disappointed
I would feel lonely, depressed and mentally disturbed.
'I might as well commit suicide.'

If I woke up tomorrow as a boy
I would not ...
bully others
impregnate a girl and run away
(Commeyras and Montsi, 2000).

Communicating findings in poetic form is a strategy compatible with communication systems in African cultures. As a writing strategy, it brings urgency to the problems and appeals to the emotions. Most development problems in adult education in Africa are urgent and need the passionate involvement of researchers. It is important that researchers working with communities begin to embrace the poetic strategy so that they can communicate with urgency to readers and the researched.

SUMMARY

You can see that carrying out a qualitative research study requires as much preparation as a quantitative study. There are concerns about credibility and the general trustworthiness of the research study just as there are concerns about validity, reliability and objectivity in quantitative research. Analysis in qualitative research takes time and is more complex than in quantitative research. Qualitative research, however, gives the researched more voice and, if carried out cautiously, provides space for the inclusion of people's experiences in the context of their histories, experiences, value systems and ways of perceiving realities.

KEY POINTS

- The need to establish rigour.
- Emphasising interpretation and communicating themes, main points and interpretation back to the researched for validation purposes.
- Studying, analysing and interpreting data in the context of African experiences and ways of perceiving realities.
- Creating space for evidence and interpretation embedded in African ways of knowing to repair the historical record of continuous distortion of African identities.
- Rendering the previously invisible vis-

ible through the active involvement and recognition of the researched in the production of knowledge.

▦ ACTIVITY

The research extract on gender and the construction of femininity and masculinity (Chilisa, 2005) in Example 9.4 includes data that illustrates the influence of culture on the construction of gender. Researchers obtained data through interviews on the kind of chores boys and girls do in school and at home. Furthermore, girls and boys were observed in and out of class to see how they construct themselves as gender and sexual beings. Study the data and do the following:

1 Identify themes from the data. Key words and phrases related to the influence of culture on gender are presented in bold to help you in identifying and writing on the themes.
2 Write paragraphs on each theme to show how gender is constructed. In your writing show how data from the three data-gathering techniques was triangulated to build credibility of the study.
3 Illustrate some of the themes with a poem.
4 Write a paragraph explaining how your personal background might have influenced your writing and presentation of the themes.

EXAMPLE 9.4 (Examples from field notes for the study by Chilisa, Dube-Shomanah, Tsheko and Mazile, 2005)

Diary notes

Girl 1: On this day my mum made me very happy because when I got home, from

Mary's house, I found a wrapped parcel and my mum told me that it was mine. I excitedly unwrapped the parcel and found that it was a big chocolate and some roses. When I asked her why she bought these things for me, she said I **had cleaned the house to my best in the morning** … I was the happiest person on earth.

Observations: site 1, 10 April 2002

Students were observed during cleaning, feeding time and during extracurricular activities. During cleaning it was obvious that girls and boys assumed different roles. Girls **swept and mopped classrooms**, boys **cleaned windows, moved and lifted desks**. The moving and lifting of desks was looked upon by both as a **heavy task and more suitable** for boys, who are viewed as naturally **stronger than girls**. One young, thin-looking boy at school C said: 'mopping is a girls' job because they are too **weak to lift up the tables**, we are strong' (making fists trying to show muscles). Outside boys **cleared the grass** and some girls raked for them.

Boys' and girls' individual interviews, 10 March 2001

Interviewer: Do you think there are roles that should be performed by boys or girls only? If so, why?
Boy 1: Yes. Boys can look after **livestock and stay in the bush starving** while looking after livestock while girls cannot endure such conditions.
Girl 2: Roles should be divided amongst boys and girls since boys can do **rough jobs**, which girls cannot do.
Boy 4: Roles depend on one's masculine and femininity. Girls are **weak** to do tough jobs while boys are **rough**.
Girl 2: No. The girls are not punished in the same way as boys. Girls for example, will be

beaten on the hands, while boys are **beaten on the buttocks**. This is a common practice among the male teachers. The girls just tell the teachers that **they are in menstruation periods**, thus they cannot be beaten on the buttocks.

Mixed group interview

Interviewer: Do you think boys and girls are treated differently or the same in class? If different how? Give examples. What do you think about this?
Girl 5: Academically speaking no but socially yes. Like in our Setswana lesson girls performed better than the boys, one time the teacher gave back our test papers and said that girls had performed better than boys, she told the boys she was going to **beat them because they were not supposed to be led by girls and went ahead and beat them**. I think this is being gender insensitive, **telling boys to perform better and yet we are taught about equality yet teachers don't practice it, it is unfair.**

Interviewer: What do you think about this?
Girl 6: I think it is okay **because girls are fragile**, however it is unfair to boys as they are always punished since they cause more trouble.
Boy 3: They are treated differently especially during **corporal punishment**, boys are beaten on the buttocks while girls can be excused. **Behaviour-wise it is seen as normal if boys become rascals, and girls are supposed to behave nicely.** It is the same treatment in all subjects.
Boy 1: **Boys do not care, and seem to enjoy the attention, and they feel masculine about it, and they feel girls should not be beaten, as they are weak.**

FURTHER QUESTIONS

1 What do you think will be the most challenging tasks in carrying out a qualitative study among adults in your communities?
2 How would you prepare yourself to address some of these challenges?

SUGGESTED READINGS

Meloy, J. M. 2002. *Writing a qualitative dissertation: Understanding by doing.* Mahwah, NJ: Lawrence Erlbaum Associates.

Chapter 10

Combining methods

OVERVIEW

It is still common practice for quantitative and qualitative researchers to work in isolation from each other. Yet there are many advantages to be gained from a combined approach to studying the same problem. This chapter discusses the contrasting features of both paradigms, and shows how quantitative and qualitative methods can complement each other in adult education research. It also discusses how African indigenous knowledge can enhance a combined-method approach. You may like to revisit Chapter 6 (quantitative design), Chapter 8 (qualitative inquiry), and Chapter 3 (African philosophies) when reading this chapter.

LEARNING OBJECTIVES

By the end of this chapter, you should be able to:

1 Examine the strengths and weaknesses of combining quantitative and qualitative methods.
2 Evaluate the relationship between qualitative and quantitative methods and African indigenous knowledge sources.
3 Justify, and use, a combination of methods in African adult education research.

KEY TERMS

deductive Drawing particular conclusions from general premises.

dominant/less dominant Either the quantitative or the qualitative will be the lead method throughout the research design.

indigenous knowledge Knowledge that comes from local expertise and experience.

inductive Drawing general conclusions from particular instances.

mixed methodology Using aspects of qualitative and quantitative characteristics at several stages throughout the study questions.

qualitative Based on interaction and dialogue with the research participants.

quantitative Based on statistics.

triangulation Using different methods to reinforce, complement or cross-check data findings.

two-phase Two separate phases for qualitative and quantitative aspects of the study, keeping two separate sections for each part of the design.

⊞ BEFORE YOU START

1 Summarise for yourself the distinctive features of quantitative research and qualitative research.
2 What are the disadvantages and advantages of each approach?

THE DEBATE

Opinions about the value of combining *quantitative* and *qualitative* methods are divided. Some people feel that both paradigms come from such different epistemological starting points (assumptions about knowledge and the ways of accessing it) that it is simply not possible to conduct the same piece of research using both methods. Others say that the methods complement each other and the issue is one of practicality, rather than philosophical differences. The debate about whether one method is more suitable than the other for educational research purposes has been raging since the 1960s. Prophet and Nyati-Ramahobo (1994: 6), for example, emphasise that educational problems are complex. As such they require a complex array of methods to provide a holistic view of the problem. In particular they defend the advantages that qualitative methods can bring to a purely statistical database:

> *Good description is vitally important in providing a basis for enabling policy makers to make sound decisions as it provides details about what is actually happening in a particular setting* (Prophet and Nyati-Ramahobo, 1994: 6).

They advocate a multiple methodology that

> *not only allows for different perspectives to be brought to bear on old problems but more importantly […] widens the range of research questions which can be asked and solutions offered* (Prophet and Nyati-Ramahobo, 1994: 6).

This position is strongly defended by Reinharz (1992: 213) on behalf of feminist research: 'Multi-method research creates the opportunity to put texts or people in contexts, thus providing a richer and far more accurate interpretation'. In African contexts, these issues are important if the inaccuracies of external researchers are to be counteracted.

The argument that quantitative and qualitative methods can complement each other is gradually becoming more acceptable, though it is important to understand the concerns that people raise before you attempt a combined methods approach yourself. An additional feature of this chapter, and the book as a whole, is the contribution that African indigenous knowledge sources can make to a combined qualitative and quantitative study. The next section looks at the contrasting features of the two paradigms in more detail. This is followed by a discussion on the contribution that African indigenous knowledge sources can make to adult education research agendas.

CONTRASTING FEATURES

Quantitative methods

Chapter 6 has already discussed quantitative methods in detail, so only a short summary is presented here. The principal feature of quantitative research is that it is about numbers and statistical analysis. Research questions test theories, measure causal relationships between variables, use predefined and, where possible, representative samples, and present findings in table form. The questions are designed in advance of the study. As mentioned in Chapter 6, however, research questions and sampling processes can be developed through community participation. This will ensure the questions are relevant and avoid Eurocentric use of language. Nevertheless, quantitative research is based on a predefined view of the problem.

The research is based on scientific methods, is more highly formalised and is more explicitly controlled. It essentially presents a static picture of a certain point in time (De Vos, 1998). Typical examples of quantitative studies are social surveys, experiments with control groups or structured observation.

Qualitative methods

Chapter 8 has indicated that qualitative research in itself often uses a multi-method approach known as *triangulation*. Qualitative data collection is generally less structured. The focus is on understanding people's interpretation of their own social reality in a given situation – how they feel, live and act (Bryman, 1988: 8). Rather than test a theory, the theory often emerges or evolves during the data collection. The methods used range from observations and informal interviews to discussions, videos or diaries or any number of methods outlined in Chapter 3 (African perspectives) and Chapter 8 (Qualitative research), and includes some identified in Chapter 11 (Action research) and Chapter 12 (Feminist research). The principal feature of qualitative research is that it is about words and a search for contextual understanding. Whilst the main research question defines the topic of investigation the ensuing research questions are less formalised and more open ended. They rely more on what the respondents want to talk about during the data collection, rather than a predefined agenda. Sampling is purposeful and results seek to analyse through the eyes of the researched. The researcher is more willing to empathise and get involved with the people they are studying. This form of research is sometimes called humanistic.

Epistemological principles and modes	Quantitative	Qualitative
Use of theory	Test a theory/hypothesis	Explore/develop a theory
Sampling process	May involve communities in initial sampling process	Involve communities throughout evolving sampling process
Researcher's view of topic	Establishes causal relationship	Asks why there is a relationship
Researcher role in relation to subject	Formal, but in consultation with the researched community	Informal and often as part of researched community
Research questions	Predefined, static	Flexible, may evolve during data collection
Form of analysis	Statistical measurement	Interpretive
Presentation of findings	In numbers	In words
Nature of data	Large-scale, representative, fixed patterns broad in scope	Small-scale, localised, in-depth, attention to detail

Table 10.1 Contrasting qualitative and quantitative research

Typical examples are small-scale, in-depth, ethnographic, or case studies.

Table 10.1 provides an outline of the main contrasting features. There are criticisms of both methods. On the one hand, quantitative research is seen as ill suited to studying the complexity of people and their social situations. It is too focused on finding patterns and may fail to capture the situations of minorities. The emphasis is on the big picture. Moreover, while surveys may describe relationships between variables, they don't explore the why factor – what accounts for those relationships (Bryman, 1988: 101). On the other hand, qualitative research is seen as too unstructured, less rigorous and not easy to generalise. It usually deals with small numbers and can be very time-consuming. The emphasis is on the micro-situation in detail.

Arguments for and against combining research methods in one study

The justification for producing both quantitative and qualitative studies is not difficult. The paradigms present different ways of seeing the world and those viewpoints complement each other. Qualitative research is able to challenge practitioners and policy makers to pay attention to detail. Quantitative findings are useful for planning resources and predicting future trends. The question is, can they be combined in a single study? Some say that the methodologies present incompatible ways of viewing reality. Also, the process and presentation of findings require expertise in both methodologies by the reader and the researcher. Furthermore, in practical terms, a combined study is costly, time-consuming and would take up too much space for most academic reports.

Nevertheless, there are good reasons for combining such approaches. Bryman (1988), De Vos (1998) and Creswell (1994) all offer

rationales for doing this. They are summarised here:

- *For triangulation purposes*: As mentioned in Chapter 8, researchers often use more than one research instrument to enhance the validity of their findings. One technique enables the researcher to get information that is not otherwise available using the other method.
- *For developmental reasons*: Qualitative and quantitative methods can mutually facilitate the formulation of a problem, the development of a research instrument, and the checking of discrepancies in findings at different levels of data collection.
- *To engage both insider and outsider perspectives*: Quantitative research is concerned with the questions asked by the investigator. It collects the perspectives from the viewpoint of the subjects. A dual approach enables both insider and outsider perspectives on a problem.

In many ways, a combined approach fits easily into African perspectives that seek to both uncover hidden truths and persuade policy makers to act. A combined approach is particularly suited to adult education projects such as programme evaluation, participatory rural appraisal and mass intervention studies (De Vos, 1998). Reinharz, in summarising the advantages from a feminist perspective, makes the point succinctly:

The multi-method approach increases the likelihood that these researchers will understand what they are studying, and that they will be better able to persuade others of the veracity of their findings. Multiple methods work to enhance understanding both by adding layers of information and by using one type of data to validate or refine another (Reinharz, 1992: 201).

⊞ ACTIVITY

Think about these arguments for and against combining quantitative and qualitative research methods, and do the following:

1 Organise a classroom debate.
2 One team defends the argument that methods should not be mixed.
3 The other team argues that they should.
4 Let the two teams present their arguments to the rest of the class audience.
5 At the end of the debate, invite the audience to say which arguments they support, and why.

DESIGNS AND INDIGENOUS KNOWLEDGE

It is often assumed that quantitative research is value free and that qualitative research is value laden. It is the premise (assumption) of this book, however, that any method risks being both value laden and biased, particularly if studies are using findings from previous research that has not taken account of African contexts. So quantitative research may suffer from sampling error, and from a bias in the researcher's view of the problem that blocks *indigenous knowledge*. Similarly, qualitative research may misrepresent the local voice. Interpretation of the African voice may make that voice disappear if local contexts are misunderstood or data gathering has been hampered by incompatibilities between the researcher and the researched.

One way of guarding against such biases is to use participatory methods to comple-ment sample selection procedures and to focus the research questions. An additional strategy is to include African indigenous knowledge as a data resource in both methodologies. As Chapter 3 has already shown, these represent values that are transmitted through an oral tradition. They are a resource for constructing, and drawing on, community-based knowledge. Pongweni highlights the function of African oral literature in contemporary contexts. Fables, for instance, often use animals or anonymous human characters. This serves a purpose:

The distancing and anonymity serve to tell us that the behaviour being portrayed is universal. Commentary on society can be made from a vantage point that is parallel to that from which metaphor evaluates conduct, by analogy and implication (Pongweni, 2001: 156).

Such texts represent a particular cultural view of the world. They provide researchers with contextual data that tell them whose voices and values are being represented in a particular situation:

… the actions, events, motives, rewards and sanctions presented in the texts are part and parcel of their knowledge of what it is to be a member of their society, or what constitutes heroism or villainy, or what a typical father or mother, uncle or nephew, husband or wife, and so on, is obliged to do (Pongweni, 2001: 158).

So oral literatures demonstrate the way in which people learn to view the world. In most cases such stories contain representations of the past that are not documented in conventional texts. As such they 'open the way to interpreting previously hidden mechanisms and meanings' (Field, 2001: 250).

There are a number of ways in which the three methodologies can be combined. Creswell (1994) offers three models for combining qualitative and quantitative designs. They will be summarised here, using the additional feature of drawing on African indigenous knowledge sources for extra validity.

Two-phase approach

This is the most straightforward strategy. The two-phase approach entails two separate phases of research: one phase for the quantitative and one for the qualitative study. This enables the researcher to keep strictly to the epistemological principles and modes of doing each kind of research. African indigenous knowledge sources could inform the quantitative phase as part of the literature review and people's own language will frame the problem that influences the research questions. African indigenous knowledge sources could also inform the qualitative phase as part of the data collection process during, for example, focus group discussion or participant observation. In each case, they would inform the researcher of the value systems that need to be considered in presenting findings. In the design process quantitative and qualitative studies vary slightly. This would be reflected in the two-phase model. So Creswell (1994: 179) explains that the research design section might provide two introductions – each introducing a separate phase of the study. The literature review would also have to be presented according to each methodological paradigm. So the quantitative phase would require literature and theory that is used *deductively* to advance precise research questions, while the qualitative study will allow further literature to emerge alongside the data collection phase (*inductive* approach). The statement of purpose and research questions in a two-phase design would be presented as two sets of statements and research questions, each related to the relevant phase of the study in its respective style and format.

An example of such a model might be a study of attitudes to adult education amongst older adults. Proverbs will give a clue as to embedded cultural beliefs about older adults and learning, such as: *thuto gae go lelwe* (there is always something to learn no matter how old one is) and *kazena ua kuatua rune zena ua kengeza rune* (do not say that because you were born long ago you know everything) (Youngman, 1998). The quantitative phase of such a study might use such proverbs within a survey questionnaire to establish the strength of influence on current attitudes amongst different age groups (the relationship between proverbs and participation). The aim in the quantitative phase would be to explore a conceptual framework that predicts no difference in attitudes to adult education amongst older adults and to find a statistical relationship between language of the proverbs and attitudes. The qualitative phase might seek further clarification of the proverbs' influences on attitude, followed by discussion about events that could change existing attitudes, or discussion of additional proverbs that might be used to influence participation in adult education.

Dominant/less dominant model

In this model either the quantitative or qualitative aspect will be the lead method. The introduction, literature review, purpose statement and research questions will be theoretically driven by the lead paradigm. The *less dominant* method will simply be a small segment of information on methods, perhaps to expand on one aspect of the research. Its secondary purpose might be described accordingly in the language of the less dominant paradigm. Methods and results are written in the style of the *dominant* paradigm with a small section for the less dominant methodology.

An example of a dominant/less dominant qualitative model might be as follows. In a qualitative study on choices of medical practitioners in rural villages, the introductory, quantitative feature could provide a large-scale statistical comparison of choices between traditional and modern medical practitioners in several rural villages. The results would inform a more detailed, qualitative, purposeful sample from the quantitative picture that draws on oral literature concerning herbal medical practices by traditional doctors. A Yoruba doctor in Nigeria, for instance, 'encompasses the physical, spiritual and mystical aspects of the patient, unlike the western medical system, which largely focuses on the physical aspect of the patient' (Olawale, 2001: 75). In ascertaining the rationale behind such practices the Yoruba verses of a practising doctor can serve to illuminate why people choose a certain source of treatment. Olawale offers the following incantation:

> Words are thoughts,
> Thoughts are words;
> If we critically reflect over it [word],
> Everything becomes straight;
> Once everything is straightened,
> Whatever we want it [word] to do is easily
> done (Olawale, 2001: 77).

He explains it as follows:

> Incantations can be used in emergency cases, such as in the treatment of headaches, expulsion of poison or snake's venom from a patient's body, or reviving a fainted person or a convulsing child. In this case the incantations serve as a palliative, or first aid treatment. It is usually followed by the necessary herbal medication (Olawale, 2001: 77).

An empirically based study that draws on African indigenous knowledge sources alongside quantitative data can inform international funding agencies such as the World Health Organisation (WHO) about strategies for national health care systems. Indeed, Olawale states that the WHO are looking to herbal medicine as an alternative health resource for the majority of the population in several developing countries (Olawale, 2001: 73). A closer understanding of the causal relationships between rural participation in health care and what is deemed valuable about the experience of traditional medicine can provide a more holistic basis for future planning in terms of provision and adult education strategies for information sharing.

Mixed methodology

Mixed methodology studies include aspects of qualitative and quantitative characteristics at several stages throughout the study. This would entail presenting two purposes for the research, which would be recorded in the language of both paradigms (Creswell, 1994: 183–184). The findings would include themes from both qualitative data and statistical analysis. This means working back and forth between inductive (for quantitative studies) and deductive (for qualitative studies) analyses for each set of findings. The introduction might focus on only one paradigm but would make it clear that both paradigms will inform the study. The literature review will probably be presented quite fully, but rather than introduce a set of propositions to be tested they would be propositions to be modified (Cresswell, 1994: 180).

Alternatively, the theory might present a tentative model to be developed or refined during data collection. (Cresswell also discusses other literature review models.) The statement of purpose and research questions will probably be presented twice – once qualitatively and once quantitatively. The questions could be presented first in terms of variables for the quantitative part of the study, and later as descriptive questions with sub-questions for the qualitative focus. The purpose of such research could be for triangulation or to elaborate on results of one methodology, or to extend the enquiry or discover contradictions. The results would be presented qualitatively in terms of themes and quantitatively in terms of statistics.

Two studies that demonstrate this approach chose to use a mixed methodology because the desired statistical data was deemed inadequate by itself. In the first instance, Assie-Lumumba (2000) used a historical, qualitative analysis alongside quantitative data from UNESCO and the African Development Bank to assess the impact of economic factors on women's access to higher education in Africa. The qualitative analysis located the study in its global and historical contexts of colonial administration attitudes to female education. Assie-Lumumba also used a dependent variable for her quantitative analysis that was measured in terms of the female enrolment ratio in higher education in any given year. This was not an empirical study because it used existing data. But the results provided useful preparation for further work:

> *Time series and longitudinal studies with fresh and sufficient data will help refine the analysis of the trends of female enrolment in various socio-economic categories and higher education fields of studies* (Assie Lumumba, 2000: 105).

The second study, by Kachur et al. (1999), assessed the use and perceptions of insecticide-treated bed-nets and curtains by villagers in western Kenya. This study was exploring the impact of malaria protection intervention strategies. The researchers used a household survey and focus group discussions. The quantitative aspect was designed to record individual responses, but was limited by an outdated sample frame. The focus groups enabled the researchers to obtain general attitudinal and behavioural patterns towards the intervention strategies. By understanding how and why use of curtains declined in relation to bed-nets the researchers were able to suggest strategies for improving the sustainability of current and future efforts. This information could then be passed on to extension workers for use in their health education work.

▦ ACTIVITY

Brainstorm some research problems:

1 **Let different class groups choose one problem and select some research questions.**
2 **Each group must then identify some African indigenous knowledge sources that might be useful data sources to situate the research problem.**
3 **Each group should then identify some African indigenous knowledge sources that could inform their study.**

SUMMARY

In this chapter you have seen arguments for and against combining quantitative and qualitative research methods. There can be epistemological and practical reasons for keeping the two paradigms separate. However, a combined-method approach can also strengthen adult education research, particularly for policy and planning purposes. There are different ways in which qualitative and quantitative methods can be used together – a *two-phase* approach, a dominant/less dominant approach, or as a mixed method. This chapter has also argued that your research will be further strengthened if you include African indigenous knowledge sources in your methodology. This ensures the research is situated in African realities.

KEY POINTS

- Combined quantitative and qualitative studies can increase the likelihood of gaining scientific credibility and research utility with policy makers.
- In spite of some epistemological objections to combining methods, quantitative and qualitative methods can complement each other to produce a more holistic study.
- While African contexts require statistical data to facilitate planning, the inclusion of African indigenous knowledge sources and rich qualitative data ensure the data is situated in local realities and that plain statistics are not misinterpreted.

You have already read that adult educators often use combined qualitative and quantitative methods in participatory, intervention and evaluation research. The previous example was from an intervention study. Chapter 11 will show that a variety of methods can be used in participatory action research using community knowledge bases. In the next activity, you will discuss how to put together a combined study for programme evaluation.

⬚ ACTIVITY

Write a combined methods research proposal for an evaluation of an adult education programme. You can refer to the book by Gboku and Lekoko (2006) in this

series for a detailed description of programme planning and evaluation in adult education. Here are the evaluation stages outlined by De Vos (1998). You can choose to undertake either a quantitative or qualitative investigation for each stage. The ones suggested here are just ideas:

- *Needs assessment*: This may be a quantitative and qualitative review of learner needs.
- *Evaluability assessment*: This might be a qualitative investigation of the strategies used by adult educators to evaluate the programme.
- *Programme monitoring*: You could choose to ask some qualitative questions about how people are recording day to day progress of the programme. What aspects are looked for as quality criteria?
- *Impact assessment*: This may be quantitative and qualitative in terms of what outcomes are measured and recorded.
- *Cost-effectiveness and cost benefit*: A quantitative investigation could identify how the programme is budgeted and how spending is monitored.
- *Utilisation evaluation*: Qualitative questions could ask what kind of values the users and stakeholders place on the programme.

In your research proposal, prepare a literature review that reflects your combined methodology.

1 List your research questions for each evaluation stage, and the method you choose for each stage.
2 Include a section on how you would utilise African indigenous knowledge sources to situate your study and facilitate the research questions.

FURTHER QUESTIONS

1 How can you write up quantitative and qualitative findings in a way that ensures the reader understands both aspects of your research?
2 Are there research topics that are not suited to combined methods? Why not?
3 Suppose you are commissioned to do a combined-methods study for an adult education topic. What arguments will you give for including African indigenous knowledge sources?
4 What are the additional costs (financial and human) in doing a combined-methods study? How can you justify those costs?

SUGGESTED READINGS

Creswell, J. W. 1994. *Research design: Qualitative and quantitative approaches.* London: Sage Publications.

De Vos, A. S. (ed.). 1998. *Research at grass roots: A primer for the caring professions.* Pretoria: J. L. van Schaik.

Chapter 11

Action research

OVERVIEW

In this chapter, the rationale for action research as a common adult education research tool is discussed. The chapter then explains how to develop the conventional action research process so that it becomes more empowering for those being researched. As you will see, there are different perspectives on this process. A particular action research approach that is often used in African contexts is participatory rural appraisal. This process, described here under the broad umbrella of emancipatory action research, can be used as an empowerment strategy for grass-roots participation and as a means of developing community action plans.

LEARNING OBJECTIVES

By the end of this chapter, you should be able to:

1 Analyse the role of action research for adult educators in African contexts.
2 Explain the typical stages of an action research approach.
3 Critically distinguish between action research and emancipatory or participatory research.
4 Undertake a participatory rural appraisal.

nsaa

KEY TERMS

action research   A research cycle of plan, act, observe or record, reflect and revise plan.

community action plan   A record of the community's development priorities and potential based on the findings from the participatory rural appraisal with assigned responsibilities for follow-up action.

community data   Data collected about a whole community.

daily calendar   Time-tabled list of daily activities undertaken by men and women in a household.

emancipatory research   Research that privileges marginalised voices.

farm sketches   Drawings that depict farm management practices.

livelihood map   List of all the resources a household needs on a daily basis.

participatory research   Research that involves the researched in the whole research process.

participatory rural appraisal   A data-collecting exercise involving a whole community and leading to a community action plan.

spatial data   A visual representation of the whole community landscape.

technical data   'Expert' information, such as soil analysis.

timeline   List of key events in the history of the community.

transect map   Cross-section of the village that plots landmarks and associated problems and opportunities.

Venn diagram   Visual representation of how institutions interrelate.

BEFORE YOU START

Think of an activity you learned as a child. Maybe it was learning to ride a bicycle, cook a meal, milk a cow, or tan skin. Write down how you learnt it. Did you get it right the first time? How did you perfect your skill?

The chances are that you perfected your skill by experimenting, thinking about what you did wrong or how you can improve, and then trying again. In this case you were engaging in what is known as experiential learning. Such learning is a form of *action research*.

ACTION RESEARCH CHARACTERISTICS

The principles of action research originated as far back as the 1940s, with people like Kurt Lewin (a pioneering behavioural psychologist from Germany), as a feature of experiential learning. Experiential learning, simply described, is continuous learning. It is a process of doing, reflecting on the action, drawing conclusions, re-doing based on these new conclusions, and then reflecting again on the doing. Adult educators often follow this process as a matter of course. For example, if an extension worker is encouraging new farming techniques with a group of farmers, different farmers may experiment with different methods, then discuss their findings with each other and the extension worker, and subsequently agree on a common method that seems well suited to the local conditions.

Action research follows a similar process. It has developed into a professional model of systematic inquiry in response to other, more predefined approaches to research. It became popular as a research process for practitioners during the 1980s. The argument put forward by practitioners was that some forms of inquiry need a continuous cycle of practice and reflection, based on real-life experience (see Figure 11.1). This is because most social issues cannot be tested in the laboratory.

An additional argument was that such practice-based research inevitably required involvement by the practitioners themselves, rather than simply relying on an outside expert to observe, analyse and solve the problem. So action research became a way of demystifying the research process for the layperson (such as the farmer or the caregiver). It was seen as a form of inquiry where practitioners could work together to solve their own, practice-based problems. The nursing and teaching professions, for instance, have been strong advocates of action research. The opportunity to devise a research process that involves the non-academic has led some researchers to see its potential beyond just improving effectiveness. It has also emerged as a tool for engaging ordinary people in a process of collective inquiry with the aim of empowering them to have greater control in decision-making about various aspects of their lives. It will be shown later in this chapter just how much this concept has developed for community-based adult education.

Whatever the research goal, there is a basic sequence that all action-oriented studies follow. This chapter will describe the basic model for action research. It will then look at an empowerment model before moving more specifically to the participatory rural appraisal approach.

Winter (1996: 13) identifies six principles that all action research initiatives adhere to. These are:

- *Reflexive critique*: a self-critical thinking process whereby awareness of one's own biases is developed
- *Dialectic critique*: an emphasis on the role of context in understanding the problem
- *Collaboration*: a basic acceptance that everyone has something worthwhile to contribute
- *Risking disturbance*: a willingness to change as a result of the research process
- *Creating plural structures*: acknowledging that there is more than one interpretation
- *Internalising theory and practice*: a willingness to see the link between the two in order to develop new insights and practices.

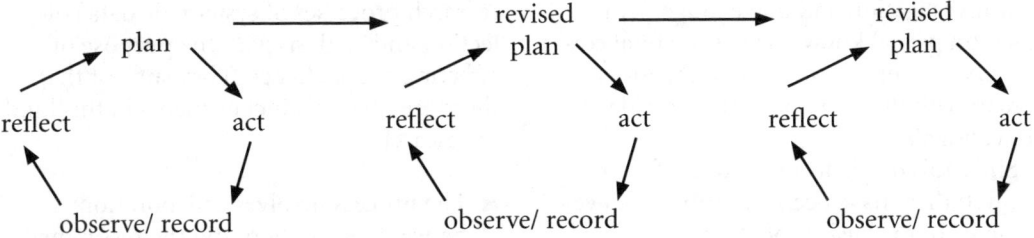

Figure 11.1 The basic action research cycle

Data-gathering methods are usually multiple. They can be both qualitative and quantitative and may involve techniques such as diaries, testing practice, observation, video recordings as well as interviews and focus groups or discussions. Action research is seldom done in isolation from its environment because the context of the research setting is an important feature of the study. So consultation and acceptance of a variety of viewpoints become both ethical and methodological principles. Already you can see why such an approach is relevant in African contexts where it is important to ensure everyone's voice is heard. Traditional action research, however, may not go far enough in this respect.

The research outcomes of traditional action research may have a number of audiences. Winter (1996: 26) suggests there are three: colleagues with whom the researchers have collaborated; interested colleagues in similar institutions; and the researchers themselves, since writing up the report is also an act of learning. It might, however, be argued that a context-specific study has no transferability value – a key requirement for research validity (see Chapter 9). On this matter Winter argues that, as long as the study has been systematic and analytical, it will inevitably have value for audiences who experience similar professional practice issues:

The suggestion that the primary audience for an action research report comprises the members of the situation from which it was derived may trigger the fear that the action research does not lead to the discovery of truths which are of a broader relevance than to the situation from whence they came. However, what enables one specific situation to be relevant to many other situations is a similarity of structure. If our research report has managed to go beyond descriptive detail, and grasped the structure of the situation, there is every chance that the report will be of value to a wider audience than just our immediate colleagues (Winter, 1996: 24).

While action research claims to be of value to practitioners, and also claims to make research more accessible to people outside academia, there are still problems associated with this basic model, particularly for adult educators working with marginalised or poor communities in African situations. The main criticism of this approach is that it does not automatically address the imbalance of power between the researcher and the researched (sometimes described as the subjects and objects of research). From an African perspective this could mean that outsiders ('post-colonial elites or their Western allies' [Mulenga, 1999: 2]) come into local communities, perform their investigation and make judgements based on partial knowledge of the total context. Ownership and control of the ideas remain with the more powerful outsider professional.

Since this original conception of action research there have been a number of developments of the basic model. These have been variously named as participatory, emancipatory and feminist action research. Chapter 12 talks more specifically about the nature of feminist research in African contexts. The purpose of all these emancipatory styles of action research, however, is broadly similar. That is, they aim to address problems that are rooted in oppression. From this realisation the oppressed are better able to understand and respond to the oppressors who control their lives. The following activity will look at some of the ingredients for this kind of action research and see how it is a development from the above model.

🎴 ACTIVITY

Discuss in class some examples of experiential learning. Take the following points into consideration:

- How similar to the basic action research cycle in Figure 11.1 are they?
- How can the experiential learning process become an action research process (for example, by including in the process systematic recordings of findings, reflection with others on the action, etc.)?

EMANCIPATORY RESEARCH

Green et al. (1995: 53) emphasise the participatory nature of emancipatory action research and the fact that it links the research processes of systematic data collection and analysis with the purpose of effecting social change. They suggest that there are three distinct elements in this kind of research:

- The process involves collaboration between researchers and the researched community at all stages of the process.
- The result is a reciprocal learning experience for researcher and researched.
- The intended outcome of the study is new action.

There are also three ways in which the community involved in the study should benefit:

- New knowledge
- New skills
- Participation in, and therefore a sense of ownership over, decisions made as a result of the research.

A common theme running through this book is the concept of knowledge and whose knowledge should be trusted. *Participatory research* says that the knowledge that should be trustworthy comes from the communities themselves and not from an interpretation imposed from above. This does not mean that professionals or experts have no place in participatory or *emancipatory research*, but it does mean that the relationship between researcher and researched should be treated more equally:

Rather than pre-supposing absolute equality between the researcher and the community participants, more recent descriptions of participatory research emphasise unique strengths and shared responsibilities. This gives community participants active involvement in all stages, from identifying the problem to data analysis and dissemination (Green et al., 1995: 58).

The focus in participatory research is on involving the community. This means seeing the community as co-researchers, ensuring dialogue and discussion with community members throughout the process, and using methods of data collection that enhance their participation and understanding. The community is encouraged to research their situation systematically in cooperation with a community change agent (such as an extension worker), reflect on the findings, take action and liaise appropriately with relevant change agents. De Vos (1998) and Mulenga (1999) show that this philosophical approach evolved in African contexts in response to development problems that were overshadowed by neo-colonial interference:

> Critics of African development such as Julius Nyere of Tanzania argued that any meaningful development could only be achieved if the people's culture and popular knowledge were integrated into the process (Mulenga, 1999: 3).

So, for example, a police training officer might be responsible for developing a community watch scheme in a village in order to involve the residents in helping to prevent crime. The model is often introduced by Western police officers who bring their own cultural expectations for both the training style and community liaison techniques. In order to devise an appropriate community watch scheme, it will be necessary for both local and Western police trainers to discuss with local police officers and the relevant community how they should plan the training, how to monitor results and what community liaison strategies should be advocated in the particular village context.

There are problems with the term 'participatory research' in African development contexts, however. Increasingly the word 'participation' is being used indiscriminately because projects that include this word are likely to attract donor funding. The project itself may not always, in practice, address issues of power and often does not take account of gender power differences. Token participation leaves the disempowered without real ownership of the research process or its outcomes. More detailed discussions on this and similar emancipatory action research issues are available in the book by Zuber-Skerritt (1996).

In African contexts there is also a growing awareness by some governments that top-down methods of development have failed to facilitate community sustainability. Development models that came after political independence in Africa largely followed colonial administration methods, which had already dismantled indigenous community institutions in favour of centralisation. As a result of such practices the rural poor have become increasingly dependent on public provision, and have lost a sense of ownership over their own destiny. There is now a drive to transfer decision-making responsibility and control back to communities. This requires, in most cases, retraining of extension workers and institutional officers to build confidence in community leadership structures. The Botswana Government, for instance (Ministry of Finance and Development Planning, 1997), has a community-based strategy for rural development that promotes social mobilisation and advocacy. This involves a community-based development programme and *community action plan* with the goal of reducing poverty in rural areas by encouraging communities to use their local knowledge and skills to find solutions to their own problems. It was from such observations that participatory rural appraisal was born in many African and other low- and middle-income countries.

⌗ ACTIVITY

1 Consider the problem of income generation in a local village.

■ Who has the most knowledge of the problem?
■ How can an expert research the problem using the participatory research approach?
■ How does this participatory research differ from the traditional action research approach?

2 Discuss how traditional doctors or diviners consult with their patients. Are there similarities in approach with participatory research?

PARTICIPATORY RURAL APPRAISAL

Participatory rural appraisal (PRA) is a holistic, all-encompassing data-collection exercise concerning a whole community. The research process is put as far as possible into the hands of ordinary people. Although 'experts' are involved, their role is to facilitate, not take over, the investigation. It has very practical goals. The aim of the inquiry is to obtain a detailed understanding and analysis of a specific local context, then for local people to prioritise their needs based on this enhanced understanding. The outcome of this process is a community action plan, devised with a view to helping local communities solve their own problems through different local initiatives.

The PRA embraces diversity. It can be applied in a range of adult education contexts, such as health, agriculture, biodiversity and urban planning. It is used to address specific African problems such as desertification, low food production, declining productivity and fuel wood short-

ages (Egerton University, 2000). PRA, then, is 'built on the premise that participation by the beneficiaries in any project is fundamental' and that 'locally developed technologies are more likely to succeed' in building community confidence and capacity (Egerton University, 2000: 4). Its strategy is to encourage the use of local cultural values, organisations and knowledge systems for solving problems. The community is involved in every stage of the PRA process. Sometimes members of the community may raise a particular problem themselves, as in Example 11.1. At other times a change agent takes the first step, as in Example 11.2.

EXAMPLE 11.1 (Printed with kind permission from the Trust for Community Outreach and Education, 2001. Participatory Action Research: a facilitator's manual. Cape Town: TCOE (p. 85))

We are a group of women from the Umzekelo community [South Africa]. We want to organise ourselves better to fight the lack of proper sewerage facilities in our community, because this has become a health problem and our children especially are getting very sick too often. We have met with the local council and the Government's Director of Health for this district. But without a strong organisation, and broader community participation and better information about the problem and what possible solutions there are to our problems, our argument with the council remains too weak… and so we have not been able to change our problem situation here.

EXAMPLE 11.2 (Printed with kind permission from the Trust for Community Outreach and Education, 2001. Participatory Action Research: a facilitator's manual. Cape Town: TCOE (p. 86))

You are the [participatory research] facilitator and your organisation is not situated in the community, which experiences health problems and lacks an adequate sewerage disposal system. You are not known to the community. But the health worker at the district clinic knows you and your organisation. She has consulted the local women who have been bringing their sick children to the clinic and suggested that you be invited to visit their community. They agree and you are invited to meet the women.

The participatory rural appraisal process usually involves a team of people, rather than an individual researcher. A range of people-friendly research techniques ensure understanding, ownership and commitment by all members of the community where the research is taking place. These techniques include role playing, drama, charts, diagrams and, of course, discussions. One of the main theoretical influences on this approach is Paulo Freire. You probably already know of him as a renowned adult educator who advocated dialogue and mutual learning between facilitator and participants. He believed that through dialogue people can move from an individual sense of oppression about their situation to a collective awareness of the causes of injustice and the potential of collective action to redress the power imbalances that kept such injustices in place (Freire, 1972).

The word 'community' appears often in this chapter. It is not an easy term to define. For the purposes of this chapter, think of community as all the members of a village or ward. It is now time to look at some of the practicalities of the PRA process. You can see how it builds on the action research cycle of plan, act, observe and reflect.

The PRA start-up process

Although participatory rural appraisal itself encourages diversity and flexibility, there is a recommended approach that maximises community involvement. The Trust for Community Outreach Education (2001: 89) in South Africa calls this process participatory action research and they propose five steps:

1 Identifying a shared community problem and preparing for the action research
2 Gathering information through group reflection
3 Collecting additional data through fieldwork
4 Analysing and interpreting information
5 Planning and taking action.

The PRA Field Handbook (2000: 14), produced by Egerton University in Kenya, elaborates on this process slightly and proposes eight steps to include the community action plan and some preparatory steps by the PRA facilitator:

1 Site selection
2 Preliminary site visits
3 Launching
4 Data gathering
5 Data synthesis and analysis
6 Preparation of a community action plan (CAP)
7 Adoption of the CAP and strategies for its implementation
8 Participatory monitoring and evaluation.
The approach in the Egerton University handbook takes account of the fact that a change agent who initiates the research process may not be familiar with the community. Therefore, preparatory site selection and visits are likely to be undertaken. The

Egerton University handbook looks at PRA from the perspective of a facilitator. The Trust for Community Outreach Education (TCOE) manual is aimed at training the local community itself. But the philosophy of both documents is very much the same – that of encouraging full community participation, with involvement of relevant technical support only when appropriate. As a research student it is likely that you are going to play the role of an expert or facilitator, even if you are doing the study in your own village. So this chapter will take you through the eight steps.

Site selection and preliminary site visits

An extension worker, local leader or NGO might decide to select a certain locality and introduce the idea of PRA to community leaders. Example 11.2 showed how an external professional can decide to conduct participatory research in a village. But in order to build a trusting relationship the researcher needed an intermediary, the village health worker, to introduce the villagers to the researcher. The next step is to develop a local support committee that ultimately becomes part of the PRA research team.

Once initial contact has been made, PRA initiators need to familiarise themselves with the local community. The community-based 'research' phase can only take place after trust and confidence have been established between all participants. So this stage could take some time. After familiarising themselves with the area, the outsiders (which could be yourself) should hold some formal meetings with community leaders, with a view to recruiting some of them as PRA team members – and also to enlist their support in selling the research idea appropriately within the locality. It is important to ensure all relevant groups are involved in these meetings and that there

is ample opportunity for discussion. The research team will consist of both local villagers and relevant practitioners, such as extension workers. It should be as representative as possible in terms of gender, social class and ethnicity. At this stage you may need to run a training workshop so everyone is clear about the goals of PRA. Once the PRA idea has been accepted, it is time to hold planning meetings and agree on the allocation of tasks. Now you are ready to launch the whole project.

Launching

At this stage the whole community must be informed through public meetings organised by community leaders. Depending on how widely spread your community is, you may need more than one meeting to ensure everyone has been introduced to the idea. You can see, already, how different this approach is to the traditional research activity that may take place over a few days with just the minimum of preliminaries for permission. If research is to be participatory and inclusive, it must be introduced to everyone and it must be given sufficient time. Only when trust and confidence have been established can you start the data-gathering phase.

Look at Example 11.3 – a case study from Ethiopia. It demonstrates some of the complexities of getting information and subsequent decision-making.

EXAMPLE 11.3
(Taken from Burckhart, 2003: 310–311)

The PRA was so conducted that the women were always questioned separately from the men, and held discussions in their own groups. Even in the closing session, the women started off talking about their problems among themselves. It was no surprise that the problems which the women raised were different from those of the men. Shortage of wood for fuel is a major problem for the women, for example, as they often have to spend many hours searching for it, and they were therefore very interested in economical stoves. Traditional harmful practices, such as circumcision, were also mentioned by the women.

The men were more interested in training in non-agricultural fields. In both villages in Oromia, almost half the population no longer have enough land to be able to live off what it produces. These men, most of whom are young, have to hire themselves out as wage labourers on other farms, assuming that they find work at all. Strictly speaking, there is no private ownership of land in Ethiopia. Under the communist regime of the 1970s and 1980s, land was handed over to be used by individuals on the basis of size of family. Since then, their descendants have sub-divided the land among themselves, but because the plots have become too small, most 'lease' their land (illegally) to the better-off among them, or even to the 'rich people' in the towns. The fields of training are, however, very limited, as indicated above, and seldom lead to a hoped-for job. House building might be one area that could improve employment. …

In the other village in Oromia, the water supply was the greatest problem. There are no springs, and the nearest river is 3–4 hours away on foot. The local population have therefore dug ponds which fill with water in the rainy season. When this season ends, the ponds become empty in about six months, however. Moreover, the water in the ponds is impure, as animals are also taken there to drink, causing disease. The local people were asked whether they were interested in information about means of purifying the water by filtering it through

stones and sand, or boiling it. Consideration was also given to enlarging the ponds or digging new ones. One of the main problems is disagreement within the village. If all were to agree, everyone working together could manage the work to be done on the ponds. But conflict management is not always easy.

Gathering and recording of community data

Community data is normally readily available, but is fragmented. The purpose of PRA data-gathering exercises is to help the community to make sense out of their scattered information. Because data is collected over an extended period, it is necessary to have a system of arranging the data so collected each day, in a format that ensures each day's data builds on the previous one (Egerton University, 2000: 20).

It is likely that the PRA team will already have collected secondary data (documents and reports) during the preliminary introductions. This will give statistical information about people and resources or land use in the area. The community members collect the field data. They collect these in many ways and from different sources. This acts as a form of triangulation (see Chapter 8) as well as a means of ensuring maximum participation. Field data are clustered into spatial, temporal, social, and technical data. These are based on local knowledge. Findings are usually pooled at the end of each day by the PRA team so that they can organise the information and avoid omissions.

Spatial data

A community sketch map is a visual representation of what the community perceives as their community space. This includes showing the shape (appearance) of the community, boundaries and all the major resource and social features as understood and known by the community (Egerton University, 2000: 22).

Where researchers would normally draw their own map by walking around the site, it is the community members themselves who draw their map on the ground. People may use sticks, stones, foliage or any locally available materials to create landmarks and identify facilities. During this process participants can discuss problem areas, differences in land use or access to resources. A follow-up to the sketch map could be a transect map. The transect map takes a route through the village and identifies various changes in the physical environment that might affect livelihoods:

> *Transect data should be able to enrich information provided on the sketch map, such as data on cropping patterns, trees and other vegetation, and average farm size, land use practices, status of socio-economic infrastructure, community problems and opportunities among others* (Egerton University, 2000: 25).

The transect map provides a cross-section of the community or village landmarks – where the hills, rivers and soil changes are. Underneath the sketched-out cross-section the villagers list some details about the activities in that part of the village, such as crops grown, types of trees and buildings and the main problems and opportunities in that section of the village. These issues are then recorded on the map, directly underneath the area that the villagers are talking about.

EXAMPLE 11.4 (Adapted from Egerton University PRA Manual (2002: 27))

First the cross-section of the village is drawn, showing hills, rivers and buildings, say from east to west:

Cross-section from east to west:

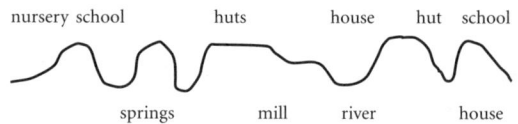

Then the village is divided into sections so that if you were looking across the top of each section you could identify the kind of soil and crops grown from one end of the village to the other. At the same time you can plot particular problems and opportunities in that part of the village (see Table 7.1).

Time-related data

It is important to know about significant events in the community's history that may influence current attitudes and behaviour: 'A historical timeline is a list of key events in the life of the community that helps to identify its past trends, events, problems and achievements' (Egerton University, 2000: 28). The timeline is achieved through discussions with groups of all ages and sectors of the community. The community decides which events are important and the PRA team documents those events. This information helps the community to understand the underlying causes of its problems and possible solutions based on past experiences. Similarly, a seasonal calendar records monthly activities and highlights particular stresses or environmental issues during the year.

By now you will have a fairly clear understanding that this process is very different

	Nursery school, springs, huts	Mill, house, river	Hut, school, house
Crops	Maize, sorghum, sweet potatoes, beans	Maize, beans, cassava, bananas, sweet potatoes	Maize, beans, cassava, sweet potatoes
Soils	Mixed gravel and clay; sandy loam, red clay; patches with hard pans	Alluvial soil along river valley; loam, sandy soils; patches of gravel	Alluvial soil along river valley; loam, sandy soils on highest ground
Vegetation	Lantana, acacia, mango, sausage tree	Natural bushes, wild guava trees, lantana	Natural bushes with scattered manure trees
Water	Springs, rivers	River Sese, Nyamboyo stream, wells proposed	Seasonal rivers and dam
Socio-economic	Few permanent buildings, bicycles, roof water catchment	Posho mill, health centre and churches	Permanent buildings, shops, school, iron sheet roofing
Problems	Poor crop yield, lack of drinking water, tsetse fly menace, pests, soil erosion	Poor crop yield, lack of drinking water, lack of crop variety, stock theft	Soil erosion, low food production, lack of clean water, and lack of sanitation, health and recreation
Opportunities	Building bore holes, crop rotation practice, use of composite manure	Rocks for ballast-making, coffee and cotton	Terracing, agroforestry, community leaders educated through seminars and workshops

Table 7.1

from the structured question-and-answer sessions that traditional research methods adopt. The emphasis here is on eliciting indigenous knowledge and a sense of ownership over what is recorded. This is important groundwork for the community action plan. The process is not as easy as it seems here, however. Critics say that PRAs are very formal events. It is sometimes doubtful whether ordinary village people do truly participate. Local communication systems are not always efficient in this respect. Even if people do attend meetings, there are question marks about how truthful people are prepared to be in such a public process. Such concerns provide strong arguments for seeing people on an individual basis in addition to these community gatherings. Individual or household interviews are often used as part of the social data collection exercise discussed next.

Social data

Social data include household interviews, drawings that depict farm management practices (farm sketches), and time-tabled lists of the activities undertaken by men and women in a household (daily calendars). It may also include a livelihood map – a list of all the resources a household needs on a daily basis and where they collect them. The above research has shown that many household members are not present at the kind of public gatherings where you have been collecting spatial or time related data. In any case it may be that men, or old people, have dominated those gatherings. It may also be that some information will only be revealed in small meetings. The Egerton PRA Field Handbook identifies each scenario in detail.

The interview process itself will probably be conducted by an experienced interviewer, with involvement of local villagers in selecting households. The farm sketches and daily calendars can follow a similar procedure to that adopted for the spatial data. Data about institutions will also be based on community perceptions of how those organisations interact and what they do. One way of representing their interrelationships is through the use of Venn diagrams (Figure 11.2).

Technical data

The nature of the *technical* surveys required will depend on the community data. It is possible, for instance, that information on improved water management or soil erosion is required. It is at this stage that the community participants might agree that some technical knowledge would supplement their local data. Such 'expert' information would focus on opportunities and potential for development.

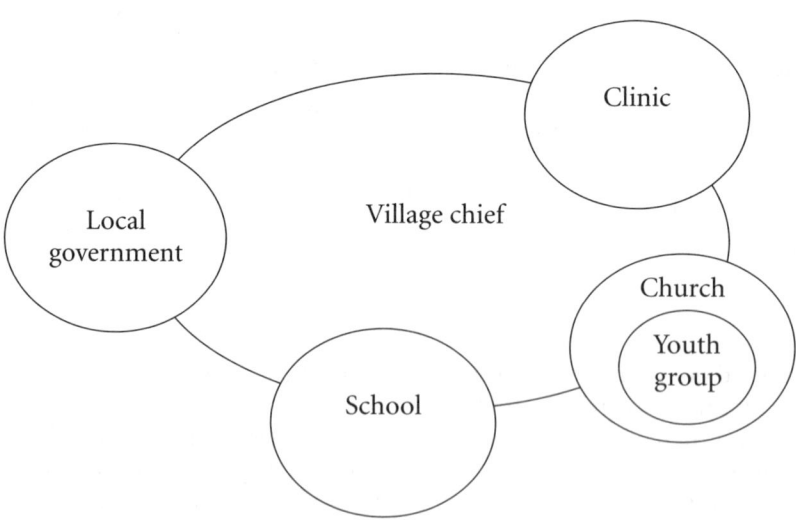

Figure 11.2 Venn diagram example

Once all these various sources of data are collected, the community must systematically analyse them to prepare for their action plan.

Participatory rural appraisals depend on securing the trust and support of the community. Consider this story of a community meeting with the People's Rural Development Organisation in Kei village, South Africa.

EXAMPLE 11.4 (Reproduced with kind permission from the TCOE manual, pp. 118–119)

Recently a development organisation working in East London received a request to visit the Village of Kei to help them identify and prioritise their development needs. The person who initially made the request for them to visit Kei organised a community meeting in the village. On our arrival in the village we were received by the chairperson of the residents' association, who introduced us to a gathering of Kei residents. During the meeting, which was chaired by the person who introduced us, we identified ourselves as members of the People's Rural Development Organisation based in East London. We explained that we did not provide funds, but that our task was to help the village community to identify and prioritise their development needs. The community was divided about the usefulness of our possible cooperation and unclear about what they expected from us. It was decided that they needed time to discuss our involvement and a date was set for another meeting.

The next community meeting, chaired by the same person, was well attended and our involvement was agreed upon. We reiterated our mission and introduced the meeting to our [participatory research] approach to development. We outlined the broad

principles and process. The remainder of the meeting was used to brainstorm needs, problems, expectations and questions with all participants. By the end of the meeting a profile or general picture of the conditions of life in the community had been established. This provided a foundation for identifying some of the main problem areas in the community and which could form the basis for a [PRA] process of personal and social transformation.

By the time all this information has been collected the PRA team should have a fairly clear idea about how a particular community is thinking, behaving, and surviving. There will also be a clear list of issues and problems. If the discussions have been facilitated effectively the causes of and potential solutions to those problems will also be emerging. It may now be necessary to support the community data with some technical data.

✜ ACTIVITY

The following questions (taken from the TCOE Manual pp. 118–119) are based on the experiences of the People's Rural Development Organisation in Kei Village (see Example 11.4):

1 Write a short paragraph in which you explain why a second meeting had to be called. Describe briefly what you think could have been done to avoid having to call another meeting.

2 Write a short paragraph explaining how you might respond in a situation like this, in which you are a [PRA] facilitator and someone stands up and says: 'Many people before you who posed as researchers and developers have come to this village, discussed matters and went away never to return; they did not really

listen to what the community had to say. You can see why we ask ourselves: 'What are the motives of this researcher? And how can your presence in our village be of relevance to us?'

3 'Don't start your contact-making with a public meeting.' Set up a debate with some of your colleagues where you present arguments for or against this statement. Based on the debate and your own experience, record what you think the purpose of a community meeting is. List what its strengths and limitations are.

DATA ANALYSIS

The purpose of analysing and synthesising data is to make sense out of disaggregated information, showing the relationships, their root causes and possible solutions (Egerton University, 2000: 56).

As has been the case throughout this process, the community must be fully involved in identifying problems and solutions. The most effective way is to create thematic groups. The role of the PRA team is to facilitate and guide the community to ensure they include minority and women's issues, and that they look for solutions and opportunities as well as causes of problems. Once the lists are complete, the problems are ranked in order of priority. This is a critical stage in community development. It allows planning to remain with the beneficiaries and not the adult educators and other development workers. So decisions are owned by the community. The PRA team facilitate decision making by drawing attention to trends and situations in the past that were already identified through the data collection. They also seek explanations for trends, discussion of solutions that may have worked in the past and identifi-

cation of opportunities for the future. The following issues all have to be taken into consideration: sustainability, productivity, equitability, cost, technical feasibility, socio-cultural acceptance, timescales, who should take responsibility for implementing action and what resources are needed. When all these details are finally completed, the community action plan can be started.

Creating a community action plan (CAP)

The CAP 'is a record of all the community's development priorities and potential, and is used as a basis for sustainable development planning' (Egerton University, 2000: 71). Whilst the community takes the lead in developing the CAP, all relevant stake-holders (NGOs, donor agencies, technical officers, extension staff) are involved. The emphasis throughout this process (as it was for the appraisal) is on dialogue and discussion. Facilitators ensure completion of a list of tasks, roles and responsibilities, a timeframe for action and a strategy for monitoring progress. From here the ownership of decisions remains with the local community, though extension officers and others will facilitate progress.

Implementation

At this point the research process is almost complete, and development takes over. Local groups need to be organised to carry out particular tasks and a designated local leader coordinates activities. It may well be that others, such as a school head, an NGO or a church can use the CAP to raise financial support from donor agencies. In all cases the goal is to facilitate grass-roots empowerment and self help. This is a daunting and ambitious goal, however. Therefore a final participatory phase is recommended: monitoring and evaluation.

Monitoring and evaluation

Traditional evaluation is usually undertaken by outside agencies, using the rationale that true evaluation can only take place from an external, objective viewpoint. However, the argument throughout this model of research is that local, indigenous knowledge is the key to self-actualisation and community empowerment. Traditional evaluations will not take cognisance of the detailed context or the relationships that have led to the existing situation. PRAs and CAPs are about empowering local communities and are not about generalising findings. It is an action-learning-action process:

> By involving communities in the Partici-patory Monitoring and Evaluation process, the communities are kept aware of the status of all their developmental activi-ties, so that they are jointly responsible for revising the implementation strategies before it is too late (Egerton University, 2000: 77).

So, evaluation is carried out by teams from within the community. Monitoring is an ongoing process conducted by a local com-mittee. They keep track of progress and actions related to the implementation of the community action plan. Evaluation is a one-off process. However, since there are likely to be many smaller projects that need to be evaluated, the evaluation may be ongoing. The evaluation committee will draw on monitoring reports to assess the effectiveness of a project. It will also agree on performance indicators against which to measure objectives and outcomes.

SUMMARY

This chapter has discussed action research as a particularly appropriate research approach in adult education settings. This is because it puts the research process in the practitioners' hands. It is particularly suit-able for adaptation to community-based contexts in Africa where the trend is to decentralise control over decision-making that affects ordinary people's lives. One way in which that can be achieved is by emphasi-sing the participatory nature of the action research cycle. Participatory rural appraisal or participatory action research has been developed to suit African situations where a diversity of people need to be involved in solving their own problems. Two African texts have been used extensively in this chapter to take you through the processes and considerations of participatory action research for empowerment. Their details are listed below if you want to study them further.

KEY POINTS

- Action research aims to demystify the research process so that it does not remain in the hands of the experts. It can be about improving effectiveness or emancipating the oppressed.
- Participatory action research or partici-patory rural appraisal aims to maximise local, indigenous knowledge. It assumes that local people are best placed to solve their own problems.
- Participatory research approaches are about doing research by and for the people, not on the people.

✠ ACTIVITY

Plan your own participatory rural appraisal. Do this exercise in small groups or individually, and follow these steps:

1 **Decide on a PRA site.**

2 Decide who you will speak to at the site regarding preliminary site visits.
3 Outline how you will launch the PRA process.
4 List the data-gathering methods you will use.
5 Do a plan of how you will organise data synthesis and analysis.
6 State how you will set up a CAP.
7 Propose an activity in which the CAP will be adopted.
8 Identify some procedures for monitoring and evaluation.

FURTHER QUESTIONS

1 Imagine a village gathering where people are discussing the problem of teenage pregnancies or the problem of poor crop yields for the village. What kind of problems and solutions might they come up with?

2 How would you as a PRA facilitator ensure all ideas are recognised? What is the best way to ensure a high attendance?
3 When conducting community meetings for data-collection purposes, whose voices are most likely to be heard?
4 Community meetings are likely to produce opposing views. How can you ensure a consensus is reached?

SUGGESTED READINGS

Egerton University, 2000. *Egerton PRA field handbook for participatory rural appraisal practitioners*. 3rd edn. Njoro, Kenya: Egerton University

Trust for Community Outreach and Education (TCOE). 2001. *Participatory action research: A facilitator's manual*. Cape Town: TCOE.

Zuber Skerritt, O. (ed.). 1996. *New directions in action research*. London: Falmer Press.

Chapter 12

Feminist research

OVERVIEW

Feminist research is another example of the emancipatory research paradigm. Like action research, it uses multiple data-gathering methods, but with a focus on gender as the main variable of study, and privileging women's voices as the goal. Feminist research ideologies have a particular resonance with African research agendas because both attempt to challenge dominant values. However, dominant Western feminist ideologies can also fail to acknowledge perspectives that are relevant to Africa. This chapter explains the basic principles behind feminist research approaches. It also shows how feminisms that derive from post-colonial contexts are more inclusive of race and class, and are informed by the influence of imperialism on struggles by men and women against oppression. You will recog-nise a number of overlapping ideas with previous chapters, such as issues of empowerment, valuing indigenous knowledge, and attempts to avoid naming the researched as 'other'.

LEARNING OBJECTIVES

By the end of this chapter, you should be able to:

1 Distinguish between Western feminisms and post-colonial feminisms.
2 Identify methods that can be adapted or used to privilege women's voices.
3 Apply African feminist perspectives to relevant adult education research topics.

sesa woruban

KEY TERMS

feminism   The exposure of gender inequalities and gender-oppressive behaviour.

genealogy   Tracks female friendship groups and networks.

liberal feminism   Focuses on gender as an equal opportunities issue.

post-colonial feminisms   Problematise Western feminisms for ignoring issues of race and colonial interpretations of women and gender.

post-structuralist feminism   Focuses on the role of language and power in defining women's oppression.

radical feminism   Focuses on the equal, but different, biological and psychological characteristics of men and women.

socialist feminism   Focuses on the social construction of gender through class and race in determining oppression.

Third World feminisms   Alternative term for post-colonial feminisms.

BEFORE YOU START

Before you start reading, it is worth exploring in class what you understand by the following concepts:

- Feminism
- Gender
- Gender bias.

Then discuss ways in which you think 'gender' influences what is taught, how it is taught, and what is learnt in different social contexts.

UNDERSTANDING FEMINISM

The word 'feminism' often stimulates nega-
tives feelings. It is associated, for instance,
with being anti-male and it is assumed
that feminist writers are only writing for
other feminist or women readers. It is true
that feminist research is usually research
that is done by women with or about other
women because it is usually women who
are attempting to redress previous gender
biases in research about women. Or they
are trying to present women's perspectives
where women's voices have been silenced.
But those goals resonate with the purpose
of this book, which is to give voice to
African perspectives.

In the same way that African voices have
been silenced in the past, so have women's
voices – in Africa and elsewhere. So is this
chapter just for women? Certainly not. In
the same way that this book speaks to the
West as well as Africa – but from African
perspectives – so this chapter speaks to men
and women, but from women's perspectives.
It emphasises that feminist research is a
consciousness-raising approach, an opportunity to challenge oppressive practices
that uphold particular versions of truth
(De Vault, 1999). An understanding of this
approach, therefore, can help the researcher
give voice to a range of marginalised sectors
of society, such as people with disabilities
and minority ethnic communities. It is a
way of reminding society that all people
have biases. As Hayes and Flannery (2000)
assert, we must be sensitive to our own personal biases and be open to challenging our
assumptions and perspectives about the
world we live in.

This chapter serves a number of purposes:

- To recognise the complementary nature
  of feminist research approaches with
  African research approaches
- To correct some misconceptions in
  Western feminist research in relation to
  African contexts
- To give appropriate recognition to
  African feminist scholarship and thereby
  broaden the minds of men and women
  to potential gender biases in adult educa-
  tion research
- To encourage an understanding of how
  African feminist research approaches can
  give voice to the marginalised in adult
  education contexts and make the invisi-
  ble become more visible.

In order to fully understand how you can
translate the ideas of various feminist perspectives into your own situation, it is
necessary to gain a basic understanding of
feminist research and how it has evolved.

FEMINIST RESEARCH

As already stated, feminist research is an
approach, or perspective, rather than a
methodology. It uses research methods
that were discussed in Chapters 6 and 8 but
also adds some new methods that are perceived as privileging women's voices. Some
of these additional methods are particularly relevant for African adult education
research and will be discussed later. Nevertheless, the ideologies (because there are
many feminisms) behind this approach
have often been criticised for their insensi-
tivity to African contexts. The first part of
this chapter briefly describes various phases
of feminist ideas. It shows how African and
other women from post-colonial contexts
have developed a more inclusive feminist
philosophy, and have produced new forms
of feminism that are more sensitive to the
socio-political contexts of formerly colonised countries.

Feminisms

The principal concept of feminism is that its focus is on women and their gendered position in society. Gender is the category given to the social roles that men and women are expected to play as a result of culturally, socially and institutionally internalised values (Nafukho, Amutabi and Otunga, 2005). Feminism seeks to expose these normative assumptions about men and women. In doing this it has a political goal to redress power imbalances and inequalities that are based on gender. The way in which inequalities are exposed aims to privilege women's experience and their interpretation of how they are marginalised by dominant male practices. In adult education this will mean recognising women's experiences of learning in relation to teaching, curriculum, interpersonal relationships, training opportunities, social class, ethnicity, locations of learning and ways of knowing. However, there are many feminisms or perspectives on gender relations. You can read about these from many sources, such as Preece (1999), and Hayes and Flannery (2000). This is a brief summary of the main ones.

Liberal feminism

Liberal feminism views gender as an equal opportunities issue. Liberal feminists do not challenge existing social structures. That is, they do not suggest that men or women should relearn how to behave towards each other. They are simply saying men and women have an equal right to the same opportunities and that obstacles should not be put in their way. They emphasise the equal right of men and women to jobs, choices and decision-making through democratic processes. In adult education situations this would mean that both men and women are entitled to go on the same training courses, and that men and women

should be allowed to study the same subjects, such as computers or science. Liberal feminists would ensure that men and women are asked the same questions at an interview for entry into a programme of study. They would also examine, for instance, whether women are ostracised by men during a learning programme. But once women have been accepted onto the course liberal feminists are less likely to examine more subtle differences. For example, whether women prefer to learn in a different way from men and whether the teaching style itself affects women's learning achievements.

Radical feminism

Radical feminists have tried to raise the profile of women's marginalisation by emphasising the biological and psychological differences between men and women. So, for example, women are seen as having particular characteristics that are associated with nurturing, intuition and caring; men are associated with aggression and objectivity. Radical feminists say that these characteristics have equal value. Learning opportunities should accommodate all these characteristics. A learning programme on management in adult education, therefore, should emphasise the equal importance of being both nurturing and objective. Another example of radical feminist perspectives is in the way people learn. Learning, it is argued, does not always have to be scientifically based (and associated with male-derived ways of producing knowledge). It can also recognise the role of experience in producing knowledge. If you compare these ideas with the African perspectives mentioned in this book, you can see that radical feminism is beginning to introduce the idea that there is more than one way of knowing and presenting knowledge. Radical feminism has a tendency to generalise about women and men, however, so it has its limitations.

Socialist feminism

During the 1980s, women of colour and women of working class origins began to challenge what seemed to be selective women's voices from elite, white, middle-class experiences. A wider literature evolved that challenged the unitary (all-embracing) category of 'woman', arguing that gender is socially, rather than biologically, constructed. The concept of 'difference', for socialist feminists, recognises the impact of race, ethnicity, class (and more recently) disability on how women are differently marginalised or oppressed. Socialist feminists often use Marxist concepts of production, capitalism and class to explain gender oppression. Socialist feminists, therefore, are interested in challenging the way the education system itself promotes middle-class, male-dominated values about knowledge. This type of feminism gives researchers a framework to understand how different groups of women have different experiences that are affected by class-, race-, ethnic- or disability-based oppression.

Post-structuralist feminism

Many women became dissatisfied with the focus on 'difference' as the unifying explanation for women's oppression. This has often meant, for example, that the dominant, white, middle-class voice has named and labelled women based on a normative comparison against themselves. So different women have simply become 'other' than themselves. They are 'essentialised' (fixed) as having different, but particular characteristics under the label of class or race, for instance. One solution to this problem has been to theorise once more. Post-structuralism shifts the focus on labelling to an analysis of the relationship between language and power. This shows how discourse (a culturally and socially contextualised way of seeing the world expressed through language and behaviour) defines difference. The language used, and the user, create a relationship of power between the person doing the labelling and the person being defined.

By theorising difference in this way one can see how groups of women become oppressed and their voices marginalised, but also how those oppressions are not fixed in time and space. If people are defined by language and power relationships, then they can, arguably, change the power dynamics and produce their own language. This opens up possibilities for resistance and change. A disabled woman can be labelled as not worthy of, or not in need of, anything more than basic education because it is assumed she would never get a job. Yet she can ultimately resist this definition of herself and challenge those who are controlling (have power over) her by producing her own language that says she is capable of, and entitled to, learning. One example of this kind of resistance (though not defined as post-structuralist) is a book by Amadiume (1987). Here she challenges the dominant literature about women and men's roles in the Igbo community in Nigeria. The post-structuralist framework of analysis has also been used by men to analyse and explain how men are socialised into particular forms of behaviour that may oppress women, but also how different groups of men and boys are involved in social class oppression (Mac an Ghaill, 1994).

There are still problems with post-structuralism, however, for formerly colonised people. The dominant voices in these debates continue to come from white people. So definitions of marginalisation are usually from a white perspective. Moreover, the emphasis on language and power as defining factors merely enables several different viewpoints to be heard. While this is a step forward for marginalised communities, it does not provide them with the space to be heard more loudly than the dominant voices. And since the dominant voices are still labelling and naming difference, there is an imbalance in what is being heard and whose knowledge actually counts. So women of colour do acknowledge the progress of post-structuralism in viewing feminism in a more fluid way (Hooks, 1991; Ntseane, 1999). But they have also sought to claim their own definitions that represent more accurately the experiences and priorities of women in the formerly colonised countries. These feminisms are categorised here as post-colonial feminisms. At one and the same time, they challenge normative definitions and aim for a 'strategic essentialism' (taking a fixed position on purpose to show its opposition to the dominant one) that defends values of the marginalised 'to affirm that which is denigrated' (Dube, 1999: 216). They also place feminism within a more relevant socio-political context.

Post-colonial feminisms

In African contexts there has been considerable debate about the word 'feminism'. The issue for African women is that the experience of colonialism is a central experience of both men and women in Africa. The second issue is that culture should be seen as dynamic. It should therefore be possible to challenge oppressive cultural practices in relation to gender sensitivity without rejecting one's culture per se. Both men and women should work together for positive change. However, the word 'feminism' is too closely associated with Western concepts of gender equality and is sometimes rejected by African writers. In Mohanty, Russo and Torres (1991) a number of women writers

from the non-European Third World critique the conventional meanings that are attached to feminism. The issues centre around its association with cultural imperialism and a narrow definition of gender that is framed by middle-class white experiences in the West. Mohanty (1991: 11) points to the fundamental difference for women of colour as being 'the contrast between a singular focus on gender as a basis for equal rights, and a focus on gender in relation to race and/or class as part of a broader liberation struggle'.

In other words, for many women of colour, and especially those in the former colonies, there are additional forms of oppression that that need to be taken into account when examining relationships between men and women (Johnson-Odim, 1991: 315). For example, Western-style adult education material on HIV/AIDS prevention has assumed that women simply need to be given the message: 'Say "no" to men – you have the power'. But this position ignores the local understanding by men and women of the causes and origins of HIV/AIDS. It denies men and women the opportunity to explore together how they can find shared solutions. So the message divides, rather than unites, men and women in the fight against AIDS. It assumes HIV/AIDS is simply a gender power issue. Furthermore, as the following quote shows, women in less industrialised nations need to define themselves differently from the way they are perceived in the West:

A homogeneous notion of the image of women is assumed, which in turn produces the image of an 'average Third World woman.' This average Third World woman leads an essentially truncated life based on her feminine gender (read: sexually constrained) and her being 'Third World' (read: ignorant, poor, uneducated, tradition-bound, domestic, family-oriented, victimised, etc.). This, I suggest, is in contrast to the (implicit) self-representation of Western women as educated, as modern, as having control over their own bodies and sexualities, and the freedom to make their own decisions (Mohanty, 1991: 56).

So post-colonial feminisms need to both problematise Western feminisms and at the same time present alternative Third World feminisms within the realities of life experiences that include the ongoing struggle against colonial interference, racism and the micropolitics of work, home and family (Mohanty, 1991: 20–21). As a result of this debate, a number of words have been used to try to capture the particular stance that African women wish to portray when they choose to challenge the oppression of women without alienating African men or rejecting African cultures. Post-colonial feminisms are sometimes called Third World feminisms. These umbrella terms include concepts such as African feminism, womanism, and Africana womanism.

African feminism is defined by Mekgwe as a discourse that

> takes care to delineate those concerns
> that are peculiar to the African situation.
> It also questions features of traditional
> African cultures without denigrating
> them, understanding that these might be
> viewed differently by the different classes of
> woman (Mekgwe, 2003: 7).

One of these differences is to recognise men as partners in the struggle against gender oppression, rather than the enemy (Mekgwe, 2003). This is in recognition that 'we are all trapped in a patriarchal system, but it's the way in which we deal with those gender issues that makes us different' (Hudson Weems in Yaa Asantewaa Reed, 2001: 169). The desire not to separate women's issues from male struggles is a significant depar-

ture from Western feminisms that hold male gender power relations as central to the feminist position. The African position is often defended by African women writers by the use of proverbs and folk tales. Dube (1999) draws on a Setswana myth about a hen scratching the ground for a lost needle as a way of highlighting the complexities, dangers and possibilities of defining feminist endeavours in post-colonial Africa. Yaa Asantewaa Reed (2001: 169) refers to the proverb 'it takes a village to raise a child' as demonstration that men and women together come from a communal past where responsibilities are collective.

Womanism has been adopted by some African feminists to signify their rejection of the term feminism because it is associated with Western ideologies.

Africana womanism is a term given to the particular experience of people of African origin, both diasporic (living outside of their country of origin) and indigenous. This includes understanding how colonial ideologies have imposed Western patriarchal gender discrimination on societies that were not, prior to colonialism, necessarily identifying with such power differentials. For example, Amadiume (1987), Mohanty (1991) and Ntseane (1999) point out that women in Third World countries have played a far more equal role in the production of food and livelihoods than middle-class white women. This contradicts the common assumptions that are made in Western feminisms about public/private divides for gender roles. The Africana womanist position is explained by Yaa Asantewaa Reed (2001: 169) in a discussion with Hudson-Weems. Hudson-Weems argues that Africana womanism claims the solution to gender inequality is seen as already lying within African philosophy:

> Essentially the Africana womanist position is that the framework for a world free

of patriarchal oppression already exists within the traditional African philosophical worldview – *if only the Africana woman will claim it* (Hudson-Weems in Yaa Asantewaa Reed, 2001: 175).

This implies that African philosophies, rather than cultural practice, should be the starting point for repositioning gender power relations.

In short, Mohanty sums these arguments up as follows:

Third World feminists have argued for the rewriting of history based on the specific locations and histories of struggle of people of colour and post-colonial peoples, and on the day-to-day strategies of survival utilised by such peoples (Mohanty, 1999: 10).

You can see, from this brief introduction, that feminism is not a fixed position. While its central theme is women's experiences of gender power relations, there are many ways of addressing this issue, and the researcher's own theoretical position influences how they undertake their research, even in the name of feminism. African women's struggles have influenced how women organise themselves. Organisations such as WIN (Women in Nigeria) and WAND (Women's Association for National Development) in Sierra Leone, among others, are often the starting point for women's activism in Africa.

⊞ ACTIVITY

Discuss, in groups, situations from your own experience that demonstrate gender inequalities and oppressive practices.

1 Think, for example, how proverbs and folk tales, or the use of certain words in your language, help to reinforce gender stereotypes.

2 Look at pictures in children's reading books. See how the pictures of boys and girls, men and women reinforce assumptions about their role in society.

3 Discuss whether common law in your society allows equal access to land rights or property rights between men and women.

Consider the following idea. Suppose the practices, representations and laws that you have just discussed were applied to distinguish access to rights between black and white people. No doubt you would feel such discrimination is unacceptable. Now consider why such discrimination still continues between men and women and how adult educators can address such issues.

THE FEMINIST RESEARCH PROCESS

For the purpose of this book, it can be said that African feminist research methods focus on research that seeks to challenge dominant assumptions about sexism, gender and power relations that are implied in language and social behaviours in African adult education contexts. Many methods are those adopted by researchers in any context. But the way those methods are used is crucial to the feminist emancipatory paradigm.

Feminist researchers define the process according to a number of principles that centre around the relationship between the researcher and the researched. Reinharz (1992) emphasises that feminist research strives to represent diversity and aims to create social change. So, like adult education, the research has a scholarly and practical basis. Moreover, as has been stated earlier in this chapter, the process can also be applied more generally to research about marginalised groups. The point here is that every effort must be made to privilege the marginalised researched voice and not your own. This means encouraging the researcher to speak through the voice of the marginalised. The following principles guide that approach.

- Experiences of the researched are key data sources, with the goal of representing how the world is experienced and understood by women.
- An acceptance that neutrality or 'objectivity' is not possible. The researcher cannot be separated from the researched.
- Researchers should acknowledge their own situatedness (where their value base is coming from) from the beginning of the research initiative.
- There is often continuity between the researcher's life and the experience being researched; that is, the researcher makes personal connections with the research topic.
- The researchers' reflexivity includes a process of continually exploring their own experiences and feelings – how they are interfacing with the research process and how research relationships are affecting the data collection and findings.
- Self-disclosure (revealing aspects of one's life, values or experiences) by the researcher to the researched can facilitate a rapport with the researched, though it cannot be assumed that sameness of gender or race alone will create the rapport.
- The research aims to be collaborative and participative; that is, research questions and data findings are developed collectively with the research subjects.
- The analysis looks for hidden meanings and implied assumptions in the data; what is not said is often as significant as what is said.
- When writing up the research,

researchers should make their methods and experiences transparent.

To this list McEwan (2001: 94) adds the anti-colonial stance that the researcher should 'destabilise the dominant discourses of imperial Europe, including "development". These discourses are unconsciously ethnocentric, rooted in Western cultures and reflective of a dominant, Western worldview.' Afrocentric approaches are concerned about situating African identities within their specific locations, as discussed in earlier chapters.

▓ ACTIVITY

Think about how you can increase the degree to which your research 'speaks through the voices of the marginalised'.

AFRICAN FEMINIST PERSPECTIVES

Feminist research in African adult education contexts must embrace analytical frameworks that take account of African histories and contemporary post-colonial experiences. African feminist research draws on a variety of methods – including those outlined in previous chapters in this book. What makes the research itself feminist is the perspective or set of values that influence how you approach a topic and how you interpret existing studies. This part of the chapter looks at feminist perspectives using common research methods such as interviews, surveys, ethnography and content analysis. It then identifies some additional methods that are particularly associated with feminist studies. You can read more about these methods in Reinharz (1992).

Surveys

From a feminist perspective, a survey usually studies social change and social problems. Such a survey combines the scientific method with sensitivity to how gender-specific issues are portrayed. It might aim to counter the sexist influence of previously conducted quantitative research. It might simply interpret secondary data, through the lens of a feminist perspective. The following example shows how one feminist writer, Razavi (1999: 411) critiqued data and criteria for measuring poverty in standard household surveys used in developing countries.

EXAMPLE 12.1
(Taken from Razqui, 1999: 41)

The reliance on poverty lines and household expenditure data has profound implications for how gender issues are analysed. Measuring poverty on the basis of household expenditure data effectively ignores the long-standing feminist concerns about intra-household distribution. It is very rare to find standard surveys, such as those carried out in the context of the PAs [Poverty Assessments], embarking on a qualitative exploration of intra-household poverty. Per capita and adult equivalent measures make assumptions about equal intra-household distribution of resources. Hart's (1995) interrogation of the claims made by those using collective models of the household to be able to recover intra-household distributional patterns from household surveys, using sophisticated econometric techniques, also reveals that they are for the most part exaggerated. In other words, if household surveys are to become useful tools for capturing and monitoring gender differentials in poverty, then intra-household distribution issues need to be addressed at the very early stage and specifically built into questionnaire design.

The reliance on household expenditure data also means that one of the easier ways to make gender visible is by dividing the households into male-headed and female-headed ones, given that the characteristics of household heads (their gender, age, etc.) are invariably collected through these surveys and form a ready basis for sorting the data.

The tendency to equate female headship with poverty has, however, been queried on both empirical and methodological grounds. The trajectories leading to female headship are clearly divergent, and the category of households labelled 'female-headed' is a highly heterogeneous one. It includes lone female units, households of single women wage earners with young dependants, households in which women earners receive significant remittances from absent males, and so on. Some of these conditions may constitute what can be reasonably thought of as poverty risk factors, such as households with young children maintained by women alone (Folbre, 1990). But by aggregating these distinct categories of households generated through different social processes (e.g. migration, widowhood, divorce), and constructing a simple dualism between male-headed and female-headed households, it becomes impossible to interpret the evidence in a meaningful way.

The implications for adult education research of such distinctions could have an effect on how adult education is provided. Statistics that portray all female-headed households as poor with young children may mean that providers decide only to offer educational programmes on childcare to women in a certain location because it is assumed that this is all that is needed. This will discriminate against other female householders who are looking for different educational opportunities.

Interviews

The feminist interview aims to uncover previously neglected or misunderstood experiences. It may analyse the interview process itself for gender power relations or use the interview to expose new experiences. A woman lawyer, for instance, might describe in an interview how she is always being taken away from important cases simply because a woman is needed elsewhere for less important tasks. These experiences might affect her promotion opportunities. The experiences have implications for the training of the legal profession, to make it more gender sensitive. The interviews described by feminist researchers Dillard (2000) and Erasmus (2000) in Chapter 14 provide good examples of a self-reflective analysis of how the interview process itself is a power relationship that is influenced by who the researcher and researched are.

Ethnography

Feminist ethnography aims to understand situations and analyse experiences from women's points of view. It exposes oppressive behaviour in its social context. Ethnography involves in-depth analysis of social situations, conversations and human interaction (see Chapter 8). Gender is the focus of analysis in Thetela's (2002) description of 'sex discourses and gender constructions' in a study of police interviews with rape victims in Southern Sotho. Her discussion is concerned with the way language and linguistic codes of language used between men and women serve to reinforce gender power imbalances and reinforce inequalities in the way the legal system deals with rape cases. Discourse here is described as a social practice – the behaviours and use of language – in controlling

norms and beliefs about gendered behaviour and sexual morality:

> *I use evidence from this study to suggest that one of the key issues in examining language and the law in southern Africa is that of the relationship between language, culture and the police interview rooms and courtrooms since these institutions are not only legal domains but also domains where cultural power relations are contested* (Thetela, 2002: 180).

Thetela identifies the Sesotho words that describe sexual intercourse (*ho arolelana dikobo*, meaning 'to share blankets'; *ho bapala*, meaning 'to play'; *ditaba tsa motabo*, meaning 'activities of *motabo*' [a form of snuff]). She points out that women are culturally discouraged from using explicit language about sex, while men have access to a different vocabulary. This places women in a passive, accepting role without the means to even describe the process of rape. In the police interviews, Thetela shows how both behaviour between police and the rape victims, as well as the language they use, conveys an image that the woman has no case to claim she has been raped. The victim, in her description to two male police officers, is embarrassed to use explicit words because it is not culturally acceptable. The following interview translation shows how the police officer chides her when she asks if her mother can explain for her:

> *Look here young woman, you are the complainant, and not your mother, or was she present when the two of you were having sex? An allegation of rape is a very serious matter and not a joke. Tell us in his own words as he said them* (Thetela, 2002: 183).

Thetela explains that the police officer's response to the victim's reluctance to use embarrassing words is his own description of the rape by

use of the swear word kota [meaning sex] ..., by means of which he holds both the victim and the alleged rapist equally responsible. This allegation does not only embarrass the victim, but also discursively reproduces rape as a non-criminal activity (Thetela, 2002: 184).

Language is a rich source of analysis for exposing culturally accepted norms in gender power relations. Thetela also demonstrates how language is an implicit reinforcer of oppression, discrimination and domination in her content analysis of documents.

Content analysis

Feminist content analysis of texts includes books, research publications, billboards, proverbs, fashion, clinical records and any visual product of social or cultural norms. Feminist researchers interpret texts through the lens of feminist perspectives to expose gendered themes that are often hidden, or implicit, in the language used (Reinharz, 1992). Thetela (2002), in her description of sex discourses, uses police newspaper reports on cases of rape and murder to show how the language of male reporters fails to reflect the violence of rape because the reporters use cultural expressions 'that carry the underlying sense of consensual sex, while underplaying the criminal element and the violence involved in the rape event itself' (Thetela, 2002: 181).

She points to different rape case descriptions (translated into English) as follows:

An eight year old girl was turned into a woman by one man in T- ... .

A man of about forty-six years of M- ... is alleged to have turned his 29-year-old daughter into a woman by forcing her to engage in activities of motabo during the absence of her mother ....

The Leribe police found the body of a six-year-old child in one house in the village of .... The postmortem shows that the child had been interfered with through matters of motabo.

Thetala continues her analysis by saying: 'The authors of these reports enter into a negotiation of cultural meanings with their readership, and in this way, ensure social acceptability' (Thetela, 2002: 81). These examples, which are used for content analysis, demonstrate the power of language. The language conveys messages that undermine women's right to social justice and that implicitly accept, thereby condoning, male rights to dominate women by portraying their violent acts through non-violent images. Such studies have a significant role to play in the training of police officers in gender sensitivity and consciousness-raising of the impact of seemingly normative behaviour on gendered social justice.

Reinharz (1992) discusses a range of other consciousness-raising methods which she associates particularly with feminist research. Space does not permit expansive discussion of them here so just two are mentioned, with the goal that they can be explored more fully as class activities.

Drama

Reinharz (1992) suggests that drama is a particularly useful emancipatory and participatory data collection method. Through the process of role play women can construct or reconstruct scenarios that demonstrate their social circumstances.

The scenarios, identified as data, can then be analysed by the women to make sense of their experiences and find their own voice. Role play is concrete and specific to local experiences. It is a common medium of communication in African villages and a powerful adult education resource.

Genealogy

Genealogy conventionally consists of tracking family lineage and representing a family tree, showing where people have come from through the generations. Genealogy for feminist research is identified by Reinharz as a way of tracing female friendships and other relationships. This is done through constructing diagrams that reveal the kind of relationships and networks that may otherwise be hidden in ordinary biographical research. This kind of genealogy could be used to compare and contrast the relationships that men and women have in different social settings. It might be useful when planning adult education programmes that aim to target particular social groups, for instance.

⊞ ACTIVITY

1 Discuss in class research situations where role play might be used as a form of data gathering in order to expose gender inequalities.
2 Do your own gender-specific genealogy of friendship networks and relationships in class. Discuss your findings. What does the genealogy reveal about social behaviour in your student community?

SUMMARY

This chapter has explored the relationship between Western feminist research and post-colonial feminisms. Feminist approaches stem from the emancipatory research paradigm. There are many interpretations of feminism and some Africans have chosen alternative terminologies to distinguish themselves from the association of feminism with Western ideologies. African feminist discourses focus on gender-based concerns that are relevant to African situations with the goal of questioning oppressive features of African culture without denigrating them. African feminist discourses recognise that women need the cooperation of men to effect change. They aim to resist colonial discourses in solidarity with their male counterparts, while at the same time raising consciousness of gender oppressions that manifest themselves both prior to, and as a result of, colonialism. Feminists often embrace conventional research methodologies but they study issues from a critical feminist perspective in order to challenge dominant assumptions about sexism, gender and power relations that are implicit in language and social behaviour. Researchers reflexively situate their position within the write-up of the study in order to address the ethical question of bias and help the reader understand how this position affects the study.

KEY POINTS

■ African feminist research uses multiple methods, including those that embrace oral traditions.
■ The researcher-researched relationship attempts to break down power differentials through the use of self-disclosure and often choosing to share the same ethnic or cultural identity as the researched.
■ Feminist researchers are self-reflexive, constantly reviewing their own situatedness in the research process. This

informs the data collection and analysis.

- African feminist research is situated within a larger liberation struggle against imperialism. As such, it seeks to involve men in the same struggle.

⊞ ACTIVITY

Consider the extract from Ntseane (1999: 28–32) in Example 14.3, where she describes the plight of small business entrepreneurs in Botswana. After you have read it, devise your own research question and methodology that attempt to understand women's learning patterns for entrepreneurial training, and that can lead to recommended strategies for future learning. Consider:

1 What sort of researcher-researched relationship should you have, and how will you achieve this?
2 What methods will you use and why?
3 What questions should you ask in order to obtain women-friendly perspectives for this context?

EXAMPLE 14.3
(From Ntseane, 1999)

Women's involvement in business is largely confined to small-scale activities in the informal sector. In recognition of these limitations, Government has made various efforts to improve women's chances in business. The Financial Assistance Policy (FAP), for instance, has a component targeted to the development of a small-scale citizen business in manufacturing. The programme makes special provisions for women, offering them easier eligibility terms than men. The striking thing is that only 15% of these funds have benefited women, and it has quite limited impact on the develop-

ment of the projects so financed. A major reason is that women are too constrained by various other factors, such as access to business premises.

Some women have, however, used government assistance from FAP, the National Development Bank, and non-government training and financial support to build up sustainable businesses, venturing into areas such as brick making, food packaging and small manufacturing. Some have even advanced from street hawking to regular enterprises like dealerships, supermarkets, butcheries, and import/export businesses. However, they face serious limitations due to insufficient access to funds, inadequate access to business space, insufficient effective markets and lack of entrepreneurial skills. One entrepreneur, Mrs Mosinyi, shared the following with the participants of a National Seminar on the informal sector and small-scale enterprise development in Botswana and was quoted by Somolekae:

> As an entrepreneur, I feel that the training we receive does not address our felt needs. I request … closer cooperation between our trainers and us to ensure that we will tell them what we really need. I don't know how to write but every time I attend training workshops I am given books and pencils and asked to keep records. Of course when they visit they don't find anything in their book. That is why they say we are not interested' (Somolekae, 1992: 78).

With this background it is proper to provide very practical directions to individuals who might deliver training in the context of Botswana women described above. … Trainers in particular have to understand why women are in business, what their problems are, and how they think they might be helped. Business concepts are new in a culture that has a history of sharing and group solidarity.

Individual measures have been implemented to promote women in the informal sector, such as ... courses ... loans ... and ... credit. ... But there is a lack of programmes that allow women to transform the awareness into strategic gender needs, such as developing their position in society into action, aiming to create more rights for women and creating control for resources.

FURTHER QUESTIONS

1   How can you apply the feminist approaches in this chapter to adult education issues in relation to disability or ethnic minorities?
2   Can you think of any new data-collection methods that have not been mentioned here? Justify your choice.
3   If you were trying to justify an African feminist position to a Westerner, what kind of examples would you produce to illuminate your position?

SUGGESTED READINGS

Hayes, E. and Flannery, D. D. 2000. *Women as learners: The significance of gender in adult learning.* San Francisco: Jossey Bass.
Mohanty, C. T., Russo, A. and Torres, L. (eds.). 1991. *Third World women and the politics of feminism.* Bloomington and Indianapolis: Indiana University Press.
Reinharz, S. 1992. *Feminist methods in social research.* Oxford: Oxford University Press.

Chapter 13

Research ethics

OVERVIEW

This chapter describes ethical concerns that arise in carrying out research in African contexts. Ethical issues discussed are of two dimensions. First, ethical issues of confidentiality and consent are discussed. Emphasis is on the psychological harm, humiliation, embarrassment and other losses that occur when research participants, communities and the researched suffer because consent and confidentiality principles are violated. Some examples of unethical practices in research in Africa are given. Second, validity or claims about true knowledge as ethical issues are discussed. The chapter demonstrates how the criteria for evaluating the legitimacy, credibility or validity of knowledge differ depending on the research paradigm that informs the research methodology. The emphasis is that every study should be designed to produce accurate, valid, credible and legitimate research findings. Ethical concerns in quantitative, qualitative and participatory research designs are discussed.

LEARNING OBJECTIVES

By the end of this chapter, you should be able to:

1 Understand the different concepts involved in defining ethics
2 Apply ethical principles to the evaluation of research practices in Africa
3 Formulate ethics guidelines to inform research practice in an institution or a community.

bese saka

KEY TERMS

confidentiality Safeguarding the interests of the research participants by ensuring that their identities are not revealed in the research study.

covert research When researchers in qualitative research conceal the fact that they are carrying out a study.

ethical principles A set of standards that guides researchers on how they should interact with research participants.

validity When the research process empowers the researcher and the research participants to bring about meaningful change with regard to the issue under investigation.

BEFORE YOU START

Are you aware of any research that has been carried out in your communities? Have you carried out any research before? Are you aware of any concerns that the people in the communities where the research was carried out have raised? Do you have any concerns regarding the way research has been carried out in Africa in general? Some of the concerns on how to carry out research have been raised in the chapters you have already read. Brainstorm the concerns and list them. After you finish reading this chapter, compare your list to the list of concerns described as ethics in this chapter.

ETHICS

How is it possible to de-colonise (social) research in/on the non-Western developing countries to ensure that the people's human condition is not constructed through Western hegemony and ideology? How is it possible to create a climate in which intellectual discursive and political practices are sensitised to the socio-environmental demands and needs of the people in creative, adaptive and productive ways? (Elabor-Idemudia, 2002: 231)

Ethical principles for adult educators are necessary to help indicate the professional responsibilities of the researcher. These responsibilities include the obligation of the researcher to empower and emancipate the research participants so that they can actively engage in the formulation of research problems, choosing research designs appropriate to their needs, and participating in the analysis, interpretation and reporting of the findings in ways that ensure that knowledge is not constructed through Western hegemony and ideology.

Flew notes that for the layperson the word ethics often suggests the following:

a set of standards by which a particular group or community decides to regulate its behaviour to distinguish what is legitimate or acceptable in pursuit of their aims from what is not. Hence we talk of business ethics or medical ethics (Flew and May, 1996: 41).

Ethics in the context of research refers to a set of standards that can guide adult education researchers on how they should interact with the researched and how research problems could be conceived and formulated. The standards include how data-gathering instruments are constructed and how data is collected, analysed and interpreted, and

how reports could be written and findings disseminated in ways that are sensitive and inclusive of the values and realities of the researched.

Consent

There is almost a consensus among researchers from all disciplines, including Science, Medicine, Social Science and Education, that research should be carried out on human beings only with their *consent*. The researched should be provided with information about the study, its purpose, how it will be carried out and its duration, risks and benefits to participants. The researched should be made aware that participation is voluntary and that they can withdraw from the study before its completion if they so wish. This universal ethical code has, however, been violated across time, space and culture. In most cases it is the marginalised and powerless whose consent the researchers ignore. We provide cases in which the consent of the researched was ignored.

Stealing

The worst violation of consent ethics in Africa was in the colonial era when Western researchers abducted human beings to serve as illustrations (just as researchers illustrate findings with graphs and tables) that supported their research agendas. An example of this practice is what has been labelled the 'El Negro of Banyoles', a name given to a stuffed human body that was displayed at the Francesco Darder Museum of Natural History in Banyoles, Spain, between 1916 and 1997. El Negro is the remains of a chief whose body was stolen from its grave by two brothers, Jules and Eduoard Verraux, on the night after it was buried (University of Botswana, 2000). They took the body to France in 1830. The body was sold to Francesco

Darder who deposited it in the museum in Banyole north of Barcelona in Spain. There 'the body represented all 'Negro' people, and became a symbol of Spanish exploitation and enslavement of black Africans' (University of Botswana, 2000). It was removed from public exhibition in 1997 after protests by Africans and people of African ancestry, and later repatriated to Africa where it was re-buried in Gaborone, capital of Botswana, on 5 October 2000. The following are excepts from reports on El Negro. Read them and discuss the questions that follow.

Two young people, Messieurs the Verreaux brothers, have recently arrived from a voyage to the ends of Africa, to the land of the Cape of Good Hope. One of these interesting naturalists is barely eighteen years old, but he has already spent twenty months in the wild country north of the land of the Hottentots, between the latitudes of Natal [Port Natal 30 degrees South] and the top of St Helena Bay [33 degrees South]. How can one possibly imagine what deprivations he had to endure? Our young compatriots had to face the dangers of living in the midst of the natives of this zone of Africa, who are ferocious as well as black, as well as the fawn-coloured wild animals among which they live, about which we do not need to tell. We want to speak only about the triumphs of their collecting, and do not know which to admire more, their intrepidity or their perseverance. Humans, quadrupeds, birds, fish, plants, minerals, shells – all of these they have studied. Their hunting has given them tigers [leopards], lions, hyenas, an admirable lubal [a scavenger], a crimson antelope of rare elegance, a host of other small members of the same [antelope] family, two giraffes, monkeys, long pitchforks [fouines?], very curious rats, ostriches, birds of prey which have never

been described before, a great quantity of other birds of all sizes, colours and species. ... But their greatest curiosity is an individual of the nation of the Betjouanas (Botswana). This man is preserved by the means by which naturalists prepare their specimens and reconstitute their form and, so to speak, their inert life. He is of small stature, black of skin, his head covered by short woolly and curly hair, armed with arrows and a lance, clothed in antelope skin, with a bag made of bush-pig skin, full of small glass-beads, seeds, and of small bones. Another thing that we are rather embarrassed to find a suitable term to characterise, is the very special accessory of modest clothing worn by the Betjouanas, which we find most striking. Messieurs Verreaux have deposited their scientific riches at the stores of Monsieur Delessert, rue Saint-Fiacre, n.3. There they are generously put on display for the public, without charge. It would be well if the Jardin des Plantes (Botanical Gardens) took this opportunity to extend its collections, already so beautiful, to become even more desirable – and to use the skills which they do not already possess of Messieurs Verreaux with the time, the talent, and the energy necessary to go out to Africa to catch nature in the act (Excerpts from the 1831 press report: Le Constitutionnel, Journal du Commerce, Politique et Litteraire (Paris, rue Montmartre) no. 319, 15 Nov. 1831).

In 1830 the Verreaux brothers, Edouard and Jules [,] preserved the body of the Bechuania [sic] man using taxidermal techniques. The body had been eviscerated, and muscles, the testicles and most of the bone structure had been removed. Later the cavities in the body were filled with material made of vegetable fibre, except for the penis, which was filled with more consistent, radio-opaque materials in order to better substitute its morphology. Finally, the body was mounted on a metal structure (Excerpts from a summary of the post-mortem report on the body of El Negro, 1993).

⊞ ACTIVITY

Discuss the following questions.

1 Should a researcher steal objects or information that they are otherwise unable to access?
2 Do you think there are still researchers who steal information, artifacts or objects of interest from the researched?
3 The people of Botswana claimed and re-buried El Negro to regain self-respect for Africans in general. What should happen to the body of knowledge in the libraries, archives and museums, written by Western researchers and their Western-trained counterparts, that continue to dehumanise Africans?

CONSENT AND THE MARGINALISED

A violation of the consent ethic is when researchers do not reveal all the information about the research to the research participants. The poor, the marginalised and the less privileged often need more time and the researcher's patience to understand the research and the implications of their participation. On numerous occasions, however, researchers take advantage of the research participants' limited knowledge of Western-informed research practices and only give research participants partial information. When information on the research participants is published that causes embarrassment to the research participants, researchers are quick to claim that it was

with the consent of the research participants. Pauline Soppo's story is an example of the research participant giving consent without full knowledge of the intent of the researcher. Rosny (cited in Nyamnjoh, 2001) wrote a research-based book in which Pauline Soppo, a customs officer, appears half naked. Rosny had obtained consent from Pauline Soppo to take photographs of her undergoing a rite during which a goat was slaughtered. Little did she know that her photographs would appear in a book. She was most embarrassed when friends, acquaintances and colleagues talked about her half-naked pictures (Nyamnjoh, 2003). Pualine Soppo's story is not an isolated case. Nyamnjoh notes:

> *Most villagers and slum dwellers in Africa are unaware of the fact that the photograph which an apparently friendly anthropologist has asked to take is going to serve as slides in public lectures, dessert at anthropological meals or the cover picture of a book in a strange, distant country, where they might never go* (Nyamnjoh, 2001: 13).

Nyamnjoh goes on to pose the following questions:

> *Were the villagers as informed about the world as their anthropological researchers, would they have allowed their photographs taken, knowing that they could serve as laughingstock in the land of the so-called civilised? Is it because one is seen to be unsophisticated and uninformed, that one should be exploited? In other words, is it because one has not seen a camera before that one should pay the expensive price of appearing naked at public lectures and dinner tables or on book covers and inside pages without informed consent?* (Nyamnjoh, 2001: 13)

The adult education researcher carries out research among adults who in most cases have low literacy rates and limited exposure to the international world. This is the population of the researched that is most vulnerable to unscrupulous researchers who ignore or misuse consent ethics. The adult education researcher has a responsibility to avoid violating these ethical concerns and to ensure that others do not violate them.

Anonymity and confidentiality

Anonymity as an ethical concern can arise when research findings expose a community, institution, individual, ethnic group or nationality to public scrutiny and embarrassment. Take, for example, the case study on women in the informal sector in Chapter 10. A description of the selected samples of businesses and their owners might reveal the identity of the owners. The researcher conceals the identity of the businesses by giving them false names. The researcher also avoids those descriptions that might reveal the identity of the businesses and their owners. This makes anonymity much harder to achieve in qualitative research. The researcher also treats information from the research participants with confidentiality. *Confidentiality* refers to the fact that even though researchers can associate information with certain research participants, they do not disclose the source of the information. In survey research anonymity is achieved by asking the research participants not to disclose their names. Confidentiality is achieved by not revealing the research participants' names when the researcher is able to associate some responses with certain research participants. Anonymity and confidentiality are exercised to avoid embarrassment, pain, loss of self esteem, psychological damage and the loss of dignity and self-respect that might occur when research participants or communities

recognise themselves or are named in embarrassing descriptions in print.

Lying, deception or covert research

There are instances when researchers misinform or lie to the research participants about important information that could affect their behaviour in the study. This often happens in experimental research design studies. In Chapter 6 you learnt that one of the threats to validity occurs when research participants are sensitised to the experiment. Some researchers withhold the information that the research participants are not receiving treatment by giving them false treatment. Where this has happened, the researcher is expected to debrief the research participants and compensate for any opportunities that they may have lost by not receiving the actual treatment in the study. There is also *covert research*, which happens mainly in qualitative research. This, according to Bulmer (cited in Nyamnjoh, 2001), occurs when researchers spend an extended period of time in a particular research setting, concealing the fact that they are researchers and pretending to play some other role. The identity of the researchers and the nature of the research are not revealed to the research participants. They are also not made aware that they are being studied. A study on land in South Africa by a professor from one of the universities illustrates covert research. A white professor at one of the universities in South Africa was commissioned by a ministry to assess how a piece of land taken from the villagers during the apartheid regime to form part of a national park could be utilised. The story is narrated in Nyamnjoh as follows:

> *As part of the project, the professor was expected to visit the concerned villagers and find out exactly what they had in*

mind about using the land once it was returned to them. However, given the anger that these villagers and their chiefs had over whites (mostly academics) for the role they played during apartheid, it was unthinkable that this white fellow would be able to carry out the research of this nature. All that the professor did was to use black undergraduate students. He selected native students from the village concerned to get involved in this research. Every day he picked these students and drove them to this area, which is about 60–80 km from the university. On his arrival to the area, he would drop them by the corner, which was just a kilometre from the villages. These students would go in and get information as if it was for meeting requirements for their own degrees. On realising that they belonged to them, the villagers were happy to cooperate with the students. The villagers never saw the professor, nor did they ever know what really was the information about. Had they known, they would have been very cautious since there was (is) already a committee, representative of all villagers, dealing with this crisis.

On completion of the research, the professor wrote a report, which he sent to the ministry, recommending that the land be turned into a 'Reserve' which would be part of the Kruger National Park. On getting the news the villagers were surprised since they never knew of such a project conducted in order to know how their land could be best utilised. All they knew of were the students who came to ask them questions. Fortunate enough, one of the villagers knew one of the students. The villager reported this to the committee. The student was traced and brought to the gathering of villagers. It was this student who revealed all of this (Khaukanani Mavhungu, personal communication. Narrated in Nyamnjoh, 2001) .

ACTIVITY

Discuss the following questions:

1 What ethical issues arise in the research study?
2 Is it ethical for researchers to undertake a study for which they do not fully understand the culture nor command a mastery of the language?

VALUE OF RESEARCH

Another ethical issue concerns the significance or value of the research study, research questions asked and modes of reporting findings in contributing to knowledge or practice. It is unethical, for instance, to ask intrusive questions that cause distress to the research participants if that information does not add value to the knowledge that will contribute to the improvement of the researched peoples' lives. It is also unethical to illustrate descriptive information with pictures or objects that cause embarrassment to communities or individual research participants if those pictures do not add any value and meaning to the data obtained. For example, what value did the picture of half-naked Pauline Soppo add to the subject matter of the book? Were the pictures worth compromising her dignity and causing her embarrassment? Of what value was the display of the El Negro in the Banyole museum? Did knowing the morphology of El Negro add enough value to risk the embarrassment and humiliation of Africans? In carrying out research, you will be faced with ethical dilemmas in which you have to choose between embarrassing individuals or communities and violating individual rights to privacy, and satisfying public curiosity or academic demands for answers to certain problems. In such situations, you will have to weigh the value of the research to the researched people against the damage that the research could cause them.

The public's right to know

Dissemination of research findings to the researched communities is an ethical issue that is often ignored by researchers. This is a violation of the public's right to know what has been written about them, and what knowledge the research advances, that can help the researched communities to improve their lives. It is a way of excluding the researched people from participating in the production and consumption of knowledge for which they are the subject of research. Noting this trend, Escobar observes:

> Most conventional approaches to development implemented by Western 'expert' researchers and their local counterparts in non-Western 'developing countries' have tended to restrict access to knowledge, especially by the poor and, at the same time, have neglected to help poor, grassroots peoples to articulate their experiences to the outside world. There is a disturbing failure to recognise that these people do theorise in their communities as part of their community life, and that they are not only articulate but also able to interpret their experiences (Escobar cited in Saunders, 2002: 227).

Chapter 14 advances strategies that researchers in collaboration with the researched can use to disseminate research findings. The strategies include community-based ways of disseminating knowledge such as songs, drama, poems and stories, as well as modern communication systems such as radio, documentaries on television, newsletters and newspapers.

Efforts to address ethical issues

Stealing, lying, and abusing and exploiting research participants in Africa continued unchallenged throughout the colonial period. In Botswana at the time, most researchers were Westerners. Western colonisers also occupied the civil service and judiciary and were therefore unlikely to challenge their Western counterparts on the ethics of their research (Mazonde, 2001). It was only after Independence that the 1967 Anthropological Act was enacted to address unethical research activities. The Act states:

> no person shall conduct anthropological research by means of the physical examination of individuals including the measurement of their physical traits, or by inducing persons to submit themselves to experiment, unless with prior permission of the Minister (Botswana Government, 1967(59): 7).

Currently some non-government organisations are working to address unethical research activities on some of the most exploited minority groups, such as the San of Southern Africa, the Masai of East Africa and the Pygmies of Central Africa. The Working Groups on Indigenous Minorities in Southern Africa (WIMSA) is an organisation that has worked on a research policy that seeks to protect the San of southern Africa from the unethical practices of some researchers. Nyamnjoh cites two policy issues from the document that adult education researchers might consider in the variety of contexts in which they carry out research:

- *The San people alone shall ultimately determine what form of research shall be performed on or about them, and under which conditions it shall be performed.*

- *The San shall only permit research that is shown to be of tangible benefit to the San people or conversely that is not detrimental to the interests of the San people in any way* (Nyamnjoh, 2001).

There is a worldwide move to empower the poor, underprivileged and powerless to make decisions on who does the research and how it is done. Servaes and Arnst (cited in Nyamnjoh, 2001) argue that the poor and the illiterate who 'have always been researched, described, and interpreted by the rich and the educated' should be actively involved in the research, and even take over the conducting of the research because 'they best know their situation and have a perspective on problems and needs that no outsider can fully share'. Participatory rural appraisal (PRA), described in Chapter 11, is an attempt to involve marginalised communities in the research process.

Refer to the sample ethical approval document at the end of this chapter.

⌗ ACTIVITY

What do you think about these efforts to address ethical issues in research?

ETHICS AND RESEARCH DESIGNS

The first dimension of ethics discussed focused on consent and confidentiality. The second dimension of ethics deals with truth standards. The basic questions are: Are the research findings true? Do they satisfy the criteria for true knowledge? Are they objective, trustworthy, acceptable, legitimate or valid? Also arising from these *validity* issues is the question: By whose standards or criteria is truth or validity judged? Criteria for claims of true knowledge are informed by the research paradigms that guide the research process.

Within the positivist/post-positivist paradigm and its quantitative research designs there are standard or set criteria against which to assess the validity of research findings. These are different from the standards set by those within the interpretive or emancipatory research paradigms. Qualitative researchers (Guba and Lincoln, 1989; Krefting, 1991) have argued that because the nature and purpose of quantitative and qualitative research traditions are different, it would be erroneous to use the same criteria to assess truth claims. It should be noted that, even though ethical issues are specific to the research design adopted in a study, the choice of study design is also an ethical issue. It would be unethical, for instance, to conduct a conventional survey on adults with low literacy rates when a participatory method could result in more meaningful findings.

Quantitative research designs and true knowledge

In quantitative research, the criteria for truth claims include judging the internal validity, external validity, reliability and objectivity of the study. Even within the quantitative research approaches, some criteria will be specific to the research design adopted in the study. In experimental research, for example, credibility of the study is ensured by controlling threats to internal and external validity. In survey research, the concern is that results of the study should be generalised to the population from which the sample was drawn. To achieve this goal the researcher must select the appropriate sampling strategies (refer to Chapter 6). The researcher has to avoid sampling error by controlling for self-selection bias, non-response bias, affinity bias, termination bias and visibility bias. Another consideration is that the data collection instruments, such as questionnaires, should measure what they purport to measure and should be answered reliably. Chapter 6 suggested ways of ensuring that the language communicates the researched people's experiences and is sensitive to their lived experiences and ways of perceiving reality. To control for error due to measurement, the following were discussed:

- Wording in the instrument
- Question structure
- Length of the instrument
- Question sequence
- Layout of the instrument.

Another important validity issue is the appropriateness of the statistical analysis in the study. Any statistical analysis adopted should meet assumptions about the study design, research questions and the levels of measurement of the variables in the study. For instance, when inferential statistics are used, the assumption is that random sampling or random assignment of treatment to subjects was employed. Any use of inferential statistics on non-random sampling will be invalid. It would also be invalid to use inferential statistics when data is measured at the nominal scale level.

Correct interpretation of results is also considered one of the most important validity issues in research (Forcheh, 2003). In quantitative research, statistical significance and non-significant results need to be interpreted with care to ensure that the meaning adds value to the study.

Qualitative research designs and true knowledge

In qualitative research truth is multiple and subject oriented. Knowledge is therefore true to the extent that it represents the multiple realities as revealed by the informants.

A qualitative study is legitimate, credible or valid when it presents such accurate descriptions that people who share those experiences would recognise, associate with, claim or own the descriptions. A different criterion is thus used for assessing truth claims. Guba and Lincoln (1986) have listed the criteria as: credibility, transferability, dependability and confirmability. Mertens (1998) lists the following strategies for enhancing credibility in qualitative research:

- Prolonged and sustained engagement
- Persistent observation
- Peer debriefing
- Negative base analysis
- Progressive subjectivity
- Member checks
- Triangulation.

Refer to Chapters 8 and 9 for a discussion of all of these terms.

Trustworthiness in qualitative research

In qualitative research the notion of reliability is problematic because human behaviour is not static. Replication of a study would not produce the same results. The question of reliabity is therefore irrelevant. What is relevant is whether results or findings of a study are consistent with the data collected (Merriam and Simpson, 1995). The concept of trustworthiness replaces reliability. Researchers strive to establish a study's credibility, transferability, dependability and confirmability (Crossley and Vulliamy, 1997).

Validity and the emancipatory research paradigm

According to Lather (1986) trustworthiness, credibility, legitimacy or validity questions should support 'research which both advances emancipatory theory building and empowers the researched'. One of the validity concepts that Lather advances to support the emancipation and empowerment of the researched is catalytic validity. Catalytic validity is the degree to which the research process re-orients, focuses, and energises participants in what Freire terms 'conscientisation', knowing reality in order to transform it (Lather, 1986: 67). Catalytic validity refers to 'the degree to which research empowers and emancipates the research partici-pants' (Scheurich, 1997: 83). Catalytic validity therefore calls for adult education researchers to deepen their understanding of the social realities they are investigating in a way that enables them to assess their attitudes, views or perspectives about the research participants. It also refers to the change in the research participants as researchers gain a deeper understanding of their life experiences and the problems investigated. Studies with strong catalytic validity are those in which the researchers and the participants can recount the changes that have occurred as a result of the research study. Sparks (2002: 116) urges adult education researchers concerned with issues of ethics, legitimacy and validity of research studies to consistently address the following questions:

- How can dominant culture individuals conduct inquiry with those who have been subjugated without further pro-ducing distorted accounts?
- What are the responsibilities that the researcher has for the participants?
- Whose knowledge counts?
- How are topics to be constructed?
- How do you frame questions so that people talk about what is important to them?

There is no one answer to the questions raised. Suggestions, for instance, on making research relevant to the participants have been made in Chapter 4. Responsibilities of the researcher have been discussed in this chapter. The questions raised bring into focus ideological bias as an ethical issue.

Ideological bias

Ideological bias in research occurs when researchers use Western-informed cat-egories of analysis, worldviews, ways of perceiving reality and values as stand-ards against which they view name, label, describe, write and make conclusions about the researched. Ideological bias is the most resilient, pervasive, traumatising and dam-aging unethical practice in research. Sparks notes that one of the limitations of some adult education research is

> *the conservative hegemony that both reproduces and obscures the outdated worldviews that researchers have regarding the material realities and social character-istics of others as deviant, noncompliant, lazy, unintelligent and other constructions that maintain the status quo* (Sparks, 2002).

SUMMARY

In Africa, biases, prejudices, distortions and misconceptions about African communi-ties and their experiences are legitimised by the accumulated body of knowledge and literature in the archives, libraries, museums, cinemas, preserved bodies such as that of El Negro, photographs, and education curricula in schools and tertiary institu-tions. Addressing ideological bias should include, as an agenda, creating space for other knowledge systems. Chilisa (2001: 14) proposes that creating space for other knowledge systems could begin by recognising local languages as important sources of meaning making. In research, definitions of terms are referenced to dictionaries and then operationalised. It is important to make reference to local meanings attached to experiences. Proverbs, folklore, songs and myths should be part of the literature

---

1. **Description**
   1.1 Justification
   1.2 Objective
   1.3 Procedure for Recruiting Participants and Obtaining Informed Consent
   1.4 Procedure in which Research Participants will be involved
   1.5 Procedure for handling information and material produced in the course of the research including raw data and final research report(s)

2 **Ethical Concerns**
   2.1   Access to participants
   2.2   Informed consent
   2.3   Anonymity and Confidentiality
   2.4   Potential Harm to Participants
   2.5   Potential Harm to Researchers
   2.6   Potential Harm to the University
   2.7   Participants' Right to Decline to take Part
   2.8   Use of Information
   2.9   Conflict of Interest/Conflict of Roles
   2.10 Other Ethical Concerns

3. **Legal Concerns**
   3.1 Legislation
        Note: Indicate where applicable the relevance of any of the following legislation:
        3.1.1 Intellectual property legislation, e.g. Copyright 1994
        3.1.2 Human Rights Act 1993
        3.1.3 Privacy Act
        3.1.4 Health and Safety in Employment Act

   3.1.5 Accident Rehabilitation Compensation Insurance Act 1991
   3.1.6 Employment Contracts Act 1991
   3.2 Other legal issues

4. **Cultural Concerns**
   Note: Where applicable indicate whether you have the necessary knowledge and experience to work in a cross-cultural situation and whether you have discussed this research with the Inter-ethnic Research Committee.

5. **Other Ethical Bodies Relevant to this Research**
   5.1 Ethics committee
        Note: list other ethics committees to which you are referring this application.
   5.2 Professional codes
        Note: list all professional codes to which this research is subject.

6. **Other Relevant Issues**
   Note: list any other issues you would like to discuss with the committee.

Source: Studman, C. 2001. 'Social ethics: Too much of a good thing.' Paper presented at the OSSREA workshop on challenges and responsibilities of doing social research in Botswana: Ethical issues. Gaborone: University of Botswana.

Figure 13.1 Ethical approval document for the University of Botswana

review, sources of problem identification and meaning making, as well as assisting in legitimising findings.

Other ways of addressing this unethical research practice are discussed throughout the book.

KEY POINTS

- The researched have the right to give consent to what is researched about them and how it is researched, and to participate in the construction of the knowledge that is produced about them.
- The public has a right to know and the researcher has an obligation to disseminate the findings in ways that the researched understand.
- The criteria for judging knowledge as legitimate, valid, credible and acceptable vary depending on the research paradigm that informs the methodology.
- Every study should be designed to produce accurate, valid, and credible research findings.
- African communities continue to suffer humiliation, disrespect and embarrassment from researchers who violate ethical principles of confidentiality and consent and, in addition, adopt an ideological bias that uses Western values and standards as criteria against which to judge Africans.

Figure 13.1 illustrates a hypothetical ethics document that covers most of the ethical principles raised (Studman, 2001).

⌘ ACTIVITY

1 Identify a research proposal in your department or institution. Using the points made in this chapter and the ethics guidelines in Figure 13.1, evaluate the proposal for appropriateness.
2 Identify professional associations that you belong to. Critically evaluate their research ethics guidelines, if any.
3 Imagine that your research association, department of adult education or association of adult educators does not have ethics guidelines. In groups, design ethical guidelines for any one of these. Your guidelines should address the following:

- Consent and confidentiality
- Value or utility of the research as an ethical issue
- Choice of research design as an ethical issue
- The public's right to know
- Ideological bias as a concern
- Validity and credibility of the research study.

FURTHER QUESTIONS

1 What do you think are the most common violations of ethics in adult education research?
2 Why do you think these types of ethics are violated? What do you think should be done to address the problem?
3 What would you do if you came across studies in adult education in which you suspect ethical standards were violated?

SUGGESTED READINGS

Sparks, B. 2002. 'Epistemological and methodological considerations of doing cross-cultural research in adult education'. *International Journal of Lifelong Education*, Vol. 21, pp. 115–129.

Chapter 14

Writing up and disseminating research

OVERVIEW

This final chapter helps you present your findings in a clear and accessible way. The first part takes you through the standard format for writing up research findings. It also discusses the issues that need to be considered if you are planning to present your findings to different types of audiences. In particular, it looks at how you incorporate African perspectives at each stage of the report. The second part discusses the relationships between adult education research, policy, practice and community action. It discusses some of the sensitivities of dissemination in African contexts where a variety of stakeholders are involved. We look at different strategies for disseminating to diverse audiences, including to those who provided your research data in the first place. You will probably find it useful to refer to Chapters 1, 3, 7, 9, 10 and 13 when working through different parts of this chapter.

LEARNING OBJECTIVES

By the end of this chapter, you should be able to:

1 Complete a research report in a style and format appropriate for its intended audience.
2 Situate an African perspective at the centre of your presentation.
3 Articulate the relationships among research, policy, practice and community action.
4 Anticipate the sensitivities of different stakeholders in funded research.
5 Produce dissemination strategies that can reach those who contributed as participants in the research.

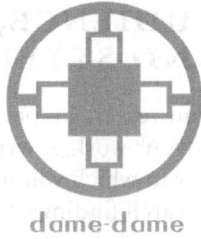

dame-dame

KEY TERMS

abstract   Summary of research.

acknowledgements   Thanks to individuals and organisations who have contributed to the study.

dedication   Written recognition of one or two people who may have nothing to do with the report but have special meaning for the report writer.

dissemination   Making research findings public.

preface   A personal statement about the research.

stakeholders   All the people who have a vested interest in your work.

table of contents   List of different sections of the report, in the order in which they appear.

BEFORE YOU START

Look for some completed research reports in the library.

1   Make a list of the headings each report uses.
2   Look for similarities across the reports regarding headings and chapter layouts.
3   Consider what kind of audience these reports have been written for. Who is most likely to read these reports?

AUDIENCE, PURPOSE AND STYLE

Your research report is an important record of your work. A written document is one way in which you inform others about your research findings. While the second part of this final chapter discusses some other dissemination strategies, both conventional and not so conventional, the first part concentrates on the writing-up process. In fact, earlier chapters in this book have already prepared you for the kind of information and viewpoints you need to consider in your final report. It is never an easy process, however. A good report requires an initial outline plan and then several rewrites. While most research reports contain similar kinds of information, the way you write depends on whom you are writing for. Indeed, it is quite possible that you will write several versions of your findings for different purposes. In addition, the different audiences who might read your report will affect your writing style.

Before you start, ask yourself who is going to read this report. If the study was commissioned or sponsored, then one audience will certainly be the funding agency. Chapter 1 discussed how donor ideologies may influence what you want to say and how. It also pointed out that research is never neutral. Apart from the influence of your own standpoint, the hypotheses or research questions may have been influenced by policy makers, practitioners, other researchers and so on. At the same time all the chapters in this book have reminded you that research with an African perspective has a responsibility to serve the needs of local communities within African value systems. Furthermore, the writing must be sensitive to colonial and post-colonial influences on adult education policy and practice. You therefore need to consider first

and foremost the original purpose of your research.

The goal of any research is to raise awareness and contribute to the knowledge base. This in turn should influence policy and practice. In the case of Afrocentric adult education studies, there is an additional responsibility. It is time for Africa to be active, rather than passive, in relation to donor aid, globalisation and lifelong learning debates. In many cases, this process includes redressing earlier misconceptions and securing sustainability for development. Moreover, as Chapter 3 has emphasised, you have a responsibility, as a researcher, to ensure that the research outcomes are acceptable to those who have been researched, while at the same time situating new knowledge within the global knowledge system.

Some readers of your report may have an academic understanding of research methods themselves, others may have only practical experience. Your potential readers, therefore, could be:

- Academics from across the world
- Colleagues from where you work
- The research participants and their communities
- The commissioners or sponsoring agency
- Policy makers
- Planners
- Practitioners or professionals in adult education.

The purpose of your report could include any or all of the following:

- To redress earlier misconceptions
- To put African perspectives into the global arena
- To give voice to the marginalised
- To improve practice
- To influence policy decisions
- To raise awareness of indigenous knowledge systems

- To serve the needs of local communities.

In all cases your writing style must be accessible, accurate, honest, concise, well organised and understandable. Use vocabulary that the intended audience will understand; explain any jargon or new terminology. Be true to yourself. Many research textbooks (Kumar, 1999) say that you should write in the third person only. Even in academia nowadays this is less frequently a requirement, particularly in adult education contexts. From an Afrocentric or feminist perspective, the opposite is positively recommended. Also, the researcher cannot be separated from the researched. The researcher should acknowledge his or her own situatedness within the research process and research experiences should be made transparent. However, the degree to which you discuss the research process depends on the amount of writing space you are allowed in the report.

ACTIVITY

1   Before you start, ask yourself:
    - Who is my intended audience?
    - What are their expectations for this report?
    - What are my goals for the report?
2   Do a rough outline of the content and themes that you propose to cover.

Ways of ensuring African representation will be discussed later. The standard structure of a formal research report, which might be presented as an academic report or to professional audiences, can be divided into preliminary material, the main body and reference materials. While different organisations may request variations on the exact format and style, the expectations are broadly similar.

PRELIMINARY MATERIAL

Preliminary material may include the following:

- Title (with author names and date of writing)
- Abstract
- Preface (optional)
- Acknowledgements (optional)
- Dedication (optional)
- List of contents
- List of tables and/or figures (if present in the text).

The *abstract* is a short summary of the whole report and is usually no more than a page. This introduces the research problem or topic, the methods used to study the problem and a statement of the results and recommendations.

The *preface* is normally found only in books or dissertations. Kane (1990: 179) describes this as 'a personal statement, telling, for example, what interests and reasons brought you to the subject, problems you had with the material, sources, techniques'.

The *acknowledgements* is usually a short paragraph thanking individuals and organisations that have, personally or professionally, enabled you to complete your study.

The *dedication* is usually short – a personal dedication of the finished product to one or two people who have special meaning to you. This may happen in dissertations or books, but rarely in commissioned reports.

The *table of contents* should enable the reader to see at a glance all the main themes and sub-topics of your study. Its goal is to take the reader through the logical steps of the research itself. You can see from the example (in the activity that follows this section) that there are six main chapters in the main body of the report. Usually the findings and discussion sections are separate chapters. In some cases there are only *five* chapters, where the findings and discussion are presented as one chapter, and interpretation and further literature review are woven into the results. The main advantage of combining these two chapters is that complex theoretical analysis can be discussed sequentially alongside presentation of data. If the data itself is complex, however, a separate chapter dedicated to findings alone may enable the reader to see key issues more clearly. In any case, each chapter has an introduction and conclusion of its own. As with the literature review described in Chapter 4, it should be possible to read the introduction and conclusion of each chapter and know what the content is about without reading the whole text. That will be your goal for the final draft. The chapter sub-headings indicate the themes present in the study and almost tell a story in themselves. The reader has already learned something about the study from the table of contents.

⊞ ACTIVITY

Study Example 14.1, a table of contents adapted from a study by Mogome (undated) on Village Development Committees (VDCs). Make sure that you note all of its parts and keep them in mind as you read the rest of this chapter.

EXAMPLE 14.1
(Mogame, undated)

Abstract
Acknowledgements
List of tables
Dedication
Abbreviations

Chapter 1: Introduction
Statement of the problem
Purpose of the study
Limitations and scope
Definition of terms
Community consultation
Significance of the study
Chapter summary

Chapter 2: Literature review
Introduction
Emergence of grass-root participation
Concept of grass-root participation in Botswana
Assumptions about grass-root participation
Chapter summary

Chapter 3: Methodology
Introduction
Study design
Population
Sample
Data collections
Data analysis
Chapter summary

Chapter 4: Findings
Introduction
Description of the study area
Study findings
Demographic data of the study participants
VDC participation at national level
Problems encountered by VDCs in their work
Extension worker views as regards VDC non-participation in DDP
How VDCs ensure development of their communities
Chapter summary

Chapter 5: Discussion of findings
Introduction
VDC participation in the DDP/VDC
Lack of participation in the implementation of DDP
Low educational standards

THE MAIN BODY

Merriam and Simpson (1995) divide the main body into the pre-results part of the report and the results part. Depending on how detailed or academic your study is, the following headings will be present, usually as chapters, in the pre-results part:

- Introduction
- Literature review
- Methodology.

Introduction (Chapter 1)

The introduction explains what your study is about. It presents the research problem; the purpose of the research; the nature and scope of the project; and the need and rationale for, or significance of, the study (Merriam and Simpson, 1995). It may also explain the theoretical perspective or experiences that prompted the study. You can see that your introduction is very similar to the research proposal itself (Chapter 5 in this book). You may even be able to use most of the material from your proposal for the introduction chapter. It is here that you will insert any definition of terms. You will include the hypotheses (if this is a quantitative study), or objectives or broad research questions (if this is a qualitative study).

Literature review (Chapter 2)

The literature review may divide into two chapters or sections, depending on the size and theoretical base of your project. Merriam and Simpson (1995), for instance, suggest that you have a second chapter or section devoted to theory (such as globalisation, lifelong learning or postcolonial theory). The first section would explain the history of the problem under consideration and provide an overall conceptual framework. That is, it situates the study within an African adult education context, such as literacy, health education, environmental awareness issues or policy debates.

Methodology (Chapter 3)

The length and detail of the methodology chapter depend on whether you are writing an academic study, journal article or report for practitioners or policy makers. An academic study will provide more of a literature review about methodological theory or issues. A report will focus on the practical details, such as the research design, sample selection, data collection and analysis procedures. Again, this is similar to your research proposal. You would update that here to describe the procedure. Here, too, you should try and situate yourself as researcher in relation to the researched.

There are many examples of how this might be done.

Dillard did a qualitative study of three American women leaders. She explicitly stated her standpoint as an African-American woman within her own 'African-centred cultural identity and community' as an explanation of how she would produce knowledge as an insider, rather than distancing herself from the research subjects. Some of the more complex words in her report are adapted for the purpose of this chapter:

This necessitates a different relationship between me, as the researcher, and the researched; between my knowing and the production of knowledge. This is also where Black feminist knowledge provides a perspective from which to construct an alternative version of this relationship. This means moving us away from detachment with participants and their contexts and using them as 'ingredients' [data that can be manipulated] in our research recipes [analysis and report]. Instead we move towards an epistemological position [knowledge base] that is more appropriate for work within such communities (Dillard, 2000: 664).

Erasmus provides another example. She discusses how different levels of power can impact on the research process in relation to her interviewing a 'coloured' woman in South Africa:

I was introduced to Mrs Benny by Colleen Crawford-Cousins, the interlocutor, who knew of my search for informants. My intention to combine journal writing and a life history interview as methods of collecting data shifted with Mrs Benny's preference for speaking to me over writing a journal. This shift was shaped by power dynamics in the research encounter.

The second interview with Mrs Benny revealed her perceptions of me as researcher. While writing in her journal, she consulted her sister about her age at the time of an incident in the family. On hearing about the research project the sister 'freaked out' (interview 2) and warned Mrs Benny to write about herself, not the family. … Mrs Benny presented me with these possibilities of abuse of power in our relationship. I reiterated the ethics of my research, asked whether she wished to proceed and whether she felt comfortable with my response.

… This account reveals the fluidity of power in the research encounter as well as the ultimate power held by the researcher in her representation of the narrator's story. It shows how power is negotiated by both parties to the research (Erasmus, 2000: 74–75).

In traditional research reports such personal details are usually omitted, in an attempt to distance the researcher from the researched. If you are trying to represent an African voice, however, it may be useful to situate yourself explicitly in relation to your research subjects. The extent to which you go into the details presented in the above two examples will depend on the nature and length of your report.

The remaining chapters relate to the results of your findings. They are usually divided into the following chapters:

- Results or findings
- Discussion or interpretation
- Summary, conclusions and recommendations.

Results or findings (Chapter 4)

The way your findings are written up depends on whether you are reporting quantitative or qualitative results. Whether you have conducted a library study, data set analysis or collected empirical data, a quantitative study will present its findings through statistics. Chapter 7 in this book has already given details of this. Suffice to say here that data can be presented in the form of tables, graphs, pictures, numbers, or even formulas. While they should be clear enough, with relevant titles that speak for themselves, you should also summarise their main message in words. Qualitative findings (see Chapter 9 in this book) will usually be presented as direct quotations from interviews, observation notes or diaries, or historical documents. The most common way of presenting qualitative data is to summarise similarities or patterns in responses, then give an example or two of direct quotes to illustrate your point. In both cases, include only selected, essential data. The important point to remember is clarity of expression. Your findings are your contribution to new knowledge. Make sure you are clear about what you are presenting and what is, or is not, interpretation.

Discussion or interpretation (Chapter 5)

In your discussion chapter (if you have kept it separate from your findings) you have the opportunity to present your own ideas about what you have seen, heard or discovered. This chapter links your data to the literature review. Kumar (1999: 248) provides a succinct summary of how you might organise your thoughts to analyse or write about a variable. Example 14.2 is adapted to an adult education context from his suggestions.

EXAMPLE 14.2
(Adapted from Kumar, 1999: 248)

The study explores whether prison education programmes are effective for rehabilitation purposes.

- Why did you think it is important to find out whether prison education programmes are effective? What effects, in your opinion, could the adequacy or otherwise of prison education programmes have on the rehabilitation chances of prisoners? This is the rationale for studying the variable.
- What have other studies in your literature review said about the adequacy of prison education programmes?
- What did you expect to find out from your study population in terms of their feelings about the adequacy of prison education programmes? If you formulated a hypothesis, you should specify that here.
- What did you find out about the adequacy of prison education programmes? What proportion of the study said it was adequate? Provide a table or graph showing the distribution of respondents by their response to the question regarding the adequacy of prison education programmes.
- What does your data show? Interpret the findings. What are the main findings? How do these findings compare with other studies you reviewed in your literature review? Does your study support or contradict them?
- What conclusions can you draw about the adequacy of prison education programmes?
- What explanation can you provide for the findings? Why do you think those who said that prison education programmes were either adequate or inadequate feel that way?

- What are the implications of what you have learned for future prison education programmes?
- Do your findings suggest the need for further research? If so, in what area and why?
- What community value systems are guiding your interaction with your treatment of the data? What worldviews inform your interpretation?
- How are you centring African perspectives?

New researchers, however, often make the mistake of inserting discussions or interpretations that go way beyond their findings. If you have not mentioned something in your findings, you cannot discuss it. The same applies to the final chapter: summary, conclusions and recommendations.

Summary, conclusions and recommendations (Chapter 6)

De Vos (1998: 125) cites Bailey and Powell (1987) as suggesting that the summary of a report serves two purposes: 'it summarises the main points and suggests the idea of finality to the reader.' Your summary should briefly walk the reader through the whole report, recapping the main message of each chapter. From these you make suggestions or recommendations for action. This could be in the form of further research, ideas for policy implementation, suggestions for improved practice, or to emphasise a crucial element of interpretation. However, Kane (1990: 187) warns us: 'Do not present conclusions which you cannot support, and do not omit conclusions which are contrary to what you had expected or desired.'

Example 14.3 contains extracts from an evaluation by Ntshangase (1997: 50–52) of the impact of an extramural penal employment scheme (EPE). This was run by the Swaziland Council for the Rehabilitation of Offenders (SACRO) in Swaziland. Notice that each new point is prefaced by a number.

EXAMPLE 14.3
(Extracts from Ntshangase, 1997: 50–52)

6.0 **Introduction**
This chapter summarises the entire study, draws conclusions based on the objectives and the data (discussion chapter), and it also makes recommendations for implementing the findings.

6.1 **Summary**
6.1.1 *The problem*
The evaluation study was prompted by the fact that since the first group of offenders was released into the Extramural Penal Employment scheme in 1991, no evaluation had been done to ascertain whether or not the scheme was achieving its objectives. A lot of resources were involved in the running of the scheme and yet no formal evaluation study was carried out to assist in decision-making and the formulation of policies by SACRO.

6.1.2 *Methodology*
A survey research method, which included self-administered questionnaire and a structured interview, was used to collect data from a sample of 87 respondents. The respondents were made of 24 current EPE clients, 31 former EPE clients, 23 EPE supervisors, 7 Probation/Welfare officers and 2 EPE officers.

6.1.3 *Evaluation results*
6.1.3.1 The rehabilitation of EPE clients
The findings show that the EPE scheme was able to rehabilitate the EPE clients by changing their behaviour patterns for the better.

6.1.3.2 The standpoint of the community members concerning the release of petty offenders into the EPE scheme

The findings indicate that the community members were positive about the release of the EPE clients into the scheme, and the relationship between the community members and the EPE clients was good. ...

6.2 Conclusions

6.2.1 *Objectives of the EPE scheme*

Based on the research results, it is concluded that all the objectives of the EPE scheme were accomplished. The EPE was able to provide: an alternative to prison for petty offenders; work experience for offenders selected for the scheme; community service by placing offenders in the community projects; supervision of petty offenders by community members and EPE officials ...

6.2.2 *The rehabilitation of EPE clients*

Based on the information gathered from the current EPE clients, former EPE clients, supervisors of EPE clients, Probation/Welfare Officers, and EPE officers, it is concluded that the EPE scheme was able to rehabilitate the petty offenders who were released from prison into the EPE scheme. This conclusion is supported by Donald Luhlanga as quoted in SACRO (1991) when he said, 'My observation has been that while we benefited from them (EPE clients)... they also got rehabilitated as normal human beings' (p. 2). ...

6.2.3 *The standpoint of community members towards the EPE clients*

Based on the data collected from the current EPE clients, former EPE clients, supervisors of EPE clients and the EPE officers, it is concluded that the community members were positive about the release of petty offenders into the EPE scheme. The community members were able to realise that sending petty offenders to prison does not reform them, but makes them to be more corrupt; hence they were positive about their release into the EPE scheme rather than staying in prison.

6.3 Recommendations

In view of the findings of the evaluation about the success of the EPE scheme, the following recommendations are made:

6.3.1 SACRO should expand the EPE scheme to become a national programme and the major 'flagship' scheme of the organisation rather than operating in only three regions of Swaziland.

6.3.2 SACRO should lobby with the Swaziland Government so that petty offenders who are serving a sentence of 12 months or less, or for non-payment of a fine of E200.00 or less, are allowed to participate in the EPE scheme rather than limiting the EPE scheme to the offenders who are serving a prison sentence of six months or less or for non-payment of a fine not exceeding E100.00.

6.3.3 SACRO should allow EPE officers to visit the EPE placements on a weekly basis rather than fortnightly in order to give rapid support to the supervisors of EPE clients.

⊞ ACTIVITY

Make your own summary of each of the parts or chapters of the main body of a research report and what it focuses on.

OTHER IMPORTANT COMPONENTS

References and appendices

References, as stated in Chapter 4 in this book, represent the whole list of resources that you have used in your study. They should be listed alphabetically according to author family name or the most common name by which the reference is known, or numerically if that is how you have cited them in the text. Kane (1990: 187–198) provides a very comprehensive list of how sources should be presented. It is also worth looking at recent books (including this one) or journal articles to see how sources are listed.

Appendices usually contain material that would otherwise interrupt the flow of your report if you placed it in the text itself. Usually the questionnaire or interview schedule is placed in the appendix. Sometimes additional statistical information or examples of raw data, such as interview transcripts (verbatim written versions of taped interviews), can be put here too. But you should keep your appendices to a minimum.

There may be a particular style or format that your university, organisation or funding agency requires you to use. So check this before finally submitting the finished document. These things all belong under the heading of editorial style.

Editorial style

Editorial style usually refers to the way footnotes are used and punctuation is styled for referencing, whether you reference your text with numbers and footnotes, the way tables and figures should be presented, and the amount of line spacing, margins and so on that are permitted. For internal reports there is usually a 'house style' that lists the requirements for such things. If you are given no guidance, the important thing is to be consistent, accurate, neat and clear with the material you are presenting and what you are trying to say.

Since this is a research report that is looking at adult education research from an African perspective, you also have to double-check your content for epistemological bias,

misrepresentation or Eurocentric interpretation.

Checking for African representation

Chapter 5 in this book provides a checklist against which you can judge a research proposal. It invites you to look for both quality of design as well as sensitivity to African representation. It is worth looking at again in relation to your report. The following questions, for instance, can be used to monitor your own work for African representation:

- Does the introduction adequately convince the reader of the global and/or local significance of the problem?
- Does the background give sufficient information on the African context of the problem?
- Does the discussion framework create space for including African voices, ways of experiencing realities and ways of knowing?
- Is the significance of the study discussed in terms of its contribution to the empowerment of the adult research participants?
- Does contribution to new knowledge include the development of indigenous knowledge systems?
- Is the place, inclusion or exclusion of African epistemologies and worldviews covered in the literature?
- Do literature sources include materials that privilege African contexts, ways of perceiving realities and ways of knowing?
- Is the design sensitive to African contexts?
- Is the sample selection appropriate for African contexts?
- Are data-gathering instruments inclusive of African community-centred techniques?

Early in this chapter it was mentioned that you may have to write more than one research report if you want to reach an audience that is not conversant with academic procedures and language. Once you have written your academic or technical report, it is not too difficult to write a shorter and more reader-friendly version that conveys the main points and shows how you arrived at your conclusions. The next section discusses the features that might influence such a report.

⊞ ACTIVITY

Read through the checklist on African representation and discuss how well this book matches the checklist. Give at least one example of how the book fulfils each item on the checklist.

GENERAL REPORTS

Language and style

The spell-checking facility on most computers will check for complexity of sentence structures. The most effective method, however, is to put your work to one side for a few days. Then read it afresh, from the perspective of someone who has had basic schooling. Alternatively, ask someone else to read your work and identify all the sentences or words they find difficult to understand. A rule of thumb is to keep most of your sentences fairly short. See if there are sentences that could be split into two sentences. Check for jargon words. Talk to your friends about what you have said in your study. Explain in conversational terms what each section is about. Then use those words as the framework for writing your 'general report'.

Presentation

It is much easier to read text that is written in large font, and is broken up by line spaces or sub-headings that are written in bold and a different font size. Keep statistics very simple; use graphs or bar charts to portray the statistical information where possible. Create a one-page summary sheet that identifies all the key points in the report.

Length

Most reports can be cut down. Look for sentences or paragraphs that are just 'padding' and delete them. Ask someone else to identify sections that do not seem necessary. It is always easier to critique someone else's work rather than your own. Look at your outline and calculate how much space to allocate to each chapter or theme.

The first part of this chapter has taken you through the stages of completing your final report. Throughout this process the emphasis has been on privileging African perspectives that are relevant to adult education contexts. Report writing entails considering its purpose, the intended audience and appropriate style. Writing should be clear, concise and well organised. You may choose to write in the first or third person, though it is now common practice for the researcher to situate him- or herself within the text itself. Normally there are five or six main chapters to the report, which takes you through each stage of your research, from problem formulation to conclusions and recommendations. Your list of contents provides the framework for drafting content, sub-headings and themes. Your findings need to be compared with the literature review and analysed with sensitivity to the worldviews that are informing your interpretation. We have also offered suggestions on how you can tailor your report to suit an ordinary person. Report writing is only one way to disseminate your findings, however. The second part of this chapter discusses how you can tailor your study to suit a variety of audiences and needs.

⊞ ACTIVITY

1 Read an undergraduate research report.
   ■ Identify the main points and decide what is just 'padding'.
   ■ Now adapt this report for a person who has completed only basic education.

2 Prepare an outline for your own research report.
   ■ Decide for whom the report is intended (your main audience).
   ■ Give it a title and write some draft content for each section using the table of contents in Example 14.1 as your guide.
   ■ Use the examples in Chapters 6 or 8 to focus your results chapter.
   ■ Use the interpretation questions in Example 14.2 as a guide for your analysis.
   ■ Use the questions on p. 250 to help you check for African representation.
   ■ Provide a summary of the main points or recommendations you wish to make about your findings.

DISSEMINATION IN AFRICA

There are a number of reasons that explain why adult educators disseminate their research results beyond simply completing a research report. As Chapter 1 stated, adult education research has a responsibility to raise awareness of how Africa can be an equal player in international lifelong learning debates. On a local or national level, there is a need to provide policy makers, planners, practitioners and communities with baseline data, to redress misrepresentations, to encourage sustainable development, and to empower the disadvantaged. Chapter 13 highlights the need to respect communities as producers of knowledge. This means acknowledging them and the source of their wisdom in your dissemination strategies. Adult education research therefore has to serve more than academics. It must do more than produce a well-written report. Adult education research has to produce new knowledge and be useful to policy makers, practitioners and communities. Any dissemination strategy has to be meaningful to a variety of stakeholders. It must be seen to be relevant to local circumstances and demonstrate that new ideas are implementable and achievable. For the research to have any lasting value it must make effective links with policy, practice and community action.

⊞ ACTIVITY

1 Imagine that you have completed a research report. Make a list of all the people who would have been associated with your research, at whatever level.
2 Brainstorm some ideas about how you could produce information about your research results in a way that would be meaningful to the people on your list.

POLICY, PRACTICE AND COMMUNITY

The relationship between research, policy, practice and community action is an uneasy one. Chapter 1 has already emphasised some of the tensions between policy makers, practitioners and researchers. Chapter 11 shows the complexities of involving communities. All have their own competing agendas and spheres of influence. Practitioners and communities often feel their grass-root circumstances are not heeded; policy makers want simple, unambiguous answers, and researchers deal with ambiguities and uncertainties. Burchfield (1994) and Prophet and Nyati-Ramahobo (1994) discuss the ways in which research might influence policy. They suggest that while the 'linear model' of research leading directly to practical action is desired, the complexities of adult education prevent this from happening very often. Similarly, the 'problem-solving' model, which assumes research will solve a specific problem, sits uneasily in the adult education world, which is multifaceted and influenced by a multiplicity of stakeholders and other factors. So the most likely model for adult education is the 'percolation model', whereby research has a cumulative, trickle-down influence on policy. Since policy makers take into account a number of external factors, such as public opinion, availability of resources, political expediency and organisational capacity of relevant institutions, it makes sense to disseminate your research as widely as possible so that you can engage with all those agendas.

There are five main constituencies of stakeholders to whom you should target your research results, beyond just presenting your research report. Each of them requires a different approach. They are policy makers, funders, practitioners, community members (the researched) and other researchers.

Policy makers

Policy makers influence adult education planners and practitioners. Crossley and Holmes (2001) state that research findings

need to connect with powerful decision makers. This means identifying key individuals within government and people who have the ear of government. Crossley and Holmes also suggest that research which is cumulative and channelled is more likely to impact on policy and practice than ad hoc, disparately produced findings. Moreover, both Crossley and Holmes (2001) and Edwards (2000) propose that research is most likely to be noticed by policy makers if it can be seen to be helpful to existing policy. In other words, research findings that challenge the status quo and promote radical change that is not currently being considered are unlikely to be heard. Dissemination messages therefore need to be well planned and preferably draw on existing policy statements. Ways of doing this may be through well-written reports, but it is likely that personal invitations and face-to-face discussions with influential people will be more effective. Policy makers, however, are often influenced by funding agencies.

Funders

Funders include government agencies, charities and donor agencies. You have already read in Chapter 1 that funding agendas have a direct impact on policy and practice in the recipient countries. While this is true, there is evidence that some funders are responding to the notion that developing countries react more favourably to development policies that recognise the value of indigenous knowledge. Some donors and government funders have consequently advocated more collaborative and interdisciplinary initiatives. There are indications that funders are beginning to view such collaborations more equally:

The Netherlands Development Assistance Research Council (RAWOO), for example, supports 'genuine research partnerships aimed at mutual benefit'. It states that 'one of the starting points ... is that research needs and priorities are assessed and articulated by researchers, policy makers and end users in developing countries' (Crossley and Holmes, 2001: 400).

Since adult education is already a multi-disciplinary activity, this trend provides opportunities to exploit many of the arguments in this book. Moreover, as funders and policy makers talk to each other, it is useful to disseminate your findings to representatives from both sectors at the same time.

The partnership terminology in the above quotation provides opportunities for promoting the ethos of participatory research. Participatory research, in turn, is better able to address questions of relevance and utilisation of indigenous knowledge. Participatory research creates opportunities for involving practitioners and community members at all levels of the research process. Using a participatory dissemination strategy has particular benefits for those people who were not involved in the research process itself.

Practitioners

Practitioners have traditionally felt under-valued in the research process, with consequences for the way they respond to research outcomes. Dissemination strategies that use practitioners to engage in dialogue with other practitioners have proved effective. Ginsburg and Adams discuss decision-making, practice and institutional arrangements for a comparative educational research project in Ghana, Guatemala and Mali. Their dissemination strategy was to engage in dialogue at all stages of the research interventions with

teachers, head teachers, district-level supervisors, parents, ministry of education and other government officials, as well as representatives from bilateral and multilateral donor agencies ... During the documentation research effort, the authors developed the notion of Policy-Practice-Research-Dialogue cycles (Ginsburg and Adams, 2000: 28).

Included in these dialogue cycles were training and discussion workshops with opportunity for all stakeholders to respond to ongoing research findings and provide input into later phases. This increased the sense of ownership felt by all parties in the research itself as stakeholders were able to advise on the practical implications of the research findings. It also enabled the researchers to understand institutional and political constraints as the research progressed.

Even in participatory research, however, researchers will inevitably have an unequal power relationship with those they are researching. Dialogue dissemination methods that are targeted at adult education stakeholders are likely to use a language and an approach that ignores traditional communication methods for those at grass roots (local communities).

The researched (community members)

Disseminating research findings to the community is also an ethical concern. Chapter 13 highlights the issue of representing information accurately. It asks you to ensure that dissemination is done in a way that the researched community understands what is being said about issues that directly affect their lives.

The Trust for Community Outreach and Education (TCOE) manual (2001: 185–202) revealed that the most effective way of disseminating to community groups is through the community members' own involvement in the research analysis process. Look at this South African case study extracted from their training manual. The research facilitator, Nondwe, is facilitating an awareness-raising analysis with the research participants about research into poor sanitation in Umzekelo. The discussion leads to local decisions about how to inform the wider community of their findings.

EXAMPLE 14.4 (Reproduced with kind permission from the TOC manual, p. 185)

After a while clear patterns began to emerge, confirming their original hypothesis that poor sanitation in Umzekelo was the cause of the gastroenteritis, typhoid and hepatitis. The analysis of the water from the Klein River revealed that there was a high level of pollution by raw sewage. Maxi then stood up and said: 'When we checked the records of a survey done by the Working for Water Project we found that the levels of pollution had increased steadily over the past ten years'. Eunice then stood up and said that this confirmed what they had found in the records at the clinic. ... After a short while, Nondwe put up a big drawing of a tree on the wall. She asked people to describe the parts of the tree, and said the tree was like the society in which they lived.

The roots, she said, represented the economic aspect, the trunk is the political aspect, and the leaves represent our beliefs and values. Then she asked, pointing at the roots of the tree: 'Why is there a higher rate of gastroenteritis among children living on the south side of Umzekelo along the banks of the river?' 'Because they play in the river most often,' said someone. 'Yes, but who lives there? Do any of the rich export

farmers live there?' asked Nondwe. 'No, the poorest of the poor live in that area. Many of them are farm workers who were chased off the farms about six years ago,' said Johan. Then Eunice got up again and said: 'That's another thing our investigation revealed. Gastroenteritis is more prevalent in the areas of greatest poverty in Umzekelo.' ...

Slowly this process of critical analysis began to show a different level of understanding of the problem situation among those present. With Nondwe's careful facilitation people first began to use their growing understanding of local conditions ... to see new possibilities for the way they thought about themselves and their collective 'fate'. Then they felt further empowered with the knowledge that came with seeing the relationship between their local conditions and the broader social issues of wealth and poverty, power and disempowerment. What began to emerge out of this was a realisation that participants need to take ownership of their 'fate'...

Mrs Magodla said: 'Looking at the summaries and listening to the discussion and analysis I have become increasingly aware that there are several groups who are relevant to our problem ... I think we will need to encourage further dialogue with these groups.' ...

All that was left to do now was to plan how, and to whom, they would communicate their research findings. Several women who had joined the research team for the day stood up and said they would like to present a play based on what they had learnt at the workshop. They would like to perform it at Mrs Magodla's house and at the 'open-air hall'. Eunice said that she would like to borrow her church minister's camera and document the health and sanitation problems. Then Nondwe thanked those who had come forward to help take their analysis of the problem situation back to the community for feedback. This was a vital step in building community participation for future action. ...

Together they planned to present their research findings through the use of popular theatre using Xhosa, Afrikaans and English. The plot line had already been worked out by the group of participants who had started to attend their meetings at Mrs Magodla's house. Eunice would exhibit the photographs she had taken and carefully labelled. Mrs Magodla and Johan would make a short presentation. ... They also agreed that the exhibition, drama performance and short presentation could be taken to the schools and church meetings. Representatives from local and community newspapers and radio would also be invited.

The community dissemination strategy in this case study was to use popular theatre and the media to get the research participants' message across. Other forms of dissemination could have included songs, poetry or even new proverbs. The essential feature of this type of dissemination, however, is the level of community involvement and the fact that ultimately the dissemination ideas came from people within the community. The main researcher here proved to be a facilitator, rather than a leader. So she avoided as far as possible the conventional power relationship between researcher and researched. The whole research process in this example becomes a holistic one, which follows the ethics and ethos of respecting indigenous knowledge systems and community values within a rigorous research framework.

As professionals, however, you also have to consider dissemination to other researchers. In the context of this book, this means that you are not only disseminating your research findings, you are also disseminating the research processes and value systems that recognise and give space to African voices.

Other researchers

Aside from your research report the most common methods of informing fellow researchers about your work are through conference presentations and journal articles.

Conferences are advertised throughout the year. Some are international and advertised through adult education Internet networks, such as AEDNET. Others are more local and you may hear about them through colleagues, lecturers or leaflets. There are adult education-specific conferences that are organised through adult education associations and topic-specific conferences that have themes relevant to your research focus, or you might even decide to organise your own conference in order to establish a research forum that particularly suits your area of interest. In most cases, you will be invited to submit a conference abstract by a certain deadline. Abstracts are similar in content to the one written for your completed report, though you may have to adapt the focus of your presentation to the conference theme. If the abstract is accepted you may be asked to submit a full paper for advance distribution at the conference or to produce a final draft for the conference presentation itself. At the conference you can choose to run a short workshop or do a brief presentation. In either case there will be space for discussion and feedback on your analysis. Conferences are very useful forums for developing your professional knowledge and personal profile. You may find it useful to attend one or two conferences before attempting to submit a journal article.

Your university or college library may not be well stocked with international adult education journals. But it will probably have one or two locally produced journals which are relevant to adult education. It is advisable to do some library searching to see what is available. Journals may be academic, refereed journals that require anything between 3 500 to 8 000 words, or professional journals that require up to 2 000 words of text. In either case it is useful to select the journal before you start writing. Journals all have their own particular focus. You may choose a journal that specifically caters for adult education or you may decide that your theoretical focus is more suited to a sociological or management journal. The best way to find out where to submit your article is to read different journals. There is usually information about the required style, format and procedures for submission on the inside cover of the journal.

Once you have decided which one you prefer, a good tip is to read some of the articles already printed. This will give you a feel for the kind of material that is accepted. If possible, you should even try to quote or refer to articles from that particular journal in your own submission. Journals always receive far more articles than they can print, so your submission is always competing for space. The editor of a refereed journal will send your article out to two or more academics who have some expertise in your field of work. The referees then make comments on the academic quality and style of your submission. They will recommend whether it should be published with minor amendments or substantial revisions. Occasionally they may accept the article as it stands; often they will recommend that the journal reject your submission. Even if you get a rejection, however, you usually receive the referee comments. The comments may be sufficient to help you improve the article to resubmit to an alternative journal. A good resource for helping you prepare academic articles is Day (1996).

▓ ACTIVITY

Conduct a thirty-minute exercise in class.

1 **Divide the class into groups. Each group should identify themselves as either policy makers, funders, researchers, practitioners or community members.**
2 **Your task is to implement a new income-generation project with local farmers.**
3 **Each group should justify, in their group role, who they would communicate with and what action they would take in order to ensure successful implementation of the scheme.**
4 **At the end of the exercise, discuss how and when each group communicated with each other. What were the outcomes of such communication?**

SUMMARY

This chapter has taken you through the process of completing your final report and a variety of dissemination strategies. Report writing needs to take account of audience, format and style. Dissemination also has to recognise the uneasy relationship between research, policy, practice and community action. The most effective way to influence policy and practice is to disseminate findings widely through a variety of forums, since adult education is affected by a multiplicity of stakeholders. A partnership approach to both research and dissemination is advocated, with opportunity for dialogue between different stakeholders. In particular, the researched community needs to feel ownership over their own contribution to both knowledge and analysis of problems. Methods such as drama, presentations, radio and stories are suitable for engaging with communities. Conference papers and journal articles will reach academic audiences. Conferences provide valuable feedback and may help you formulate your journal article.

KEY POINTS

- Writing a final report requires careful planning and redrafting with attention to language and style that are suited to the target audience.
- The formal research report follows a standard five- or six-chapter format, though data interpretation and presentation vary depending on whether the data is qualitative or quantitative.
- Dialogue and partnership are key strategies for dissemination to multiple stakeholders.
- Including policy makers in your stakeholder clientele ensures that, through dialogue, a shared awareness and ownership of recommendations can be achieved.
- Including funding agencies within the dialogue process may help to raise awareness of the need to recognise indigenous knowledge.

⊞ ACTIVITY

1 Brainstorm some adult education research topics.

- Work in groups and select a topic.
- As a group, present a list of the funders, policy makers and practitioners who would be interested in your research topic.
- What aspect of the topic would they be interested in? Why?
- What concerns might they have about the dissemination of the research results?

2 Using ideas from your brainstorm for the above activity, plan a two-day dissemination workshop for a village community. Provide a detailed plan of what you intend to do, as well as when and how you will do it. Decide on:

- The dissemination topic focus
- Who to invite
- The content and timetable of activities
- Who will lead those activities
- What you want the outcome of the workshop to be.

3 Use the following layout below as a guide.

Dissemination topic: _____

Key messages to convey	Who would be interested	Who takes responsibility	Dissemination method	Activity	Timetable

FURTHER QUESTIONS

1 Not everyone agrees that the researcher should write in the first person. What arguments can you give for and against this idea?

2 If your findings demonstrate that agricultural training is failing because it does not address indigenous knowledge systems, how can you present your argument in order to stimulate change?

3 Suppose you are unable to find local or Afrocentric literature to support or compare with your findings. What can you do?

4 Is it possible that an Afrocentric study is going to offend key stakeholders or donors? How can you anticipate this in your report?

5 What happens when your sponsors do not agree with your findings? How will you deal with this?

6 What happens when policy makers fail to attend dissemination or dialogue meetings? How will you deal with this?

7 What happens when practitioners reject your research findings that suggest they must change their practices? How will you deal with this?

8 What happens when local community members disagree with your analysis? How will you deal with this?

SUGGESTED READINGS

American Psychological Association. 2001. *Publication manual of the American Psychological Association*, 5th edn. Washington, DC: American Psychological Association.

Creswell, J. W. 1994. *Research design: Qualitative and quantitative approaches.* London: Sage Publications.

Day, A. 1996. *How to get research published in journals.* Aldershot: Gower.

De Vos, A. S. (ed.) 1998. *Research at grass roots: A primer for the caring professions.* Pretoria: J. L. van Schaik.

Kane, E. 1990. *Doing your own research.* London: Marion Boyars.

Kumar, R. 1999. *Research methodology: A step-by-step guide for beginners.* London: Sage Publications.

References

Amadiume, I. 1987. *Male daughters, female husbands: Gender and sex in an African society.* London: Zed Books.

American Psychological Association. 2001. *Publication manual of the American Psychological Association,* 5th edn. Washington, DC: American Psychological Association.

Amutabi, M. N., Nafukho, F. M. and Otunga, R. N. 2005. *Foundations of adult education in Africa.* Cape Town: Pearson Education and UNESCO Institute for Education.

Ashcroft, B., Griffiths, G. and Tiffin, H. 1989. *The empire writes back: Theory and practice in post-colonial literatures.* London: Routledge.

Ashcroft, B., Griffiths, G. and Tiffin, H. 2000. *Postcolonial studies: The key concepts.* London: Routledge.

Assie-Lumumba, N. T. 2000. 'Educational and economic reforms, gender equity, and access to schooling in Africa'. *International Journal of Comparative Sociology,* Vol. 41, pp. 89–121.

Avoseh, M. B. M. 2001. 'Learning to be active citizens: Lessons of traditional Africa for lifelong learning'. *International Journal of Lifelong Education,* Vol. 20, pp. 479–486.

Baylies, C. and Bujra, J. (eds.). 2000. *AIDS, sexuality and gender in Africa.* London: Routledge.

Bryman, A. 1988. *Quantity and quality in social research.* London: Unwin Hyman.

Burchfield, S. (ed.). 1994. *Research for educational policy and planning in Botswana.* Gaborone: Macmillan Botswana.

Burckhardt, G. 2000. 'A new approach: participatory rural appraisal'. *Adult Education and Development,* Vol. 54, pp. 310–311.

Central Statistics Office. 1993. *Report of the first national survey on literacy in Botswana.* Gaborone: Government Printer.

Central Statistics Office. 1997. 'Positivist/postpositivist study'. In *Literacy Survey Report.* Gaborone: Government Printer.

Chambers, R. 1997. *Whose reality counts? Putting the first last.* London: International Technological Publications.

Chilisa, B. 2002. 'National policies on pregnancy in the education system in sub-Saharan Africa: A case of Botswana'. *Gender and Education Journal,* Vol. 14, pp. 21–35.

Chilisa, B. 2001. 'Decolonising ethics in social research: Towards a framework for research ethics'. In *Challenges and Responsibilities of Doing Social Research in Botswana, Ethical Issues,* ed. A. Rwomire. Nairobi: OSSREA.

Chilisa, B. with Bennel, P. and Hyde, K. 2001. *The impact of HIV/AIDS on the University of Botswana: Developing a comprehensive strategic response, knowledge and research.* London: DFID.

Chilisa, B., Dube-Shomanah, N., Tsheko, N. and Mazile, B. 2004. *Breaking the silence with subject-centered research methods: Gender, sexuality, HIV/AIDS and life skills education in community junior secondary schools in Botswana.* Nairobi: UNICEF.

dwennimmen

Chilisa, B., Tabulawa, R. and Maundeni, T. 2002. *Gendered school experiences: Impact on retention and achievement.* London: DFID.

Commeyras, M. and Montsi, M. 2000. 'What if I woke up as the other sex? Botswana youth perspectives on gender'. *Gender and Education,* Vol. 12, pp. 327–346.

Courlander, H. (ed.). 1996. *A treasury of African folklore.* New York: Marlow and Company.

Coy, P. 2002. 'Poverty: The news brightens'. In *Business Week,* June 17, p. 22.

Creswell, J. W. 1994. *Research design: Qualitative and quantitative approaches.* London: Sage Publications.

Crossley, M. and Holmes, K. 2001. 'Challenges for educational research: International development, partnerships and capacity building in small states'. *Oxford Review of Education,* Vol. 27, pp. 395–409.

De Vault, M. L. 1999. *Liberating method: Feminism and social research.* Philadelphia: Temple University Press.

De Vos, A. S. (ed.) 1998. *Research at grass roots: A primer for the caring professions.* Pretoria: J. L. van Schaik.

Denzin, N. K. and Lincon, Y. S. 1998. *Collecting and interpreting qualitative materials.* London: Sage Publications.

Dillard, C. B. 2000. 'The substance of things hoped for, the evidence of things not seen: Examining an endarkened feminist epistemology in educational research and leadership'. *International Journal of Qualitative Studies in Education,* Vol. 13, pp. 661–682.

Dube, M. W. 1999. 'Searching for the lost needle: Double colonization and postcolonial African feminisms'. *Studies in World Christianity,* Vol. 5, pp. 213–229.

Edwards, T. 2000. 'All the evidence shows …: Reasonable expectations of educational research'. *Oxford Review of Education,* Vol. 26, pp. 299–312.

Egbo, M. 2000. *Gender, literacy and life chances in sub-Saharan Africa.* Clevedon: Multilingual Matters.

Egerton University. 2000. *Egerton PRA field handbook for participatory rural appraisal practitioners.* 3rd edn. Njoro, Kenya: Egerton University.

Eicherberger, R. T. 1989. *Disciplined inquiry: Understanding and doing educational research.* New York: Longman.

Elabor-Idemudia, P. 2002. 'Participatory research: A tool in the production of knowledge in development discourse'. In *Feminist post-development thought: Rethinking modernity, post-colonialism and representation,* ed. K. Saunders, pp. 227–242. London: Zed books.

Emagalit, Z. 'Contemporary African philosophy', 2001, viewed 26 June 2001. http://homepages.acc. msmc.edu/fuculty/lindeman/af.htm1

Erasmus, Z. 2000. 'Recognition through pleasure, recognition through violence: Gendered subjectivities in South Africa'. *Current Sociology*, Vol. 48, pp. 71–86.

Escobar, A. 1995. *Encountering development.* Princeton: Princeton University Press.

Faure, E. 1972. *Learning to be: The world of education today and tomorrow.* Paris: UNESCO.

Field, S. 2001. 'Oral histories: The art of the possible'. In *African oral literature: Functions in contemporary contexts*, ed. R. H. Kaschula, pp. 249–256. Claremont, South Africa: New Africa Books.

Forcheh, N. 2001. 'Statistical components of social research ethics'. In *Challenges and responsibilities of doing social research in Botswana: Ethical issues*, ed. A. Rwomire. Nairobi: OSSREA.

Freire, P. 1972. *Pedagogy of the oppressed.* London: Penguin.

Gboku, M. and Lekoko, R. N. 2006. *Developing programmes for adult learners in Africa.* Cape Town: Pearson Education and UNESCO Institute for Education.

Ginsberg, M. and Adams, D. 2000. 'The politics of linking educational research, policy, and practice: The case of improving educational quality in Ghana, Guatemala and Mali'. *International Journal of Comparative Sociology*, Vol. 41, pp. 27–48.

Goduka, I. N. 2000. 'African/indigenous philosophies: Legitimising spiritually centred wisdoms within the academy'. In *African voices in education*, eds. P. Higgs, N. C. G. Vakalisa, T. V. Mda and N. T. Assie, pp. 63–83. Lansdowne, South Africa: Juta.

Grant, S. and Grant, E. 1995. *Decorated homes in Botswana.* Gaborone: Bay Publishing, Phuthadikobo Museum.

Green, L. W., George, M. A., Daniel, M., Frankish, C. J., Herbert, C. P., Bowie, W. R. and O'Neill, M. 1995. 'Background on participatory research'. In *Study of participatory research in health promotion: Review and recommendations for the development of participatory research in health promotion in Canada*, pp. 53–66. Ontario: Royal Society of Canada.

Griffiths, M. 1998. *Educational research for social justice.* Buckingham: Open University Press.

Hayes, E. and Flannery, D. D. (eds.). 2000. *Women as learners: The significance of gender in adult learning.* San Francisco: Jossey Bass.

Holloway, I. and Wheeler, S. 1991. *Qualitative research for nurses.* Oxford: Blackwell Science.

Hooks, B. 1991. *Yearning: Race, gender, and cultural politics.* London: Turnaround.

Hopfer, C. 1997. 'Empowering adult education in Namibia and South Africa during and after apartheid'. *International Review of Education*, Vol. 43, pp. 43–59.

Hoskyns, C. 1999. 'Gender and transnational democracy: The case of the European Union'. In *Gender politics in global governance*, eds. M. K. Meyer and E. Pruegl, pp. 72–87. Oxford: Rowman and Littlefield.

Johnson-Odim, C. 1991. 'Common themes, different contexts: Third World women and feminism'. In *Third World women and the politics of feminism*, eds. C. T. Mohanty, A. Russo and L. Torres, pp. 314–327. Bloomington and Indianapolis: Indiana University Press.

Kachur, S. P., Phillips-Howard, P. A., Odhacha, A. M., Ruebush, T. K., Oloo, A. J. and Nahlen, B. L. 1999. 'Maintenance and sustained use of insecticide-treated bednets and curtains three years after a controlled trial in Western Kenya'. *Tropical Medicine and International Health*, Vol. 4, pp. 728–735.

Kane, E. 1990. *Doing your own research.* London: Marion Boyars.

Kanyoro, M. 1999. 'Reading the Bible from an African perspective'. *Ecumenical Review*, Vol. 51, pp. 18–24.

Kaphagawani, D. N. 2000. 'What is African philosophy?'. In *Philosophy from Africa*, eds. P. H. Coetzee and A. P. J. Roux, pp. 86–98, Cape Town: Oxford University Press.

Kashula, R. H. (ed.). 2001. *African oral literature.* Claremont: New Africa Books.

Kaye, S. 2002. *Women in the urban informal sector: Effective financial training in Botswana.* Unpublished Ph.D. dissertation, University of Witwatersrand.

Krefting, L. 1991. 'Rigor in qualitative research: The assessment of trustworthiness'. *American Journal of Occupational Therapy*, Vol. 45, pp. 214–222.

Kumar, R. 1999. *Research methodology: A step-by-step guide for beginners.* London: Sage Publications.

Leach, F. 2000. 'Gender implications of development agency policies on education and training'. *International Journal of Educational Development*, Vol. 20, pp. 333–347.

Letshabo, K. 2002. *Breakthrough to Literacy, Volume 1 evaluation report.* Nairobi: UNICEF.

Lincoln, Y. S. and Guba, E. A. 1985. *Naturalistic inquiry.* Beverly Hills: Sage Publications.

Louw, D. J. 'Ubuntu: An African assessment of the religious order', 2001, retrieved 27 September 2001. http://www.bu.edu/wcp/papers/Afrlouw. htm

Mabongo, N. 2002. *Training needs of community home based caregivers for terminally ill people with HIV/AIDS related conditions in Old Naledi.* Unpublished research project submitted in partial fulfilment of the requirement of Master's degree in Adult Education. Gaborone: University of Botswana.

Mac an Ghaill, M. 1994. *The making of men: Masculinities, sexualities and schooling.* Buckingham: Open University Press.

Makgoba M. W., Shope, T. and Mazwai, T. 1999. 'Introduction'. In *African renaissance: The new struggle,* ed. M. Makgoba, pp. i–xii. Cape Town: Mafube Publishing and Tafelberg Publishers.

Mamdani M. 1999. 'There can be no African rennaissance without an Africa-focused intelligentsia'. In *African renaissance: The new struggle,* ed. M. Makgoba, pp. 125–134. Cape Town: Mafube Publishing and Tafelberg Publishers.

Mannathoko, C. 1994. 'The contribution of educational research networks to research capacity building: The case of BERA and ERNESA'. In *Research for educational policy and planning in Botswana,* ed. S. Burchfield, pp. 253–277. Gaborone: Macmillan Botswana.

May, T. 1996. *Social research: Issues, methods and process.* Philadelphia: Open University Press.

Mazonde, I. 2001. 'Ethical problems faced by researchers in Botswana'. In *Challenges and responsibilities of doing social research in Botswana: Ethical issues,* ed. A. Rwomire. Nairobi: OSSREA.

McEwan, C. 2001. 'Postcolonialism, feminism and development: Intersections and dilemmas'. *Progress in Development Studies,* Vol. 1, pp. 93–111.

Mekgwe, P. 2003. *Theorizing African feminism(s): The 'colonial' question.* Paper presented at the Department of English Seminar Series, University of Botswana.

Meloy, J. M. 2002. *Writing a qualitative dissertation: Understanding by doing.* New Jersey: Lawrence Erlbaum Associates.

Merriam, S. B. and Simpson, E. L. 1995. *A guide to research for educators and trainers of adults.* Malabar: Kreiger.

Mertens, D. B. 1998. *Research methods in education and psychology: Integrating diversity with quantitative and qualitative approaches.* Thousand Oaks: Sage Publications.

Miles, M. and Huberman, A. 1984. *Qualitative data analysis: A sourcebook of new methods.* Thousand Oaks: Sage Publications.

Ministry of Finance and Development Planning (MFDP). 1997. *Community based strategy for rural development.* Gaborone: Government Printer.

Mogome, G. (undated). *A study to understand the extent to which village development committees participate in the planning and implementation of the district plan in Botswana: Case of Molepolole VDCs.* Unpublished M.Ed. research essay. Gaborone: University of Botswana.

Mohanty, C. T. 1991. 'Cartographies of struggle: Third World women and the politics of feminism'. In *Third World women and the politics of feminism,* eds. C. T. Mohanty, A. Russo and L. Torres, pp. 1–50. Bloomington and Indianapolis: Indiana University Press.

Mohanty, C. T. 1991. 'Under Western eyes: Feminist scholarship and colonial discourses'. In *Third World women and the politics of feminism,* eds. C. T. Mohanty, A. Russo and L. Torres, pp. 51–80. Bloomington and Indianapolis: Indiana University Press.

Monageng, M. 1999. *Determining the nutrient content of morogo wa dinawa (vigna unguiculata).* Special research project submitted in partial fulfillment of the Bachelor's degree in Home Economics. Gaborone: University of Botswana.

Mohanty, C. T., Russo, A. and Torres, L. (eds.). 1991. *Third World women and the politics of feminism.* Bloomington and Indianapolis: Indiana University Press.

Mulenga, D. 1999. 'Reflections on the practice of participatory research in Africa'. *Convergence*, Vol. 32, pp. 33–46.

Neuman, W. L. 1997. *Social research methods*. Bacon: Allyn and Bacon.

Noel, K. L. and Ramatsui, P. T. 1994. 'Linkages between research, curriculum development and policy: Lessons from the Eighties, suggestions for the Nineties'. In *Research for Educational Policy and Planning in Botswana*, ed. S. Burchfield, pp. 199–144. Gaborone: Macmillan-Botswana.

Ntseane, P. G. 1999. *Botswana rural women's transition to urban business success*. Unpublished Ph.D. dissertation, University of Georgia.

Ntseane, P. G. and Youngman, F. 2002. 'Leadership in civil society organisations in Botswana'. In *Leadership, civil society and democratisation in Africa: Case studies from southern Africa*, eds. A. Bujra and S. Buthelezi, pp. 121–163. Addis Ababa: Development Policy Management Forum, ECA.

Ntshangase, I. M. 1997. *An evaluation of the impact of the extra mural penal employment scheme (1991–1996): The case of Lubombo, Manzini and Shiselweni Regions of Swaziland*. Unpublished B.Ed. dissertation. Gabarone: University of Botswana.

Nyamnjoh, F. B. 2001. 'Ethical challenges and responsibilities in social research: An overview'. In *Challenges and responsibilities of doing social research in Botswana: Ethical issues*, ed. A. Rwomire. Nairobi: OSSREA.

Nyamnjoh, F. B. 2002. *Epistemological considerations for endogenization of education in Africa*. Unpublished seminar paper, Department of Sociology, University of Botswana.

Odora Hoppers, C. A. 2002. ed. *Indigenous knowledge and the integration of knowledge systems*. Claremont: New Africa Books.

Olawale, A. 2001. 'The role of oral literature in Yoruba herbal medical practice'. In *African oral literature*, ed. R. H. Kaschula, pp. 72–89. Claremont: New Africa Books.

Omolewa, M. 2000. 'Setting the tone of adult and continuing education in Africa'. In *The state of adult and continuing education in Africa*, eds. S. A. Indabawa, A. Oduaran, T. Afrik and S. Walters, pp. 11–18. Bonn: DNFE Namibia and IIZ/DVV.

Omolewa, M., Adeola, O. A., Adekanmbi, G. A., Avoseh, M. B. M. and Braimoh, D. 1998. *Literacy, tradition and progress: Enrolment and retention in an African rural literacy programme*. Hamburg: UNESCO Institute for Education.

Pattman, R. 2002. *Gender, sexuality, HIV/AIDS in education training material*. Unpublished material, Lusaka, Zambia.

Pongweni, A. 2001. 'A responsive audience: Texture, text and context in Shona folklore'. In *African oral literature: Functions in contemporary contexts*, ed. R. H. Kaschula, pp. 156–180. Claremont: New Africa Books.

Prah, K. K. 1999. 'African renaissance or warlordism?'. In *Africa renaissance: The new struggle*, pp. 37–61. Cape Town: Mafube Publishing and Tafelberg Publishers.

Preece, J. 1999. *Using Foucault and feminist theory to explain why some adults are excluded from British university education*. Ceredigion, Wales: Edwin Mellen Press.

Prophet, R. B. and Nyati-Ramahobo, L. 1994. *Review of educational research in Botswana 1986–1991: Policy, paradigms and possibilities*. Gaborone: University of Botswana.

Ramokone, V. B. 1997. *An analysis of gender differences in small-scale income generating activities in Botswana: A case of Molepolole village*. Unpublished B.Ed. dissertation. Gabarone: University of Botswana.

Razavi, S. 1999. 'Gendered poverty and well-being: Introduction'. *Development and Change*, Vol. 30, pp. 409–434.

Reinharz, S. 1992. *Feminist methods in social research*. Oxford: Oxford University Press.

Rwomire, A. (ed.). 2001. *Challenges and responsibilities of doing social research in Botswana: Ethical issues*. Nairobi: OSSREA.

Samoff, J. 1992. 'The intellectual/financial complex of foreign aid'. *Review of African Political Economy*, Vol. 53, pp. 60–75.

Scheurich, J. 1997. *Research method in the post-modern*. London: Falmer Press.

Segobye, A. K. 2000. *Situating the principle of botho in Botswana society: A historical perspective*. Gaborone: Archaeology Unit, University of Botswana.

Seloilwe, E. 1997. *Family psychiatric caregiving in Botswana: Experiences, demands and social support*. Unpublished Ph.D. dissertation, University of California, San Francisco.

Smith, L. T. 1999. *Decolonising methodologies: Research and indigenous peoples*. London: Zed Books.

Snyder, M. and Tadesse, M. 1997. 'The African context: Women in the political economy'. In *The women, gender and development reader,* eds. N. Visvanathan, L. Duggan, L. Nisonoff and N. Wiegersman, pp. 75–78. London: Zed Books.

Sogolo, G. 1993. *Foundations of African philosophy*. Ibadan: University Press.

Sparks, B. 2002. 'Epistemological and methodological considerations of doing cross-cultural research in adult education'. *International Journal of Lifelong Education*, Vol. 21, pp. 115–129.

Studman, C. 2001. 'Social ethics: Too much of a good thing'. In *Challenges and responsibilities of doing social research in Botswana: Ethical issues,* ed. A. Rwomire. Nairobi: OSSREA.

Teffo, L. J. 2000. 'Africanist thinking: An invitation to authenticity'. In *African voices in education,* eds. P. Higgs, N. C. G. Vakalisa, T. V. Mda and N. T. Assie-Lumumba, pp. 103–117. Lansdowne: Juta.

Thetela, P. H. 2002. 'Sex discourses and gender constructions in Southern Sotho: A case study of police interviews of rape/sexual assault victims'. *Southern African Linguistics and Applied Language Studies,* Vol. 20, pp. 177–189.

Trust for Community Outreach and Education (TCOE). 2001. *Participatory action research: A facilitator's manual.* Cape Town: TCOE.

United Nations Educational, Scientific and Cultural Organisation (UNESCO). 1976. *The experimental world literacy programme*. Paris: UNESCO.

United Nations Educational, Scientific and Cultural Organisation (UNESCO). 1994. *Education for all: Status and trends*. Paris: UNESCO.

United Nations Educational, Scientific and Cultural Organisation (UNESCO). 1996. *The declaration on adult education and lifelong learning*. An African position paper prepared at the Africa Regional Consultation on Adult and Continuing Education and the Challenges of the Twenty First Century. Dakar: UNESCO.

United Nations Educational, Scientific and Cultural Organisation (UNESCO). 2002. Untitled paper for the Interagency Strategic Group Meeting on Lifelong Learning, Hamburg, organised by UNESCO Institute for Education and UNESCO ED/BAS. Hamburg: UIE.

Weekly Review. 1996. 'Explicating African philosophy'. Viewed 16 September 2001. http://www.africaOnline.co.ke/AfricaOnline/neswstand/weeklyvuu/august2/books.htm1

Winter, R. 1996. 'Some principles and procedures for the conduct of action research'. In *New Directions in Action Research*, ed. O. Zuber Skerritt, pp. 13–27. London: Falmer Press.

World Bank. 1988. *Education in sub Saharan Africa: Policies for adjustment*. Washington, DC: World Bank.

Yaa Asantewaa Reed, P. Y. 2001. 'African womanism and African feminism: A philosophical, literary, and cosmological dialectic on family'. *Western Journal of Black Studies*, Vol. 25, pp. 168–176.

Youngman, F. 1998. Old dogs and new tricks? Lifelong education for all – the challenge facing adult education in Botswana. Inaugural lecture, Gaborone: University of Botswana.

Youngman, F. 2000. *The political economy of adult education and development*. London: Zed Books.

Zuber Skerritt, O. (ed.). 1996. *New directions in action research*. London: Falmer Press.

Index

nkonsonkonson